RENISHAW HALL

RENISHAW HALL

THE STORY OF THE SITWELLS

RENISHAW HALL

DESMOND SEWARD

First published 2015 by
Elliott and Thompson Limited
27 John Street
London WC1N 2BX
www.eandtbooks.com

ISBN: 978-1-78396-183-2

9 8 7 6 5 4 3 2 1

A catalogue record for this book is available from the British Library.

Jacket design: Jon Wainwright, Alchemedia Design Ltd
Typesetting: Marie Doherty
Printed in the UK by TJ International Ltd

In memory of Reresby Sitwell

CONTENTS

'An ancient hall without its records is a body without a soul and can never be fully enjoyed until one has learnt something of the men and women whom it has sheltered in the past – of their lives and manners, their love affairs, their wisdom and their follies; how the oak furniture gave way to walnut, and the walnut to mahogany; how they laid out the gardens, raised the terrace, clipped the hedges, and planted the avenue.'

—SIR GEORGE SITWELL, INTRODUCTION
TO *LETTERS OF THE SITWELLS AND SACHEVERELLS*

ACKNOWLEDGEMENTS

This is a book about the Sitwell family and Renishaw Hall, where they have lived since 1625. I am most grateful to Alexandra Sitwell (Mrs Rick Hayward) for asking me to write it and to Penelope, Lady Sitwell for encouragement, as well as invaluable information.

I must also thank Christine Beevers, an archivist whose suggestions and encyclopedic knowledge of the source material at Renishaw have been of enormous help throughout – as in finding unpublished letters from Evelyn Waugh and Dylan Thomas. Others who gave me information or advice were: Julian Allason; Gillian, Lady Howard de Walden; Stella Lesser (who read the proofs); Anna Somers-Cocks; and James Stourton.

I have been lucky to have such an unusually understanding and patient editor as Pippa Crane while, as so often before, I owe a special debt to my agent Andrew Lownie for his unfailing support.

Desmond Seward
Hungerford, 2015

FOREWORD

During the 1920s three writers, Osbert, Edith and Sacheverell Sitwell, became the generally acknowledged rivals of the Bloomsbury Group. According to their friend Evelyn Waugh, they 'radiated an aura of high spirits, elegance, impudence, unpredictability, above all of sheer enjoyment. They declared war on dullness.'[1]

Behind the 'Trio' stood Renishaw Hall in Derbyshire, the family's home since 1625, which down the generations has affected everybody who lived there. In a beautiful setting, filled with treasures, it enchanted all three when they were young. 'The Sitwells might wander far from Renishaw, but they would always return in spirit,' wrote Harold Acton.[2] Rex Whistler, no stranger to great mansions, thought it the most exciting house in England, while it replaced Madresfield in Evelyn Waugh's affections. Osbert's lasting achievement was commissioning John Piper to paint it.

Unfairly, the Trio blamed their father Sir George for failing to save their beautiful, brainless mother from a prison sentence, while they resented being dependent on him for money. Osbert and Edith turned him into a figure of fun in their autobiographies, a caricature accepted unquestioningly by everyone who writes about the Sitwells.[3] So far, nobody has acknowledged just how much he formed the minds of his children. For, while undeniably eccentric, he was also brilliantly gifted – a pioneer in re-discovering Baroque art, and one of the finest landscape gardeners of his day. Above all, he was the creator of modern Renishaw.

His children's impact on the arts and their role as arbiters of taste have been forgotten (even if Edith's verse still has admirers); so too has their feud with Bloomsbury, and all the malicious gossip that accompanied it. Yet their friends included Aldous Huxley, Siegfried Sassoon, Anthony Powell, L. P. Hartley, Dylan Thomas, Graham Greene and (up to a point) Virginia Woolf. Osbert's closest literary friendship was with Evelyn Waugh.

However, the Trio are just a part of this modest chronicle of Renishaw Hall and its squires. Among the owners have been a Cavalier, a Jacobite, and a Regency Buck who added palatial new rooms. Not least was the maligned Sir George Sitwell, who, besides transforming the house's interior, created the gardens. The book's climax is Renishaw's triumphant restoration.

Chapter 1

THE CAVALIER

No portrait survives of the George Sitwell who built Renishaw Hall, but in 1900, after a close examination of the effigy on his monument in Eckington church and of his letter-book, another George Sitwell imagined how he must have looked towards the end of his life:

> over the middle height, and, as became one obviously well advanced in middle age, rather neat and precise than fashionable in his dress. He wore a long periwig scented with orange water, a slight moustache and a tuft of hair upon his chin [. . .] His face, with its good forehead and eyes, strong and clear-cut nose and well developed chin, gave an impression of force of character, tenacity of purpose, and good reasoning powers, and this impression was strengthened by his conversation, for even the most casual acquaintance could not fail to observe that he was a manufacturer who had been accustomed to think and act for himself, a man who was not only well educated, but gifted with a sound judgement and a marked talent for business.[1]

Born in 1601 at Eckington in Derbyshire, George was the son of a rich yeoman (also called George), who lived in a house on the village street and died six years later. In 1612, 'Mr Wigfall, who was then of smale estate, marryed my mother, by which meanes he raised his fortune and came to have the guidance of mine estate dureing mine minority (which was about ten yeares)', wrote George in 1653. Despite promising to leave him his property as settlement of a debt for £1,400, Wigfall married again after the death of his ward's mother and, dying intestate in 1641, ensured that it went to the children of his second marriage, much to George's anger.

With funds provided by Mrs Sitwell, Mr Wigfall had built them a house on the summit of a long, rocky promontory above Renishaw, a small hamlet near Eckington in the area then known as 'Hallamshire' – on the northern border of Derbyshire and the southern of the West Riding of Yorkshire. Six miles from Chesterfield and six from Sheffield, Renishaw lies between the Peak District and what are now called the Dukeries. Wigfall's new home, where the Renishaw stables now stand, must have alerted his stepson to the beauty of the site.

In 1625–6 (the first year of King Charles I's reign), using money saved during his minority, George built Renishaw Hall within sight of Wigfall's dwelling. A 'Pennine Manor' on an H plan, this would become the nucleus of today's Renishaw. In some ways George always remained a farmer here, eating with his servants in the hall. Even today, when you go through the north porch into the hall – which is not much changed since his day – the panelling, huge fireplace, stone floor and rough oak furniture have a distinctly rustic feel.

On three floors, the tall, gabled house nevertheless aspired to gentility. From the hall, a door at the right opened on to a Little Parlour, and another door at the right on to a buttery and kitchen. The Great

Staircase and Great Parlour (now Library) were at the left. Thirty-four feet long, twenty wide, with a bay window on to the gardens, the Great Parlour was the best room. Panelled, this had a plasterwork ceiling and a frieze of mermaids and dolphins, squirrels, vine leaves and grapes, with a large oak carving over the fireplace of Abraham sacrificing Isaac. Above the hall was the principal bedroom, the Hall Chamber, with Mr Sitwell's study next to it.

Around the house were gardens and orchards, some walled. A large south garden, wider than the house it surrounded on three sides, had green or gravel walks, box hedges, small knot gardens with aromatic herbs, yew pyramids and flowerbeds. On the left was a bowling green. The Great Orchard, south of the main garden, contained two archery butts and side alleys bordered by flowers. There was also a banqueting house of red brick that contained a tiny, oak-panelled room. A brew-house supplied the hall with beer until 1895.

For the seventeenth century the staff was small, consisting of a steward (Thomas Starkey); a housekeeper (Katherine Heays); a butler and a pair of footmen in green and yellow livery; a coachman and two grooms; a cook, a kitchen-maid and two servant-maids; a dairy maid; and two gardeners. This was in the 1660s, however, after the death of Mrs Sitwell, when the children had left home. In their day, it would have been larger. It is also likely that other servants who did not live in the house came up daily from nearby Eckington.

Yet seventeenth-century Renishaw was no lonely sylvan paradise, since a busy road (later moved downhill) ran past the main front of the house, going on to cross a bridge over the River Rother. An important highway between West Yorkshire and London, it was a road thronged with traffic – carts, pack-horses, horsemen, travellers on foot. Bolsover and Hardwick, then Derbyshire's greatest mansions, could be seen on a beautiful ridge to the east.

George came from a family long established in or around Eckington. In 1301 Simon Sitwell of the parish was recognised in a lawsuit as heir of Walter de Boys, who had died on pilgrimage to the Holy Land, while in 1310 Roger 'Cytwelle' helped to found the Guild of St Mary of Eckington. The first Sitwell of substance had been Mr Robert Sytwelle of Staveley Netherthorpe Hall three miles away, who made his money from a coal mine at Eckington Marsh and acquired the Renishaw site. A Catholic without sons, he had tried unsuccessfully to leave his fortune away from his Protestant heir, George's grandfather.

After attending the grammar school at Derby, George knew Latin and Greek, and apparently went up to Cambridge to finish his education at Corpus Christi College. In 1627 he married Margaret, daughter of Hugh Childers of Carr House, near Doncaster. We know nothing of Mr Childers, apart from where he lived and his styling himself 'gentleman' – or about Margaret, except that she gave her husband nine children, of whom several did not survive infancy, and that she died in 1658.

During the 1630s George began mining iron ore on a large scale, building a blast furnace to forge it at Plumbley, a mile north-west of Eckington, in partnership with Wigfall. The Civil War's need of iron for weaponry increased his market, which already included the West Indies and Virginia, and in 1652 he built another furnace nearer home, at Foxbrooke. This became Derbyshire's biggest ironworks, producing pig and bar iron together with castings and other iron goods. In 1656 George set up a rolling mill at Renishaw to make rod iron for nails, scythes and sickles. He also owned a forge at Pleasley, which turned out saws.

In 1641, with four other local gentlemen, George and his stepbrother Henry Wigfall sent a letter to the House of Lords urging it to petition King Charles to meet Parliament on his return from Scotland. When the Civil War broke out, George let royalist troops garrison Renishaw (no doubt from the regiment raised by his neighbour, John Frescheville) and guard the road below. Osbert Sitwell claimed that when he was a boy, old men pointed out to him the marks of cannonballs on the stone of the upper storeys, but there is no record of any siege.[2]

After the royalist defeat at Marston Moor George obtained a 'protection' from the Parliamentary commander in Yorkshire, Ferdinando, Lord Fairfax. Dated 9 August 1644, it orders that 'George Sitwell of Renishaw in the County of Darby, Gentl., bee not plundered, pillaged, or in any way Injured in any of his howses or goods'. Later, however, he was fined £400 as a persistent delinquent, which can only mean that the authorities saw him as a hard-line Cavalier. His sympathies may have been reported by his stepbrother, Henry Wigfall, who was a committed Roundhead.

George could afford to pay, as the Renishaw estates with other lands produced £800 a year, doubled by profits from his ironworks. A Justice of the Peace, eager to turn himself into a proper gentleman with a coat of arms, in 1648 he applied to Parliament's herald, 'Garter, Principal King of Arms of Englishmen', for a grant, receiving three black lions on gold and silver bars (once borne by the Stutevilles, medieval lords of Eckington). It was re-granted after the Restoration, the bars changed to gold and green. The herald noted how George, 'in the late unhappy times of distraction [had] indeavored as much as in him lay to the advancement of his Majesties just Authority, whereby he may pretend to some marke of distinction'.[3]

George Sitwell displayed these new arms on his banner at the Derby Assizes in 1653, when serving as High Sheriff for Derbyshire under

Lord Protector Cromwell. As his chaplain he brought the Eckington parson, Dr Gardiner, whose appointment to the living he had procured four years earlier and who had been his eldest son Francis's tutor at Cambridge. Gardiner preached a dangerously indiscreet Assize sermon on 'Magistracy and Ministry, the State and the Church', reflecting his patron's views. (Significantly, when the Restoration came, Dr Gardiner was appointed a chaplain to the Duke of Monmouth.)

It was a perilous time for closet royalists to air a preference for King and Bishops as opposed to Protector and Major-Generals. Sitwell and his chaplain were lucky to escape serious charges. Since the Book of Common Prayer had been outlawed, Gardiner officiated in Eckington church without book or surplice, administering the Sacrament to parishioners who sat at a long table. No doubt, he also said the illegal Anglican service at the Hall, in secret – whispering it to the family behind locked doors.

<hr />

After Mrs Sitwell's death in 1658 the housekeeper, Mrs Heays, ran the house, ensuring its tranquil routine. The servants ate with their master. Breakfast was at seven o'clock: cold meat, oatcakes, white bread and butter, washed down by small ale. At eleven Mrs Heays led them into the hall for prayers, and afterwards the butler laid the table for dinner at midday – a substantial meal, which Mr Sitwell followed by a pipe of tobacco in the Little Parlour or the banqueting house. Supper was also eaten in the hall, where the day ended with evening prayers.

The whole household went to Eckington on Sunday to hear Dr Gardiner's sermon, the preacher and his wife riding back with them for dinner. On special occasions there was dancing in the Great Parlour and card-playing in the Little Parlour, while at Christmas fiddlers came over from Staveley or Chesterfield, the hall being decked with holly and ivy.

George, who reveals a good deal about himself in his letter-book, lived an active outdoor life besides managing his estates and his iron. He bred horses, hunted with Mr Frescheville's harriers, and may have kept greyhounds for coursing. He also owned a fowling-piece, which suggests that he shot regularly, since we know he presented his neighbours with pheasants.

George prudently concealed his feelings about Oliver Cromwell's regime, destroying letters that might put him in danger. The sole exception is a note in his hand (perhaps a copy) reporting a plot to assassinate the Protector by starting a fire in the chapel at Whitehall when he was hearing a sermon, and then kill him in the confusion. George comments that while the authorities pretended it was one of 'the restless attempts of the Cavalier partie', the man behind it was a discontented Leveller, an army captain, whose aim was to discredit Royalists.

After the 'Great Rebellion' was over, George described his country's former Puritan masters as 'crafty, wicked men [who] conceave it best to fish in troubled waters, and apprehending religion to be the finest cloake to cover their intentions . . . they seem much to resemble those Zealotts Josephus mentions among the Jews a little before their destruction . . . factious, seditious, self-ended people, who when they neither care nor dare begin a disturbance in Civile affaires, then will they quarrell about religion'.

By 1659 England had grown to detest the tyranny of the 'Major-Generals' and despise the new Protector, Richard Cromwell, Oliver's incapable son. At the end of the year General Monck marched on London, reinstating the Long Parliament, which in May 1660 declared that Charles II had succeeded his father as king in 1649. We know how George, the staunch Cavalier, felt about it from a letter he wrote to his old friend and neighbour Mr Frescheville the following April.

> All honest, truehearted Englishmen are bound to render harty thanks and praise to our mercifull God, who hath miraculously restored our gracious Sovereign, and us to our right, in a calme peace, in the throng of soe blustering and unnaturall a war; wherein I cannot sufficiently set forth the worth of the good Duke of Albemarle [Monck], who was cheifly instrumental in our happiness.

George welcomed 'that great and grave Council of our Nation' – his name for the ferociously royalist 'Cavalier Parliament' – with its statutes against Levellers, eviction of Puritan parsons and savage punishment of seditious pamphleteers. 'The preservation of our laws ought to be dearest to us, for by them the crowne is kept from tottering on the head of our Sovereign.'

By this time George Sitwell had become England's biggest manufacturer of nails, reputedly producing a tenth of the kingdom's entire iron production. (It should be remembered, however, that most iron articles were imported.) During the winter of 1661–2 his furnaces turned out 1,181 tons of sow iron worth £6 a ton, when the whole country's annual output was no more than 10,000 tons. Some was sold in London, taken by barge and ship from a depot at Bawtry on the River Idle as well as by road. He also made a complete rolling mill for a client in the West Indies.

Some modern writers sneer at this association with 'trade', but George would have seen nothing demeaning. Seventeenth-century iron-making was the squirearchy's preserve, their woods providing charcoal to heat the forges, their streams powering the hammers. There were other gentleman ironmasters in Derbyshire, such as the Hunlokes of nearby Wingerworth. George enjoyed the society of neighbours like these, riding over to Chesterfield on Saturday to dine with them at the Red Lyon on fish, mutton, chicken and ale, afterwards playing shovel-board. He also went regularly to Derby for the Assizes or the Fair. Sometimes he visited Sheffield for the Tuesday market, dining at the Angel Inn near the Irish Cross.

Many letters in the letter-book are to 'Cosen ffranceys'. This was Ralph Franceys, who lived in London at the White Hart in Friday Street and acted as George's unofficial agent. George was constantly asking Ralph for small purchases, such as cinnamon water, which was good for the digestion and rheumatism. In December 1664 he wrote, 'My sone[-in-law] William [Revel] wants a ffrench hat, and I have a grand-child about six yeares old, who wants one too.' Over the years Ralph became a valued friend, he and his wife sometimes spending Christmas at Renishaw. He helped George to correspond with his sons overseas – and kept an eye on John, the youngest son and black sheep, who was half-heartedly working in London.

Two of George's younger sons became successful merchants. The second, another George, established himself at Seville, dealing in Spanish silks before retiring to London as a rich man. He regu-larly sent his father presents of red Alicante wine and sweet Malaga

– clearly much appreciated – with oranges and lemons. The third, Robert Sitwell, entered the Levant Company, exporting English woollen cloth and metals in return for oriental silks, cottons and spices. For many years he lived in Syria at Aleppo and then in Italy at Leghorn (Livorno), the Company's headquarters, eventually coming back to spend his old age at London.

The fourth son, John, was less satisfactory, losing his place as apprentice to a tailor in Derby. His father found him a new place in London, continuing to help him with money and advice. He confided to Cousin Franceys, 'John hath been a great griefe to me.'

Unusually kind-hearted, George drafted a petition on behalf of his neighbour, Mr Leigh of Coldwell Hall, who had fallen on hard times, to beg a place for him in the Duke of Norfolk's almshouse at Sheffield, besides paying for one of his sons to be apprenticed to a Sheffield tailor. He sent a letter to another of Mr Leigh's sons, telling him 'write by the next post this comes to you to hould up the hartt of the ould man'.

He asked the creditors of a former maid at Renishaw to be lenient because she had unknowingly married a man deep in debt. Twice he bailed out a debtor from Chesterfield's House of Correction, helping him again when he was imprisoned a third time.

George also did his best to aid young Whittles, 'a poore ffatherless and Motherless boy, an object of pitty to move one', rescuing him from his 'Knavish uncles', paying for his release from apprenticeship to a cruel master, and giving him clothes and money to save him from starving.

The letter-book reveals an interest in public affairs, at home and abroad. George regularly received 'news books, papers of news, letters diurnall, gazettes, royal declarations and speeches, and acts of Parliament', which were sent to him from London by Cousin Franceys. He learned of the Great Plague of 1665 with horrified fascination, noting in July, 'it's said there was 100 houses shutt up on one day in one parish, viz., St Andrew's in Holborn. I humbly pray it would please the Lord to take of[f] this heavy judgement.' He was well-informed about the Dutch war, commenting in July 1667 that 'there is a rumor that the Dutch are at sea againe with theire Navy, but I think they are not so ready'.

⌐━━━━━⌐

Every year George visited the London of Charles II and Samuel Pepys, always in the spring, in order to sell his iron. The journey took him four days on horseback, armed with a brace of pistols. Invariably he was escorted by a servant, who also carried arms.

When he arrived he lodged at the Greyhound Inn in Holborn (adjoining Furnival's Inn), where he gave dinner parties, and met friends at the Exchange, with whom he ate in nearby taverns. He saw others at Westminster, which he reached by barge along the Thames. Having settled business matters, he went shopping, leaving orders at booksellers, tailors, silversmiths and tobacconists. Each Sunday, he attended divine service at St Paul's or St Andrew's Holborn. He looked forward to these visits, telling Ralph Franceys, 'God send us a merry meeting.'

His 1662 visit was concerned with apprenticing his son John to Nicholas Delves, a silk merchant. The boy, who was clearly a wastrel, made an enemy of Delves's partner, Mr Brownsword, although for a time Cousin Franceys managed to see that John kept his place. At the end of 1663 George wrote gratefully to Ralph, 'I will not trouble you with more words about him, but will Register your great kindness in my bosome, to remaine there to minde me of the great store of friend-shipp I owe you.'

In January 1664, Delves formally complained of John's bad behaviour. George replied:

> I was much troubled when I heard my sonne was so untowardly indiscreet to cause you to write thus to me againe . . . I hope hereafter he will nether thinke Christmas nor any other time lawless to play the foole in, but when you are pleased at any time to give him leave to recreate himselfe among friends, he will make choyce of sober civell company and keepe good howers . . . Sir, I acknowledge my selfe dubblely obliged to you, first in takeing care to observe my sonne's Courses, and letting him see the danger and folly, and then for pardoning him.

In the end, the prodigal was shipped out to Seville to work for his brother George. He appears to have died young, since nothing more is recorded of him.

From what we know of Mr Sitwell's library at Renishaw, he enjoyed some very serious reading indeed in his study upstairs. Besides Homer, Aristotle and the Greek and Latin classics, it contained such fathers of the church as Tertullian, Eusebius, Augustine and Chrysostom, together with Bishop Jewel's *Apologia* and Fuller's *History of the Holy War*. Among law books were Justinian's *Institutes* and Coke's *Statutes*. On the shelves, too, were Erasmus, Machiavelli, Bacon and Milton. Science was not neglected, with Galen and Galileo as well as William

Harvey's *De motu cordis* – the pioneering study of the circulation of the blood.

Modern philosophy was represented by Descartes, while there were books on mathematics, trigonometry, logic, navigation and perspective. More frivolous was Henri Boguet's *Discours exécrable des sorciers*. There were also numerous pamphlets on current affairs, dealing with the Civil War or the Restoration, all tied in bundles.

Apart from Dr Gardiner, George had few friends with whom to discuss his reading. A possible exception, even if he saw little of him, was Richard Love, Master of Corpus Christi College, Cambridge and a former chaplain to King Charles I. It was Dr Love who in 1649 had advised George to appoint Gardiner as rector, pleasantly ending his letter of recommendation, 'Sir, be pleased to present my service to your whole family and all staying with you,' which indicates a certain familiarity. No doubt other letters were destroyed because they expressed dangerous opinions. George may have known Love at Cambridge; and perhaps it was at Love's suggestion that he sent his eldest son, Francis, to Corpus Christi.

George Sitwell had built his family's fortunes on very firm foundations indeed by the time he died in 1667. He was buried in Eckington church, where there is a monument with busts of himself and his wife. He comes down the centuries as a kindly and cultivated man, who although one of nature's entrepreneurs never lost an iota of humanity. His best epitaph is a phrase from a letter he wrote in September 1665 – 'in mine apprehension plain dealing is a jewel'.

Chapter 2

'MR JUSTICE SITWELL'

'The Squires of Renishaw in the seventeenth and eighteenth centuries were Whigs, quiet and scholarly country gentlemen who collected books and pictures, improved the farming and planting of the estate, amassed rents and royalties and married heiresses – hence the strange family names affected by later generations,' wrote their descendant Reresby Sitwell.[1]

He might also have said that they neither hunted nor shot, and were in no way sportsmen. We know a fair amount about them and their world from the letters Sir George Sitwell edited at the end of the nineteenth century. Reresby adds, 'Younger sons were put into trade and many worked so hard that they never had time to marry, so left their fortunes back to their eldest brother or nephew.'

<hr/>

Born in 1630, George's eldest son and heir Francis Sitwell was educated at Corpus Christi College, Cambridge, and then read law at Gray's Inn. Steady and hard-working, he got on well with his father. After inheriting the estate, he continued to run the forges and collieries. However, his only real achievement was marrying the sister of William Sacheverell of Barton near Nottingham, who became renowned as MP for Derbyshire. Sometimes credited with founding the Whig party, Sacheverell was a fervent anti-papist who believed firmly in the Popish

Plot. He was also a considerable orator, and Mr Speaker Onslow called him 'the ablest parliament man' of his time.

Having fathered three sons and three daughters, and been High Sheriff for Derbyshire, the second squire of Renishaw died in 1671. His wife Katherine Sacheverell apparently mourned him deeply, for on his funeral monument in Eckington church are inscribed the lines:

> Here death hath laid my treasure up.
> This earth doth cover
> My cordiall frind, my loyal
> Spouse and faithfull lover.

Francis's son George, fourteen when his father died, was lucky to have a mother who did not remarry and took good care of his inheritance. *My Rent Book beginning whitsuntide 1678* testifies to her businesslike approach. It was in 1678 that George came down from Trinity College, Cambridge. He kept happy memories of his time there, responding generously with a donation of £10 when in 1680 the Master and Fellows of Trinity wrote asking for money:

> Sir, we are engaged in building a great and magnificent library opposite to the hall in Nevill's court, and in joining it to the two sides of that building with eight new arches, a work that will not only supply our necessity and convenience, but adorn the whole university and learning itself.[2]

An oak armchair in the hall bearing the date 1679 commemorates Katherine Sitwell refurnishing the house for George's marriage to

Anne Kent of Povey Hall, who was another considerable Derbyshire heiress. As Anne was sickly, for her first lying-in the couple lodged at Derby in the house of the town's leading physician, Dr Polycarp Dakins, who duly delivered her of a son and heir, Francis. After bearing several more children, Anne died young, in early middle age.

George managed his estate carefully, enclosing common land and improving barren soil by sowing clover or planting turnips. He added a third 'orchard' at Renishaw, a kitchen garden on whose walls apricots, nectarines and peaches were grown. He also put new yew hedges into the gardens, besides planting trees on a large scale.

His main changes to the house itself were replacing the mullioned windows with sashed ones, besides building new stables and a coach house. Indoors, he added to the library, buying over a thousand books. These included a monumental work of cartography, the magnificent four-volume *The English Atlas* published by Moses Pitt between 1680 and 1683.

George had inherited the Whig principles of his uncle Sacheverell, a frequent visitor to Renishaw. In November 1688 George was among the Derbyshire gentlemen who, with their servants and retainers, escorted the Earl of Devonshire to Nottingham to show support for William of Orange's bid to replace James II. The richest Whig in England, the earl was one of the seven magnates who had invited William to come over from Holland with an army.

The following March, the new king appointed George a commissioner for the Lord Lieutenancy of the City of London. During these months he was busy making his neighbours take the oath of allegiance to William and Mary. He became a magistrate for the county in 1693, and ever afterwards was known by the family as 'Mr Justice Sitwell'.

In May 1696 the government sent him a warrant to arrest Captain Ralph Philips and 'one John Steel', Jacobites who were on the run for involvement in Sir John Fenwick's plot to assassinate William III. George was ordered to search the houses of Sir Henry Hunloke at Wingerworth and Mr Pooles, who lived near Park Hall not far off, besides those of any other suspects, and apprehend 'the said persons and all their papers.' Plainly, the authorities regarded him as a sound Whig who would do his best to prevent the return of James II.

⁕

When Mrs Sitwell died later that year, George decided to let Renishaw and live in London for a while. He arrived there at the end of 1697 and stayed there for nearly a decade instead of the two years he had intended. A portrait by Sir Godfrey Kneller during this time is of a dignified gentleman in a full-bottomed periwig, with a face memorable only for a high-bridged nose; it has the look of someone who does not possess too much imagination.

At first he lived in his brother Francis's house in Dyer's Court, Aldermanbury, but he later took lodgings with Mrs Pocock in Cursitor's Alley, and then with Mr Carlton in Fuller's Rents, Holborn, between Chancery Lane and Gray's Inn. This was the world of Joseph Addison and Richard Steele, and George frequented Will's Coffee House, which was among the essayists' favourite haunts. Conveniently, this was in Fuller's Rents, and he went there so often that he used it as an address. Coffee houses were like today's London clubs, with newspapers and good conversation, a home from home for a man in late middle age. He continued to visit London regularly even after returning to full-time residence at Renishaw in 1706.

A capable man of business, George increased his wealth without taking risks. From the 1690s the ironworks were leased out, although he kept control of the collieries. What interested him was improving the estate.

A good father, George helped his younger sons with their careers. One became a merchant, sailing on a trading venture to Jamaica in 1705. His uncle Francis wrote to his father in summer 1706:

> Some of your son George's friends have been persuading
> him to go to India about Michaelmas next, & continue
> there about two yeares, for to establish an acquaintance
> in order to have full business from the Gentlemen &
> planters hereafter . . . you must furnish him with five or
> six hundred pounds in three months, part of the fortune
> you design for him, for to purchase a cargo.

The younger George sailed to Virginia in July 1707. He later went on similar expeditions to China and India, making a substantial fortune.

Mr Justice Sitwell was closest to his daughter Alice and her husband William Sacheverell, the great Parliamentarian's second son. After marrying in 1708, the young couple lived in a fine stone mansion on Cockpit Hill in Derby – and at Barton, where they 'kept house' for William's widowed elder brother Robert, who drank too much to look after himself. 'Musters, I & Jack have been mellow a weeke together,' Robert had informed William after a drunken bout in May 1706. The Rector of Barton wrote in vain to William, living with his brother at Barton, about the 'pernicious sin of Hard-drinking . . . making Men forfeit the Felicity of Heaven and plunging them forever into the Lake of Fire with the Devil'.

William's portrait at Renishaw shows a handsome if sickly face. Sadly, there is no portrait of Alice. George's letters to William begin, 'Dear Son' and end, 'Your very affectionate ffather & Servant', while William signs his as 'Yr. Most Dutyfull Sonn'.

In July 1709 George thanked William for 'joyfull news of my Daughter's safe delivery of a son . . . I shall gladly embrace this happy opportunity of being a God-father and shall (God willing) come to Derby on purpose when you shall please to let me know the day when you design to have the Christening.'

But William's poor health was a worry. In 1711 George wrote to him, 'I was very glad to hear by James Jackson that you was pretty well in health when he came last from Barton, especially considering that a little before my Daughter wrote [to] Betty that you was much out of order.' After Alice's death in 1713 at twenty-six from complications following the birth of their second son, William's health broke down completely, and two years later he died of the ague.

❦

William's elder brother Robert had died in 1714. On 14 May, after a night's boozing, he set out at 3.00 a.m. to ride to London. Having ridden at breakneck speed for five hours, he fell off his horse shortly before reaching Northampton and died of an apoplexy within a few minutes. 'The reason why Mr Sacheverell rid so hard was that he thought he was pursu'd', wrote a friend, implying he had suffered a fit of delirium tremens – the 'Horrors'.

Following his death, his kin became involved in a protracted legal case that Mr Justice Sitwell must have watched with horror. Robert had been the son of the great Whig and, like his father, was MP for Nottingham, but there the resemblance stopped. Robert was not only a drunk, but a womaniser. Worse still, he turned out to have been a bigamist.

Three 'wives' emerged. Julian Rhodes of Nottingham came forward with a certificate of marriage, claiming a dowry and maintenance for her baby son Samuel, while Anne Marshall of Barton made the same demands for herself and her daughter Mary, producing a similar certificate. So did a Mrs Stor. In addition, Mary Castle of London wrote to say that she and her child by Robert would starve unless they received money. These were just some of the ladies on whom he had fathered bastards.

The 'Great Sacheverell Case', a succession of lawsuits, dragged on for years and entailed hearings in Chancery, the Court of Common Pleas, the Bishop of London's Court, the Prerogative Court of Canterbury, the Lord Mayor's Court, the Court of Arches and elsewhere. All this incurred heavy costs for the rest of the Sacheverells – which, after William's death in September 1715, meant two small boys scarcely out of the cradle, William and Henry. Inevitably, George became involved, in an effort to save his grandsons' inheritance.

Just after William died, however, Mr Justice Sitwell had been distracted by a danger even more fearsome than an imperilled inheritance. A fervent supporter of the Protestant Succession, he treasured a letter received by his late son-in-law in November the previous year, describing George I and his family, who had just arrived from Hanover:

> As for newes, I must tell you in the first place that 2 nights agoe I was at Court, where I first saw the King, Prince, & Princess. The King is about my size, the Prince about yours, or not so tall, & the Princess about the size of us both, tho' setting aside her being fat, she is of a fine complexion, & seems, if very ugly, very good

natur'd & obligeing. The lookes of the King answer
the character he has, and I think deserves, of being one
of the best humour'd, wisest, and honestest men in his
dominions . . .

Understandably, Mr Sitwell was panic-stricken when in October 1715
he learned of a Jacobite rising in Scotland and Northern England to
restore the Catholic King 'James III' and send the Hanoverian usurper
packing. Receiving a 'full and authentick Narrative of the intended
Horrid Conspiracy and Invasione', he rushed down to London to
ask the Lord Lieutenant of Derbyshire, the Duke of Devonshire, for
orders. He also bought swords, guns and ammunition for his tenants, including a carbine for his own use. But the weapons were never
needed, as the rising was crushed.

A letter of the same month, addressed to George at Will's Coffee
House from his steward William Hattersley, lists arms bought to
fight the Jacobites, but also gives details of more normal activities at
Renishaw. A manager has laid off the colliers too soon, while a coal pit
has been flooded, making it difficult to mine, so they have run short of
coal. Luckily, they have found other supplies, despite coal being hard
to obtain at Chesterfield. They have got the harvest in, with excellent
yields of corn and oats. The hay seed has been sown, but so far little
wheat. Ploughing has been hampered by wet weather, which has left
most meadows under water, so this will have to wait until the ground
has dried out and hardened. He has bought forty-four sheep.

The Sacheverell case dragged on. Mrs Rhodes' 'marriage certificate'
was shown to have been forged by a clergyman at Scarborough, who
confessed the marriage had not taken place – he had never even met

Robert Sacheverell, who had paid him £50 to forge the certificate after the 'widow' threatened to expose her seducer. She was lucky to obtain £200 for her son's maintenance and an apprenticeship found for him.

Anne Marshall had a better case in law than Mrs Rhodes. Her wedding certificate was the earliest, while there was no repentant parson to prove the marriage had never taken place. Even so, Mr Justice Sitwell's neighbour and kinsman, Samuel Pole of Radbourne – 'Old Pole' – was convinced he could outwit 'Mr Sacheverell's whore'. There was good reason for his trying to do so, since his son, Captain Pole (who had been with the Duke of Marlborough's army at Malplaquet), was married to Robert's only legitimate child and therefore stood to lose a lot of money.

Glad that someone else would foot the bill for exposing Mrs Marshall, George encouraged the Poles; but his influence over them was diminished by insisting that they repay a loan of £700. There was no way Mr Pole could avoid paying, George making it clear that delay meant distraint or a debtor's prison.

A hot-tempered old man, Samuel Pole was blind to any legal pitfalls. Well-versed in the law, Sitwell warned him that the case against Mrs Marshall might miscarry on technicalities and that he should proceed with the utmost care. George established contact with the 'widow', hoping to buy her off, winning her confidence to such an extent that in December 1719 she wrote to him, 'Sir, when in my power [I] shall do all reasnobel & just things you desire of me.' But Pole refused to listen to George, and unwisely agreed to a hearing before the Court of Chancery.

In 1720 the Lord Chancellor found in Anne Marshall's favour, ordering that she be paid a proper widow's dowry by the Sacheverell estate. Thunderstruck, Mr Pole refused to accept the judgement or pay her costs, whereupon the Lord Chancellor committed him to the Fleet

Prison. One of Mr Justice Sitwell's correspondents reported that Old Pole 'saies hee'l stay *durante vita* before he'll move for his discharge, and saith he will never come out till he is brought out in a coffin'.

Prison walls changed Samuel Pole's mind. He paid up and went home to Radbourne. Even so, in 1729 he wrote to George's son, Francis Sitwell, that he remained convinced Anne Marshall

> was no more married to Rt. Sacheverell as she pretends, than she was married to your father, your selfe, or me. And if I be right in my opinion, I take that whole affair to be as great a piece of knavery and villainy as any of that sort hath been transacted in the Prerogative Court of Canterbury, in the Court of Common Pleas at Westminster, and in Chancery.

The costs of six years' litigation and settling with Mrs Marshall nearly ruined the Sacheverell estate, but enough remained to provide for the upkeep of Mr Justice Sitwell's grandsons. The outcome was a blow for him even if (unlike Old Pole), he had been canny enough to lose little in legal fees. He failed to obtain the books and papers bequeathed by their Parliamentarian grandfather, despite obtaining Sacheverell family portraits that are still at Renishaw.

George had a pleasant correspondence over the years with Jane Sacheverell, Robert and William's half-sister, who, because her letters survive, is the only woman to emerge as a flesh and blood personality from the family's early history. A shrewd, high-spirited old maid born in 1682, cheerful and amusing despite her hypochrondia, Jane was devoted to her kindred. George must have enjoyed her letters, as he kept them. In September 1716, she thanked him for a present of money 'which came very seasonably to supply my wants', adding, 'I find the weather has a mighty influence over me, for, while it was warm & serene, my fitts were fewer.' Characteristically, she sends 'Affectionate Love & service to yr. Self, Dear Cousin, & all ffriends with you, who am yr much obliged kinswoman J. Sacheverell.'

In June 1718, Jane writes with the news that her stomach fits are less frequent. 'I'm so farr arrived to my former diet as to be able to eat a piece of chicken or pidgeon or a small bitt of broil'd bacon.' Referring to the great law case, she tells George, 'I'm informed Barton is too deeply ingaged to continue long in the possession of any of our familly.' She thanks him for the support he is giving while expressing uneasiness about Mr Pole: 'I don't, nor shall I like to, depend on any of his promises, that already deals shufflingly. I take him to be a man of no solidity, a mere fair speaking airy projector.' She is trying asses' milk for her weak stomach, 'which occasioned those violent agonyes'.

In August 1720 she tells her Renishaw cousin that her fits of the 'Collick' are caused by 'whetness and uncertainty of the weather'. Referring to the result of the Sacheverell case, and the conduct of Samuel Pole, she says,

> a more unreasonable man I never heard of: I cannot suspect his gaining anything but the reputation of a lunatic . . . I thought the next care would be how to make the best of poor Barton in order to clear all debts, but I am now persuaded he designs to consume all in law, & make you all beggars.

Mr Justice Sitwell's prosperous if uneventful career came to a sudden end in 1723, while he was staying with a friend at Derby. His body was brought home on a hearse, escorted by two coaches full of mourners for burial in Eckington church. He had been squire of Renishaw for over fifty years. Despite the Sacheverell case, George died a rich man with an income of over £1,000.

Chapter 3

A MATHEMATICIAN

The new squire of Renishaw was George's eldest son, Francis, who had been born in Dr Dakin's house at Derby in 1682. At only four he was sent to Mr Cooke's day school in Eckington, and at nine to Chesterfield Grammar School; at thirteen he went down to London to be tutored by Sir Isaac Newton's former secretary, Humphrey Newton (no relation) in Euclid, algebra and practical geometry. The boy stayed with a Mr Fuller at the Fleur de Luce in Little Britain, the booksellers' street, his father paying £22 a year for his board, washing and lodging.

In October 1699, Francis wrote to his father, 'I told Mr Newton I had a mind to learn something of Astronomy (which will be no less usefull than pleasant) but he told me he must first write to you about it.'[1] He did not learn it for long, however, since 1699 was the year he was admitted to Gray's Inn to study law before going up to Corpus Christi College, Cambridge.

He emerged from this lengthy education as a gentleman scholar, very different from the 'country booby squires' in Fielding's novels. He had a good working knowledge of the classics, which he read with pleasure for the rest of his life, as well as a taste for the sciences, indirectly acquired from the great Isaac by way of Mr Newton. John Milton was a favourite author, and he annotated his folio copy of *Paradise Lost* with apposite quotations from the Greek and Latin poets. Throughout his life, his hobby seems to have been algebra.

A devout Protestant, Francis took a keen interest in theology, reading the early 'fathers of the church', from whom he could quote at length. This made for a bond with his youngest brother, Dr Thomas Sitwell, a clergyman and Fellow of Christ's College, Cambridge. Francis stayed in close touch with him, corresponding regularly until Thomas's death.

His few surviving letters, nearly all to his 'Honoured Father' and ending, 'Your most dutiful son', show him as a bit of a bore. He was a Whig to his fingertips, and the people who really upset him were High Churchmen and Jacobites.

In November 1712, when he was thirty, he wrote from Renishaw to his father George about choosing a new curate for Eckington despite the rector's hostility. An extra parson was needed to run the school the Sitwells were starting in the village – 'how great an Advantage a good school will be to the Parish' – and the man they had in mind was 'very well qualified to teach to write & cast accounts . . . which will be of more use than Greek & Latin in a Country School'.

He added, 'I went last Tuesday with C. Gardiner [the rector] to wait upon my Lord Scarsdale [at Sutton Scarsdale] where I found two Jacobites & a Papist.' Less disapproving news concerns a Sacheverell kinswoman:

> My Lady Newton is extreme weak & ill, we expect her Death every day: our Ladies were all in Tears to-day at noon, as supposing she was going . . . As for Sir John & his Lady, I believe [not having to pay] the joynture will support the Spirits, & inable them to bear the Loss with Christian Patience.

At the end of September 1715, writing from Renishaw to his father care of Will's Coffee House, he showed himself equally shaken by news of the Jacobite rising – 'the horrid plot you speak of'. What angered him most was the involvement of so many churchmen. He wrote sardonically, 'The true and most genuine sons of the Church, it seems, are discovered to be deeply engaged in the Conspiracy against their King and Country, and therefore no doubt but the Rebellion in Scotland and intended Invasion of England are designed for the good of the Church,' adding that these misguided churchmen wanted to bring in 'those who are worse than Heathens and Infidels' – papists.

'As for the school,' the letter goes on, returning to life at Renishaw, 'they are now making the stairs into the Chamber, and are got almost half Way.' Very much the country gentleman, he also gives news of the home farm. 'Thos' Thomson finished the sowing of the Fallow this night: and they have plowed the better half of the Fleet, and laid the manure in the lower fold upon it . . . Will [Hattersley] has bought forty sheep to stock the Pastures now the Cattle are gone.' He wants his father to buy him a new steel drawing pen. A few days later, forgetting the impending civil war, he reports that the rooms of the new Eckington school have been built, 'and I think they are very well done'. All that remains is to put in window panes. His father had given the site and an endowment, besides collecting money for it. It provided free schooling for the locals, and was later known as 'Camm's School'.

Francis also liked to send his father news of Renishaw folk, as on 10 September 1720:

> Your tenant Vincent Towndrough is dead of the common Distemper that now afflicts the County pretty much – it is a Kind of Fever. Dixon, too, at the Lane end is in some danger. Widdow Hattersley, too, is very

ill, she was indifferent well again, but plaid the Fool by
going out too soon.

Ten days later, he reports,

> Mr Ward there died last Sunday, as did George
> Machan the quondam Clerk [of the parish] today. As
> for Widdow Hattersley she is got pretty well again, &
> Dixon is on the mending hand, tho' since I wrote last
> he fell into convulsions after he had so far recovered as
> to creep out . . . As for Towndrough, his Body swelled
> prodigiously after he was dead, so that when John
> Whitworth, on the Sunday morning when he was to be
> buried, brought his coffin, it was so much too little that
> he was forced to work on Sunday to make him another
> almost as big again.

'The late proceedings in the South Sea [stock] were owing to a sort of
political inchantment, which turned people's brains with an imaginary
shew of riches; which to be sure will end in real poverty in too many
instance,' Francis wrote to his father from Renishaw in September
1720, just after the infamous Bubble had burst.

> Well, since so great a Burden is fall'n upon the people,
> I wish it may light as much as possible on those who
> are best able to bear it; but more especially on the chief
> authors of their mischief, I mean those Knavish stock-
> jobbers by whose artifice people have been thus bubbled
> to their ruin.

He was not alone in his opinion: one MP advised Parliament that bankers should be tied in sacks filled with snakes, and thrown into the Thames.

'If you happen to walk near Little Britain, I beg you would please to ask for Wallis's Algebra in Folio,' he ended his letter. No doubt he himself regularly visited this street, where he had lived when Mr Newton's pupil – it housed all the City bookshops, and he spent a good deal of time in London. He often saw there his second brother George, the India merchant, while he enjoyed Squire's Coffee House, once the rendezvous of choice for Sir Roger de Coverley in *The Spectator*.

On entering into his inheritance, Francis made a number of small changes at Renishaw inside and out that were designed to suit eighteenth-century taste. He completed the replacement of the old mullion windows, while the hall panelling was stripped out and the hall walls painted a pearl colour; the doors to the two staircases were turned into arches with double doors. There was also a stove, with screens to keep out the cold.

The panelling in the Great Parlour, where the family portraits hung, was painted in an oak colour and given new furniture that included a harpsichord and a clock costing 11 guineas – more than a year's wages for a labourer. The Little Parlour was redecorated with old maps of France and Paris, with an oil painting of a Dutch fair over the chimney piece. A new 'Smoking room' was created, which had black, leather-seated walnut chairs and Dutch pictures.

The best bedroom, the 'Red Chamber', also received new furnishings – bedspread, counterpane and window curtains of crimson damask, an India carpet, a gilt brass pier glass and a walnut table on which stood a walnut-framed dressing glass. The next best, the 'Green Chamber', was redecorated in fine green camlet. Other bedrooms were given walnut dressing tables and glasses. Each apartment had prints of famous personages – Sir Isaac Newton, the Duke of Marlborough, and of course William and Mary – or of scenes from classical history and mythology.

'He has brought from London a great deale of verey hansom furnitures,' the steward of Dr Thomas Sitwell's little estate at Povey (an Eckington man called Dick Cowley) reported to his master at Cambridge in 1730. These included two small tables of mahogany, a wood only recently in fashion. There were quantities of china (blue and white dinner plates, gilt-edged teacups and saucers) and silver plate – notably, a magnificent punchbowl engraved with the Sitwell crest. The staff had a service of armorial pewter from which to eat, and there were steel, copper and brass utensils for the kitchen.

Renishaw had become 'altogether too comfortable a house for a bachelor who, as appears from a letter [from Dick Cowley] of the last-named year, had "declared against matrimony"', Sir George Sitwell observed suspiciously in 1900. Perhaps he suspected Francis of being a homosexual. Admittedly, Francis never married. However, he may have been courting a lady, which could explain why he refurnished Renishaw with such luxury.

Nor did Francis's two brothers marry. The only sibling who did so was Alice, to William Sacheverell. As has been seen, the short-lived couple had left two sons, the last of the Sacheverells. Both of them died young – one by drowning in the River Rother and the other from smallpox. Some of the family's lands passed to Francis, with a portrait (by a member of the Verelst family) of the boy who drowned, *The Boy in Pink*. This still hangs in the dining room at Renishaw. A tale grew up of his waking girls with a kiss and how, dripping with water and his face covered in river weed, he walked through the house at night.

The squire of Renishaw was no lonely old bachelor, however. His house was always full of cousins, young and old – Sitwells, Osbornes, Wilmots. Sometimes Jane Sacheverell was among them. When Barton was finally sold up in 1727, after complaining of 'My share in the common calamity of stubborne coughs', she firmly declined to let him have the books so coveted by his father, but insisted on their being auctioned. However, she agreed that he could keep the Sacheverell portraits.

The refusal in no way affected their good relations. In 1734 she asked Francis Sitwell for help with pettifogging laywers – 'Mr Shampante, whom I take to be Brother to Counceller Puzelcause, obliges me to give you this trouble.' Jane had such confidence in Francis that she made him her executor. In 1741 the solitary old woman left instructions for her funeral – 'a Hearse, one Coach, a Neat but not fine Coffin. I desire to be buried in Linnen. When you send my Couzin a letter, inform him what I have directed.'

⌁

Jane also corresponded with Francis's first cousin and heir, another Francis Sitwell, an attorney in Sheffield and a nephew of Mr Justice Sitwell. Inheriting his father's practice, Francis became the leading lawyer there, patronised by the Duke of Leeds and other local magnates. He acquired a considerable fortune, partly from his salary as legal adviser to the Company of Cutlers in Hallamshire – then the most influential corporate body in Sheffield – but more from investments in indigo and diamonds that brought him over £1,000 a year. He was probably the town's richest inhabitant.

It looks as if he first met Jane in 1726, at young Henry Sacheverell's funeral. At the end of November the following year, while visiting

London, she wrote to this other Francis, 'I wish yourself & family joy of your new relation,' a reference to his sister Catherine having recently married a Mr Hurt, of whom more will be heard. She says, 'Kensington Air was [so much] more agreable to my Constitution than any Country Fever, that I Bless God I and my ffriend the Widow are as well in Body as the cold season will permit.' She grumbles that 'Cousin Sitwell [of Renishaw] has not thought fitt to afford me one informing line since you left the Towne.' The real point of her letter is to seek his advice on disposing of Barton's contents without upsetting relatives.

In December 1731, again from London, we find her thanking him for 'yr Noble Present of Woodcocks'. Once more, she wants advice on managing her property. She ends, 'Our Cousin, the Esqre. [the Renishaw Francis], had a safe tho' sharp journey. Was here yesterday: says he's free from cold & better in health than he has been some time.' In autumn 1735, Francis writes, 'I doe now think it long since I saw you, but hope to give my selfe that satisfaction next this next spring.' Giving news of other cousins, he says they are at York, 'where abundance of our neighbouring gentry have took into their heads to rendezvous this winter, where they find good & cheap provisions and operas, plays, musick meetings, and I know not what, event to view with the great Metropolis.' He sent her woodcock every year till his death in 1741.

The few letters to Francis Sitwell of Sheffield from Squire Francis treat him as an attorney rather than an heir. But at least they agreed on Jane. After the last Sacheverell boy's death in 1726, the Sheffield Francis was told by the Squire, 'I had rather cosin Jane had the right of administration' than anyone else, a testimony to the respect in which she was held by the entire family.

Reserved and fastidious, Francis Sitwell of Renishaw was not an easy man to approach. In the spring of 1729, his cousin Robert Wilmot of Chaddesden wrote asking his help in finding a bride for his son – 'such a young agreeable lady as will make him happy, endowed with good sense & virtue; for he will certainly make such a lady perfectly happy'. Robert makes it clear she must be in possession of a large fortune. On the back of his letter, Francis wrote a single word – 'nausious'.

<hr/>

As one might expect of a scholar, Francis steadily expanded Renishaw's library. Eventually it numbered nearly 2,000 titles, amounting to 4,000 volumes, which he catalogued himself. Some were in bookcases in the Great Parlour.

In a letter of 1730, Dick Cowley described the Renishaw gardens as 'very handsome'. The one on the south of the house was relaid in 1728 with 3,000 yards of sods bought at Worksop, a green alley being constructed in a straight line from the new garden door out of the hall. In the middle, a flight of stone steps led up to a sundial while elaborate flowerbeds were dug for anemones, jonquils, carnations and auriculas. The centre beds sported stone obelisks, fourteen feet high. There were box borders, and yews and hollies clipped into globes or pyramids.

The next year a terrace walk was added on the east, the wall beneath it planted with cherries, plums and pears. The kitchen gardens grew artichokes, asparagus and spinach. Besides apples (Nonpareil and Golden Pippin) and pears (St Germain and Divydale), the orchards produced Red Roman nectarines, old Newington peaches, plums, cherries, apricots and grapes.

<hr/>

In midlife Francis Sitwell had his portrait painted, in 1742, by Charles Philips, a portrait painter then enjoying a great vogue. It shows a stern, stately gentleman in a bag-wig who has a surprisingly full mouth with thick, fleshy lips. He may have looked a little different in real life – a letter of 1736 from Cousin Francis to Jane Sacheverell describes 'Our Squire' as 'plump and fat as a partridge'.

Next year he lost his favourite brother, the don. 'Poor Tom is alive, but in a very bad way, as you may well imagine,' a cousin noted early in January. 'He sitts up in his Chair & is pretty Chearfull & seems strong, but has no appetite, sleeps badly, & his leggs are swell'd & turn's blackish, & the Doctor gives no hopes of him, but he seems not to think himself in so much danger.' He died a week later, leaving his estate of Povey to his brother. Francis's other brother, George the India merchant, also died before him, in 1745. He had bought land at Whiston near Rotherham, which he too bequeathed to Francis. This is still part of the Renishaw estate.

❧

Since he was a young man, Francis had abominated the Stuart pretenders and their popish supporters. The handwritten draft of a pamphlet which he wrote, *Defence of our Penal Laws*, survives, but was probably never published. (It strongly supports measures that banned Catholics from celebrating Mass or holding public office.) In 1745 he contributed £60 for defending England against Bonnie Prince Charlie. No doubt he was terrified when, in December, the Jacobite army occupied Derby for three days.

❧

Francis died suddenly in May 1753 on a visit to London, of an attack of asthma at his lodgings in Warwick Court, and was buried at Eckington. An obituary in the *London Evening Post* of 29 June describes him as 'immensely rich . . . A Gentleman in whom (as with the greatest Truth it may be said) real and unaffected Piety and Virtue, various and extensive Learning, strict Honour and Integrity, great Candour and Humanity, and the most extensive Charity, were eminently conspicuous.' The deceased had been, added the enthusiastic obituarist, 'a publick Blessing'.

Francis Sitwell had been a worthy steward of Renishaw who enlarged the estate by buying Plumbley Hall and the manor of Morton. He had also made shrewd investments, such as two entire shares in New River stock. Despite his fine mind and strong character, he is the least interesting of the eighteenth-century squires, but this may be because we do not know enough about him.

Chapter 4

THE MERCHANT SQUIRE

The man who succeeded Francis as squire of Renishaw was a younger brother of the other Francis Sitwell, the rich Sheffield attorney.

Born in 1697, a younger son of a younger son, William Sitwell can never have expected – even into early middle age – that he would inherit Renishaw, although he had other, if somewhat distant, expectations of an inheritance from his mother, Mary Reresby, who belonged to an ancient, well-to-do family of Derbyshire landowners, the Reresbys of Thrybergh. Nor can William have supposed that his elder brother Francis would die young.[1]

William had gone to London where, in the Sitwell tradition of younger sons entering trade, he was apprenticed to an ironmonger – no doubt because of his father's contacts with Sheffield manufacturers. Eventually, he became a general merchant in partnership with the fabulously wealthy William Parkin, the offices of Messrs, Parkin & Sitwell being at the White Lyon in Foster Lane. In consequence, William made a fortune, especially after Parkin's death in 1746, ending as one of the richest men in the City.

Among other business enterprises, he underwrote shipping. In about 1960, two old tin boxes bearing his name were found in the vaults of the Goldsmiths' Company in London. Among the papers they contained was a batch of documents concerning a legal action he had brought over a vessel that sank in harbour before even setting sail. He won the case with full compensation.

Plainly, he enjoyed the London of Hogarth and Canaletto – dirty, dangerous and beautiful – and liked to relax at Child's Coffee House near St Paul's Cathedral. In those days the City contained mansions besides offices and warehouses, and his residence, No. 6 Aldermanbury in Dyer's Court, was probably inherited from a kinsman. Pulled down in the 1880s, this had been a large building with a courtyard entered through a large archway with high, wooden doors that were closed after nightfall.

A prominent philanthropist, William subscribed to many charities. In 1753 he became a governor of St Bartholomew's Hospital and, two years later, of Christ's, while in 1757 he was elected honorary auditor general of the royal hospitals of Bridewell and Bethlem, a post he retained until his death. He also contributed to a fund for educating clergymen's orphans, and to another for helping crippled merchant seamen.

***

Already well into middle age, William Sitwell's prospects were transformed by the death of his elder brother. As Francis had been a bachelor, William inherited his substantial fortune as well as becoming the heir to Renishaw. For the moment, it did not make much difference to William's habits, although he regularly visited Derbyshire, and in June 1746 he organised Cousin Jane Sacheverell's funeral, sending an account of the arrangement to Renishaw.

Despite his absorbing London life, when he became squire William made Renishaw his home, although he kept on his house in Dyer's

Court. He had known Renishaw since he was a boy, having been on friendly terms with Squire Francis, who while his brother was still alive had promised to leave him £30,000. He did not make many changes, but ensured the hall and estate were well run, appointing as his land agent a Mr Foxlowe – son of the Master of Chesterfield Grammar School. Yet, while a Justice of the Peace and a Deputy Lieutenant, he took no interest in county affairs, and paid £500 to avoid serving as High Sheriff – an honour avidly sought by his predecessors.

No sportsman, his relaxations were music and the theatre – especially music. He played the flute, hautboy (oboe) and violin. Fortunately he had an heir who shared these tastes: his nephew, Francis Hurt, his widowed sister Catherine's son. On Francis reaching the age of twenty-one in 1749, William, who by then was well over fifty, formally adopted him as his son, with an allowance of £400 a year. When Francis's mother died in 1754 and he was left without a home, his uncle invited him to live at Renishaw in summer and Dyer's Court in winter.

As music lovers who played the same instruments and gave music parties, they got on well. At Renishaw they entertained the kindred named by William in a will he made in 1773 – such cousins as the Reresbys, Phippses, Allestrees, Shirecliffes, Shepherds and Stathams. The pair went regularly to the new assembly rooms and theatre at Sheffield, while from London they visited Bath or other fashionable watering places.

<hr>

William's health began to fail him in his seventies, and for the last two years of his life he stayed in London apart from rare visits to Bath for the waters. During this time Renishaw Hall was let to Mr and Mrs Clay of Bridgehouses. William died at Dyer's Court in April 1776 in his eightieth year, with the *York Chronicle* for 3 May recording that he had been buried with great pomp in the family vault in Derbyshire. 'Mr Sitwell is said to have died worth 400,000 *l*.' says the article, adding, 'He had 30,000 *l*. in an iron chest when he died.' Other reports put his wealth as high as £500,000.

Sadly, few of William Sitwell's letters survive, and no portrait, so that he is the most shadowy of all the squires of Renishaw. But he had taken excellent care of the house and the estate, besides enormously increasing the family fortunes, a legacy that would benefit succeeding generations and transform the house. A particularly attractive feature of his character was his happy relationship with his heir.

❧

Although you can still feel fairly close to the eighteenth-century Sitwells, at both Renishaw Hall and Eckington church, you can only do so up to a point. Despite all their shrewdness, benevolence and cultivation, these last members of the direct Sitwell male line are no more than ghostly phantoms in a charming landscape.

Chapter 5

PASSING ON THE TORCH

William Sitwell's heir, Francis Hurt of Hesley Hall near Sheffield, belonged to a family of small Yorkshire landowners. Until now, its sole member of note had been Francis's grandfather, employed as a land agent by Thomas Wentworth, Earl of Strafford – Charles I's great minister.[1]

An only son, born at Sheffield in 1728, Francis lost his father Jonathan Hurt when he was three and was brought up by his mother and grandmother. Medium-sized and stocky, with a noticeably blunt, no-nonsense sort of face, he grew to be a steady, capable man who had no difficulty in handling his affairs and money, although there was never any question of his earning a living. He also developed a sensitive, imaginative side, becoming the first aesthete to live at Renishaw. His taste has been underrated by later generations.

At the time of his birth his parents lived in the High Street near Sheffield's parish church, but soon after Jonathan's death in 1731 Catherine Hurt moved with her mother to a large house close to the Lady's Bridge, not far from the ruins of Sheffield Castle.

Despite being a smoke-filled manufacturing place whose prosperity came from high-quality knives – Horace Walpole called it 'one of the foulest towns in England' – Sheffield was surrounded by beautiful countryside. In winter the local gentry flocked there, renting houses or apartments, as they would otherwise have been prevented from visiting each other by the dreadful roads.

Francis received a good education in Latin, Greek, French and mathematics, probably at Chesterfield Grammar School. His uncle Francis left him £500, with the proviso that some should be used to pay for his schooling, while as a boy he often visited Renishaw. Almost certainly he was taught music, since he learned to play the 'German Flute' and the violin, accomplishments that gave him pleasure for the rest of his life. In addition, he had lessons from an art master, developing a gift for figure drawing in pen or pencil.

As a very young man he paid a subscription to the Sheffield Assemblies, to join in the weekly minuets or card games (ombre and piquet) that took place on three nights during the Sheffield Races and the Cutlers' Feast. He also subscribed to the York Assemblies. He had more serious interests, however, visiting art galleries and artists' studios, while he may have travelled in France in the early 1750s, inspired by a love of French literature.

In common with more than a few Derbyshire gentry, Francis was a secret Jacobite who drank the King-over-the-Water's health, passing his wine glass over a finger-bowl. At seventeen, he must have deplored Prince Charles Edward's decision to turn back from Derby in 1745 and withdraw to Scotland, even if not prepared to risk his life by joining him. How he derived his opinions is unknown, but plainly he kept them secret from his staunchly Whig Sitwell kindred, as they would have jeopardised his inheritance.

His adoption by William Sitwell filled an emotional void, his uncle taking the place of the father he had never known. Together, the pair travelled all over England. In the summer of 1755 they visited Portsmouth to see Admiral Lord Anson's fleet at anchor in the harbour, twenty-nine ships of the line, then attended a reception in honour of Anson and the Duke of Cumberland. Next year they went down to Surrey to view the 'encampments' of the Guards, who were stationed there in readiness for a French invasion.

Most of their expeditions were to watering-places, not only Bath and the Hot Wells at Bristol, but Harrogate, Buxton and Scarborough (the start of a long family association). Occasionally they went back to Sheffield, as in 1755 when they attended a 'grand musical entertainment' to inaugurate a new organ at St Paul's church, where William's father had been a trustee. The winter was always spent in London, where they gave evening music parties with as many as six performing sonatas, symphonies and concertos in which William played his German flute. Both uncle and nephew enjoyed going to Child's Coffee House.

In 1766, when nearly forty, while taking the waters Francis met Mary Warneford, the 'Beauty of Bath', a bluestocking or '*précieuse*' who shared his love of music. Her father was a canon of York, her uncle squire of Warneford Place, a great Elizabethan manor house in Wiltshire, and her cousin a colonel in the army. The next year, the couple were married at Clifton near Bristol.

They began their married life at Little Sheffield, a village a mile outside the town, from which it was separated by Sheffield Moor (where the races were run). They often took part in the Renishaw music parties. Three sons and a daughter were born, a relative pinning a banknote to the eldest boy's christening robe. There were others, who died in infancy.

Francis enjoyed attending York Assembly Rooms, and for the

winter of 1773 he rented a house in Bootham Bar, bringing his furniture. He was a fop, a portrait painted by his friend Nathan Drake showing him in a suit of light blue satin trimmed with silver, while he owned others of superfine green cloth, of Tyrian Bloom (purple red), of white with silver buttons and of pea-green kerseymere with silver-wire buttons. Even before succeeding to his inheritance, he dressed his servants in the green and yellow Sitwell livery.

He and his wife were often with his uncle William, at Renishaw and in London. While the young couple visited Scarborough in the summer of 1774, they kept their affection for Bath, where they had first met, wintering there from October 1774 to January 1775.

Francis got on well with his Warneford in-laws, from the evidence of a silhouette from the 1770s by Francis Torond, a leading 'profilist' at Bath. At the left, the old couple sit at a tripod tea-table; Francis stands at the right, showing his watch to his baby daughter on his wife's knee, with a small girl behind him. On the far right his young son and heir, who has tactfully been given Sitwell as a first name, plays with a dog.

⬥

Francis was with his uncle William when he died in 1776. After the funeral, he and his wife moved into Renishaw Hall. That same year a certain Mrs Bagshaw is recorded as observing, 'Renishaw may be ye most beautiful place in Derbyshire.' Yet the new squire was not entirely under its spell, since he continued to spend winter months at Little Sheffield. He also spent time in London, although his residence was no longer Dyer's Court in the City, but a smart house in Audley Square in the increasingly fashionable West End.

Next year, Francis changed his name to Sitwell by royal licence, as his cousin's will stipulated that he must take the family's name and arms. Very conscious of being the Sitwells' heir, he brought back the family portraits that had been stored at Sheffield. The only change he made to the house was adding a long-vanished servants' hall and providing mahogany doors for the upstairs drawing room (formerly the 'Parlour Chamber' or best bedroom).

Yet there was a change in the atmosphere at Renishaw. Whereas Francis's Sitwell predecessors had been steady Whigs, he himself was president of the Jacobite Church and King Club. The Hurts had always been Tories and it looks as if Francis remained a supporter of the exiled Stuarts till the day he died. The portraits of William and Mary that had hung on the walls since Mr Justice Sitwell's time were thrown into a lumber room, to be replaced by paintings or prints of 'James III' and 'Charles III' – the Old and the Young Pretenders.[2]

However proud he was of Renishaw as his family seat, Francis preferred to live in Sheffield. Very rich indeed, with £22,000 a year in rents and half a million in the funds, Mr Sitwell (as he was now styled) employed the architect John Platt to build a big, square three-storey mansion on farmland on the edge of the town. Platt, who had previously worked for the Earl of Strafford on Wentworth Castle at Stainborough, was told to spare no expense.

Mount Pleasant was bigger than Renishaw at that date and was in the fashionable Adam style: red brick, with doorways and architraves of cream-coloured stone, and a particularly beautiful window over the main doorway. Inside were massive mahogany doors and plasterwork ceilings with classical motifs. An imposing stable block flanked the house, whose name alluded to the site – a hillock with pleasing vistas. Surrounded by gardens and a small park, the mansion was a landmark for every traveller driving into Sheffield along the road from London.

It must have been at Mount Pleasant that in 1787 Francis's friend, the American exile John Singleton Copley, painted the four Sitwell children. The portrait, *A Young Lady and Her Brothers*, was exhibited at the Royal Academy the same year. (Copley's most recent commission had been a portrait of George III's three youngest daughters.) Dominated by the youthful Sitwell Sitwell in hunt uniform, and emphasising that he is the heir, Copley's painting sets its subjects against a big window of a sort that did not exist in the Renishaw of that date and was probably at Mount Pleasant. The most important portrait in the entire Sitwell collection, this takes pride of place in the dining room at Renishaw, over the chimney-piece. The hills around Sheffield can be glimpsed through the window.

While using Renishaw or his London house in Audley Square as summer residences, from now on Francis Hurt Sitwell spent the winter at Mount Pleasant. Here he was able to patronise Sheffield's new assembly rooms and theatre, and the subscription library opened in 1771, while the house was ideal for music. It was easier to find tutors for his children's education – even if macadamed toll roads were starting to replace muddy trackways, Renishaw was too far off for them to go there on a daily basis.

The influence of Mount Pleasant on Sitwell Sitwell, Francis's eldest son and heir, has been overlooked. Eight years old when the family moved in to Mount Pleasant, he grew accustomed to up-to-date architecture, making him eager to modernise Renishaw. The property also alerted him to the potential of Joseph Badger, the Sheffield carpenter-turned-architect who built the stables.

Today, swallowed up by the town and standing forlornly in Sharrow Lane in a run-down area, its grounds tarmacked over apart from a patch of unkempt grass and flanked by such amenities as a halal butcher and a hairdresser, Mount Pleasant is sadly neglected. One can only hope that by some miracle it will eventually be rescued and restored. Yet even in its present state, it remains a fine piece of architecture. It is also a monument to Francis Hurt Sitwell, telling us a lot about him and about his taste.

Francis was a keen buyer of pictures – many of which were sold at the great Renishaw sale the following century – and constantly visited galleries. Sometimes Copley accompanied him to London exhibitions. The American was not his only painter friend; Nathan Drake, the son of a Nottinghamshire parson who had painted Francis in pale blue satin, produced work ranging from landscapes to portrait miniatures. Francis also bought paintings from several leading artists including the gentleman painter Henry Walton (whose *Cherry Barrow*, purchased in 1779, still hangs in the Library at Renishaw), Henry Morland, and William Marlow, who specialised in country scenes.

Francis led a vigorous social life. In 1786, with his wife and daughter, he spent the spring and summer in London. There, besides going to art exhibitions, they went to the opera and watched displays by a 'Polish dwarf' and a ventriloquist. His evenings were spent at coffee houses, or playing cards. He had brought his carriage, which sometimes conveyed them to 'routs' (dances). In the autumn they went down to Brighton and then took the waters at Bristol and Bath, before going home to Mount Pleasant for the Cutlers' Feast.

Sir William Wake long remembered Francis as 'a gentleman of the old school'. During a visit to Renishaw early in 1789, Wake, as an idealistic young Whig, told the equally youthful Sitwell Sitwell how much he welcomed the new ideas that were about to give birth to the French Revolution. '[Old] Mr Sitwell, listening with both hands on his knees, would remark, "That's your opinion is it? Well, it isn't mine."'

In September 1789 Francis took his wife and daughter to the great ball given by Earl Fitzwilliam for the Prince of Wales's visit to Wentworth Woodhouse. In 1791, the entire family attended the races at Derby. Francis was slowing up, however, and in December that year he asked for his name to be taken out of the book at the Freemasons' Tavern, as he was seldom well enough to attend meetings.

⌥

In 1791 Francis was left further valuable estates by a cousin, Samuel Phipps. Among these were lands in South Yorkshire, Barmoor Castle in Northumberland, and Ferney Hall in Shropshire. Keeping the Yorkshire property for Sitwell, Francis left Barmoor to his second son, Francis, and Ferney Hall to his third son, Hurt. This was the year, too, when the Sitwells sold the ironworks, finally parting company with the industry that had been the foundation of their fortunes.

Francis had intended that after his death Mount Pleasant should become a hospital for the use of the people of Sheffield, but he was forestalled in this by a committee of townsfolk who founded and endowed a large infirmary. Instead, he bequeathed a large sum to the new establishment. Eventually, the house was sold to a prominent local businessman who later became Master Cutter.

Why he decided to dispose of a mansion on which he had lavished so much care, and where he had lived for fifteen years, is a mystery. Perhaps he was disillusioned by the rapid growth in Sheffield's population and the new factories that were making the air 'smokier' than ever. He may have decided that, all things considered, he preferred the beauties of Renishaw. The most likely explanation, however, is that he realised his son was a countryman who did not enjoy living in towns.

⌥

Mrs Hurt Sitwell died at the house in Audley Square in July 1792. Her husband did not long survive her, dying at Brompton, where he had gone for a change of air, on 16 August 1793. He had ensured that the Hurts would carry on the Sitwell line, and that Renishaw would be in good hands.

Chapter 6

A REGENCY BUCK

The new squire, aged twenty-four in 1793, was Frances Hurt Sitwell's son, Sitwell Sitwell – the most dynamic of them all, an autocrat bursting with energy. His 'Christian' name had been bestowed without anyone realising it would also become his surname, but he bore it with aplomb. He was middle-sized, high-shouldered, yellow-haired and handsome; we know what he looked like in the prime of life from a portrait bust by Francis Chantrey (modelled on a death mask) which gives him a great beak of a nose, arrogant eyes and a ferocious air of command. Even so, he had plenty of charm – when he cared to use it.

Although he died in the first year of the Regency, often his behaviour was that of a classic Regency Buck. *The Sporting Magazine* for November 1798 reports a characteristic exploit – how, with his harriers, he hunted down and killed a 'Royal Bengal Tiger' that had escaped from a circus at Sheffield, some hounds losing their lives. He was much admired for his stud, whose horses won many trophies. Yet at the same time he possessed impeccable taste in architecture and pictures. Above all, he was determined to cut a figure in the world.

So it was surprising that, while an Oxford undergraduate, Sitwell Sitwell should fall in love with Alice Parke, who was the daughter of an obscure Liverpool merchant. To make him forget her he was sent on the Grand Tour; but at Constantinople he received a letter from a meddling old aunt, Miss Warneford, telling him she had died, whereupon he rushed back to England – to find her very much alive. His father relenting, they were married in August 1791. In a portrait by William Beechey, Alice has fine blue eyes and a sweet expression. Clever, gentle, she charmed everybody. Two daughters were born, although it was some time before she produced an heir.

When his father died, Sitwell Sitwell contemplated buying Clumber Park, the Duke of Newcastle's gigantic mansion in Nottinghamshire; but he decided instead to enlarge and modernise Renishaw, which was very little since the day it had been built. 'This Mansion is a good specimen of the ancient mode of constructing houses,' the *Universal Magazine* for 1796 informs us, somewhat patronisingly.

'The ground plan is nearly that of an H,' it continues. 'The body of the house is embattled, and an old projecting tower is the principal doorway.' As for the setting, 'The grounds are disposed in the now exploded fashion, with obelisks placed formally at equal distances, and a fine avenue of old trees extends in a line from the house. This taste, perhaps, corresponds better with the antique appearance of the building than would the now prevailing mode of ornamenting our gardens.'

Sitwell began by giving the Library (formerly the Great Parlour) new bookcases, with carved friezes ornamented with masks and flowers. Over the next fifteen years he added a dining room, a great drawing room (nearly seventy feet long), a billiard room and a ballroom, with more rooms above. Neoclassical stables were built on the site of Wigfall's house, and in the grounds a 'Gothick Temple' and a 'Gothick Lodge' – for which his initial, hand-drawn sketch survives. Other additions were the icehouse and the dairy cottage, all probably designed by Sitwell himself and erected by Joseph Badger. Yet another was a Gothic entrance porch. The temple, originally glass-covered, served as a conservatory.

Throughout, he kept a sharp eye on the workmen. 'I know if not watched, they will put the beams near chimneys,' he wrote to his steward John Gilliatt in 1806. 'They are as prone to do it as drink at a beer barrel. I found it so when my back was turned. I know Badger's obstinacy of old.'[1] For Sitwell was terrified of fire. In 1804, he had given strict orders to the housekeeper Mrs Rotherham that she must keep the fires small in all grates – they burned coal, not wood – and ensure they were put out by 9.30 every evening, besides ensuring that chimneys were swept regularly.

The first new room to be completed was the dining room, on the site of the Green Court of the 1625 garden. Perhaps inspired by the one at Kedleston not far away, this had a semi-circular alcove that contained a crescent-shaped buffet table, an ornamental ceiling and stucco dados.

'On Friday last a very splendid entertainment was given at Renishaw Hall in the county, by Sitwell Sitwell, Esq., on the occasion of the opening of a very noble room which has lately been built in addition to his house,' reported the *Derby Mercury* for 12 November 1795. 'Among a very numerous assemblage who graced the meeting were Lord and Lady Effingham, Ladies Sherborne and Hunloke, with several of the respectable families and individuals within a large area of the place.' The report comments that

> the brilliance of the room, the fashion and taste of the
> company, the sumptuousness and elegance of the supper
> and, above all, the easy, polite and engaging attention
> shown by Mr and Mrs Sitwell to every individual . . .

were rarely exceeded, either in this or any part of the kingdom.

When the Great Drawing Room and the ballroom were completed, he installed marble chimney-pieces by Sir William Chambers (which he had bought at the Duke of York's sale at York House in May 1802), adorning them with five huge tapestries by the Brussels *tapissier* Judocus de Vos, based on allegorical designs by Charles Le Brun, Louis XIV's court painter. They 'haunt these rooms with a plumy exoticism of pearls and elephants, garden vistas and trophies', wrote his great-great-grandson Osbert.[2]

Sitwell showed no less magnificence in his choice of paintings, purchasing a Perugino, *The Three Maries*, painted about 1500. This may have come from a sale of pictures owned by the Duc d'Orléans, Philippe Égalité, who had recently perished beneath the guillotine. It was hung over the fireplace in the Great Parlour, replacing the old oak carving of Isaac and Abraham (this was later made into the back of a 'settle', now in the hall).

Another acquisition from the York House sale was a superb commode, which some experts consider to be the most beautiful piece of furniture ever made in England. The first Viscount Melbourne (father of the Prime Minister) had commissioned it in about 1774 from Thomas Chippendale, who added ormolu mounts cast by Matthew Boulton and inlaid it with vignettes by the Swede Fuhlvohg. It is now in the Great Drawing Room.[3] He also acquired two exceptionally fine eighteenth-century commodes by the great Milanese *ebanista* Giuseppe Maggiolini, who had worked for the Habsburgs.

Sitwell Sitwell's taste in pictures, furniture and tapestries was impeccable. His reliance on his own idea of what was beautiful, instead of depending entirely on the fashion of the day, would be inherited by later owners of Renishaw. It is this element of personal choice that makes the collection here so different from those at other great houses.

Sadly, his taste failed him out of doors, save for moving the road further away. The lengthened frontage created by new rooms gave the house's north side a stretched-out look, with a bleak, even sinister appearance; and he was notably unsuccessful in replacing the ancient formal gardens by what was intended to be a fashionable Capability Brown 'field'. The low walls and little courts were levelled and the flowerbeds removed, even the tiny bowling green disappearing, to give way to broad expanses of turf, the 'pleasure grounds'. The only survival from the old layout was the long lime avenue on the Top Lawn, to the south-east of the house.

Eager to become the first Sitwell to sit in Parliament, in 1795 Sitwell wrote to the Duke of Portland (who was his neighbour at Welbeck) asking if he would find him a seat. In response, the duke invited him to come down to London and discuss the matter. As a result, from 1796 until 1802 Sitwell sat for the rotten borough of West Looe in Cornwall, although it is unlikely that he ever visited his constituency.

He did not always support the government, voting at the end of 1796 for Charles James Fox's motion against giving subsidies to Britain's allies without Parliamentary approval. None of his speeches has survived, but he must have delivered a fair number, since a political journal, *The True Briton*, described him as a good man for a long debate. His name became well known at 10 Downing Street, and in 1802 Portland recommended him for a baronetcy, without success.

At the general election of 1807 Sitwell Sitwell helped Earl Fitzwilliam's twenty-one-year-old son, Lord Milton, to win a seat in the Commons as one of two MPs for Yorkshire. The two sitting members were William Wilberforce, the great slavery abolitionist, and Lord Harewood's son, Henry Lascelles. There had not been a contested election in the county since 1748, and this was the most expensive ever known, the three candidates spending £250,000 between them in an orgy of bribery.

'Though Milton is in the rear, his case is by no means lost: he has a considerable strength left, much greater than his antagonist, and sufficient to carry the election: but of course it will be hard run and a single vote may carry him the seat,' Fitzwilliam wrote anxiously to Sitwell from Wentworth Woodhouse on 30 May. 'I cannot refrain from begging you to add to the strength you have sent to his support by going to York to give your own vote. Are there any gleanings of voters in your neighbourhood to be picked up?' Wilberforce won, with 11,808 votes, and Lord Milton came second with 11,177 – only 177 more than his opponent, Lascelles.[4]

Sitwell had worked hard to ensure Lord Milton's election, which attracted a great deal of attention, and Portland, now Prime Minister, saw that he got his baronetcy the following year. However, family tradition prefers to believe it was to acknowledge a ball he gave in 1808 for the Prince of Wales (later Prince Regent), who also sent him a bust of his daughter, Princess Charlotte. No doubt, Sir Sitwell showed his guest an ornament in the new ballroom's stucco ceiling – all part of Badger's work – which had the Feathers of the Prince of Wales as its centrepiece. Later he was presented to Queen Charlotte, disgracing himself by sneezing when he kissed her snuff-stained hand.

<hr/>

He had been presented to the Prince on the racecourse, his colours of green with an orange cap being a familiar sight at every important meeting, while his stud was renowned. He 'was much interested in breeding and very successful with his horses', says his granddaughter. 'I know that he gave one horse to the Prince Regent, with whom he had some acquaintance, if not friendship.'[5] She recalls 'nine gold racing cups – real cups, the shape and size of old-fashioned tea-urns – which used to stand upon the dining-room buffet'.

Sport had replaced politics as Sitwell's road to distinction. He took his thoroughbreds' training very seriously indeed, with a private race-course at Renishaw. A letter to his trainer with instructions for engaging a new jockey reveals him at his most demanding. 'The person will have frequently to write to Sir S.S., so must be able to write himself. No hints to be given to others, of trials or of anything of the kind, or of any merits of your horses.'

He describes further essential qualities:

> The reason Sir S.S. parted with so valuable a jockey and trainer as Wilkinson, evidently shows that Sir S.S. will keep no man likely to get into scrapes or quarrels . . . Wilkinson had 40 guineas a year . . . He rode my horses and trained them but did nothing without consulting me always . . . and however he might differ from me in opinion, he always to the best of his powers rode to orders.

The letter ends, 'My house is a very regular one, and no disturbance or drinking is allowed.'[6]

This high moral tone is ironical, in view of the writer's private life. In 1797 Alice had given him a son and heir, the birth hastened by her having witnessed a violent quarrel between Sitwell and his rakehell brother Frank. She appeared to be recovering well, so her husband went off to a distant race-meeting. However, she fell fatally ill as soon as he left. Knowing she would never see him again, Alice wrote a farewell letter that overwhelmed the widower with grief when he returned to find her dead. Nevertheless, during the same year her lady's maid, Sarah Harris, gave birth to a son by him.

Fourteen months after Alice's death he remarried, choosing a bride from a sound landed background – the nineteen-year-old Caroline Stovin, daughter of the late James Stovin of Whitgift Hall near Doncaster. Tall and striking, it was said that in the classical gowns of the Regency she looked like a Sybil from antiquity. Her only child, a girl, died in infancy, so she treated her stepchildren as her own – George Sitwell was thirteen before he learned she was not his real mother. Always quoting from books, Caroline was a bluestocking; while kind to her, Sitwell shared neither her taste for literature nor her liking for literary lions.

Meanwhile, he kept on Sarah Harris as his mistress. A farmer's daughter from Slitting Mill Farm nearby, who now called herself 'Mrs Dixon', she could sometimes prove an embarrassment. When he took her to see his legitimate son George at school in 1809, the boys yelled, 'Strumpet! Strumpet!'

***

Although no letters to his wives or children survive, we have one to a brother that lets us hear Sir Sitwell's voice. The brother was Francis Sitwell of Barmoor Castle, briefly MP for Berwick, who despite an ample estate was always in financial difficulties from reckless extravagance on hounds, betting, or rebuilding his castle in the Gothic style. Neighbours called him 'Frank the Gambler'. He wrote again and again to Sir Sitwell, demanding money to pay his creditors, threatening to kill himself if committed to a debtor's prison.

On 29 August 1810 Sir Sitwell replied,

> You have sent me a letter which you call your finale, full of scurrility and only worthy of yourself and like many previous productions . . . I am now, with this, fully determined to close all future communication with you directly and indirectly. I shall, on your Solicitor certifying that the sum of £2,000 will extricate you from your difficulties (which you have stated to Mr Thomas to be your last), order such sum to be paid. But I mean it to be fully understood by you, that this sum, together with £100 sent (after deducting the £30 to Mr Milford's Bank which I have promised to pay) finally closes every communication whatever between us.[7]

Sir Sitwell liked to entertain lavishly, giving routs in Renishaw's new ballroom. One was a masked ball at which a strikingly handsome young guest in a powdered wig, wearing a rose-coloured velvet suit of George II's time, was observed to have strangely pale lips and forehead. Dancing with him, girls found themselves chilled to the bone by his cold hands despite his gloves. He never spoke a word. Next day, his partners thought he had looked like the Verelst portrait – supposedly the Sacheverell who drowned in the River Rother.

In later years, Sir Sitwell was not only a martyr to gout, but hurt his back so badly by falling off a chair that he gave up hunting. One July evening in 1811, going down to the meadows by the river to show a friend some cattle he had bought, he caught a chill. Three days later, he died at forty-two from what doctors obscurely termed 'gout in the head'. During the last few hours, he had been delirious, shouting, 'Caroline! Caroline!'

A century later, Osbert Sitwell heard how his great-great grandfather could still be heard calling for his wife as he lay dying in a great four-poster bed, curtained and plumed – downstairs, in one of the big new rooms. On the night he died, his ghost was seen at Sheffield. That night, too, when his coffin lay in the library and while the servants were at supper, a kinswoman sitting alone in the hall (next to the library) heard the bell ring faintly at the front door. Opening it, holding up a lamp, she claimed to have seen Sir Sitwell, who stared at her before vanishing into the dark.

⁕

Despite his overbearing manner, Sitwell had been much liked. 'Sir Sitwell was a very warm hearted, open handed man, very popular, though he was very strict with poachers and liked to have a great quantity of hares,' his granddaughter Georgiana was told by his physician, Dr Askham. 'He had a very strong will and a hot temper, very affectionate to his children and devoted to his first wife, and also to his second.' He was genuinely benevolent. 'The Hon. Baronet pre-eminently distinguished himself on all occasions by showering his benevolence and charity on the virtuous, needy and afflicted part of his fellow creatures,' commented the *Sheffield Iris*. 'His premature death will be long and sincerely regretted by many good men.'

Providing too generously in his will for his daughters, and for his illegitimate son George Harris (apprenticed to an apothecary) and his descendants (one of whom was receiving payments as late as 1909), Sir Sitwell left a seriously encumbered estate. Instructing his trustees to buy the manorial rights of Eckington from the crown at a ruinous price made matters worse. He had already spent too much on bailing out Frank – who outlived him by three years, despite all those threats to commit suicide, and was still in possession of Barmoor.

Yet, in transforming Renishaw Hall, Sitwell Sitwell left a lasting monument.

Chapter 7

RUIN?

Sitwell Sitwell's son, the first Sir George, inherited Renishaw in 1811 at fourteen. He was a sickly child and too delicate for Eton. Yet he grew to be six feet tall and strong enough to go up to Trinity College, Cambridge. He was protected by his adoring stepmother, who took a dramatic attitude to widowhood, wearing a veil of black gauze that hid her features and went down to her feet. Caroline did not remarry until 1821, when George had grown up and was himself married – her second husband being a Nottingham banker, John Smith-Wright.

Slender, shy and badly lacking in self-confidence, George had no trace of Sitwell Sitwell's dynamism.[1] Even so, when he contested Chesterfield – unsuccessfully, in the 1832 election – he was addressed by supporters of his Whig opponent with the words, 'Thou art the King of Tories, O Geordie, the fox-hunting son of a cock-fighting father.' This was in a book called *Figaro in Chesterfield*, which was entirely devoted to abuse of Sir George and his followers.[2]

When twenty-one, George acquired a small pack of harriers that he kennelled at Renishaw, often hunting foxes instead of hares. They were replaced in 1823 by a pack of foxhounds, and shortly afterwards he became master of a subscription pack at Whiston near Rotherham, within hacking distance of Renishaw. (A pub at Whiston is still called the Sitwell Arms.) Although an excellent horseman, with such sensitive hands that horses always behaved quietly under him, his hunting was of 'the old scientific sort', his daughter recalled; by which she meant that he preferred hound-work – watching hounds puzzle out a difficult scent – to hard riding and jumping fences.[3]

An 1820s group portrait of the young baronet with his adoring wife and small children, painted by the much-in-vogue John Partridge (who would one day become 'Portrait Painter Extraordinary' to Queen Victoria), hangs today in the dining room at Renishaw. Sir George proudly wears a pink coat, with the period's blue 'bird's eye' hunting stock. The portrait may have been commissioned to celebrate his acquiring a new pack of foxhounds; however, the family did not like the picture, and relegated it to a passage.

George preferred another sporting artist whom he had personally discovered. This was J. F. Herring Sr, who became one of the nineteenth century's great animal painters and, like Partridge, was patronised by Queen Victoria. Travelling on board a mail coach in about the year 1820, George sat next to the driver, who showed him some drawings. It was the young Herring, then a sign painter and part-time coachman living at Doncaster. Recognising the drawings' quality, Sir George promptly offered him the use of a stable at Renishaw as a studio and lent him a dog-cart to roam Northern England in search of commissions.

He commissioned Herring to paint one of his first major works. This was a picture of Sir George, with the huntsman and the whipper-in, all wearing green hare-hunting coats, mounted on their horses in front of the Renishaw harriers. The green coats suggest that it was done during George's harrier days, predating the Partridge portrait.

In the same sporting spirit George bought travelling carriages of the latest design, always drawn by high-bred bays – in deliberate contrast to the Renishaw cart-horses, which were grays. All his vehicles were painted green, and his coachmen and grooms wore green livery. His dashing 'high-flyer' phaeton, fast and dangerous with four huge wheels, was much admired. It had four bays between the shafts and two postilions wearing dark green jackets, yellow striped waistcoats and black velvet jockey-caps. Accompanied by Lady Sitwell and escorted by outriders in green, George drove it to the local race meetings.

Yet he was no mere hunting squire. 'My father had the simplest tastes,' his daughter Georgiana recalled. 'Indeed, we often thought that he would have made a capital explorer in new countries and would have been quite happy in such a life.'[4] He attended church twice on Sundays, and barely touched alcohol. His real passions were botany and geology.

As early as 1823 he began collecting plants seriously. The great Joseph Paxton sent him rare specimens from the hothouses at Chatsworth, while the botanist Gideon Mantell (better known as a fossil hunter) became a close friend. He also knew Dr Hooker, the director of Kew Gardens. Although he did not recreate the gardens vandalised by his father, he was a keen horticulturist. His gardener, Alexander Lambie, made Renishaw Hall celebrated for its hothouses' early-ripening grapes and peaches, as well as beautiful chrysanthemums. Later, Sir George and Lambie's successor, McLaurin, were particularly proud of making a breadfruit tree in one of the hothouses bear fruit. In addition, George was an enthusiastic ornithologist, assembling a collection of stuffed rare birds in glass cases.

In 1818 George had married a Scots girl, Susan Tait, whose father belonged to a family of Edinburgh lawyers, the Taits of Harviestoun. The couple enjoyed an idyllic family life, producing four sons and five daughters, although some of the children died in infancy. Susan was very pretty, pale-skinned, with large, 'happy' blue eyes, auburn curls and a light, graceful figure. She was well read, with a taste for history. She started the first Sunday school at Eckington, in which she took a keen interest, as well as encouraging a local dame's school founded by the Sitwells.

Susan introduced George to the Highlands, where he became one of the first English sportsmen to appreciate the shooting – grouse being shot over the dogs, instead of from butts. From 1830 until 1845 he annually leased houses there, first at Kinrara near Aviemore, then at Birkhall on Deeside, and finally Balmoral (before Queen Victoria rebuilt it). Each year there was a migration from Renishaw: servants, dogs, wardrobes, furniture, wine and provisions travelled by ship from Hull to Aberdeen, while the family travelled overland in a 'caravan' of three carriages.

A less happy consequence of the marriage was invasion by penniless Tait relations, who moved into Renishaw. Sir George did not have the heart to turn them out, and his generosity helped to ruin him. One of the tribe was definitely worthwhile, however: Susan's motherless, disabled youngest brother Archibald, who was four years old at the time she married and from then on lived under her care. When she died half a century later and he was Archbishop of Canterbury, he wrote that she had been a second mother to him and Renishaw his second home.[5] Sir George had found bone-setters who cured his lameness – otherwise, Archibald would have been barred from a career in the Church.

An indication of the Sitwells' standing in Derbyshire society was their friendship with the county's greatest magnate, the Duke of Devonshire, helped by a shared passion for horticulture. Godfather to Sir George's eldest son, the 'bachelor Duke' (once a suitor of Byron's mistress, Lady Caroline Lamb) often stayed at Renishaw, where a bedroom is still called the Duke's Room. George and his wife were invited to the ball he gave at Chatsworth in 1832 for Princess Victoria and her mother, the Duchess of Kent. Under the benevolent eye of the duke, who was Lord Chamberlain, the couple were presented at court to William IV and Queen Adelaide.

❦

The third of Sir George's five daughters, Georgiana (whom he called 'Georgie'), has left an account of life at Renishaw when she was a young girl during the 1830s and 1840s. It reads like an early Victorian novel, and is a testimony to the amazing spell that Renishaw cast over those who lived there. A natural writer, Georgiana had a gift for atmosphere and a touching rustic elegance. Later, the journal was given a charming title, *The Dew it lyes on the Wood*. It is the first description we have of family life at the Hall. Her father emerges as gentle, pious and scholarly, much loved by those who knew him.

Among her topics are 'mummers' – 'a village church in the 1830s' – 'the aristocratic poor' – 'governesses and other tortures of childhood' – 'the novels of Charles Dickens' – 'Frank Sitwell the rake and his two similar returns after death' – 'charades; the best actors' – 'the 5th Duke of Portland as a boy' – 'Apparition of a Red Indian' – 'the Servants' Ball' – and 'the coming of the railways'.

Georgiana's wistful nostalgia is very apparent when she describes the Sitwells rambling together around Renishaw on summer evenings. 'It was a real family walk,' she writes.

> My mother on her pony, my dear father and all the train of children with their pet lambs and pet red deer, sallied off together down the lower flower garden, across the brook, into the park, over the hill then dotted with many horse-chestnuts, flowering thorns and crab-apples, down the green lanes to Foxton Wood; or, still

more often, into the meadows by the river. Foxton Dam was then very pretty, and we often used to take lunch there and row about. The Rother then ran its natural course, twisting and doubling over acres of beautiful turf as fine as any lawn, between many fine oaks and willows. My parents came home for dinner at eight or later, but we only returned to family prayers in the hall, and then to bed.[6]

She is at her lyrical best in recalling the celebrations that she and her brothers and sisters organised for their parents' wedding anniversary:

The happiest festival of the year to us – even happier than Christmas or the New Year – was our father and mother's wedding day, on the first of June; though sometimes we celebrated it later. At that season of the year, the park and garden were all ablaze with flowering shrubs, rhododendrons, white, pink and scarlet haw-thorn, white and scarlet horse-chestnut blossoms, lilacs, laburnums, syringas, snowballs and wild crab, which scented the air with their fragrance. Of these we made garlands interspersed with roses and honeysuckle, and covered up with them an old summer-house, the scene of the festivity. This stood in the park beyond the elms and lime avenues, against the wood through which a carriage drive leads to Chesterfield. The old sycamores and limes behind the arbour were hung with wreaths, and tethered to them with long lines were to be seen our pet lambs, of which we usually had two or three, and our graceful red deer hinds. Suspended from the branches were numerous cages of turtle doves, canaries and any other pet birds we happened to possess. Late in the afternoon our father and mother came to the bower, in which was a table covered with our little presents, some of which had taken half the year to prepare – drawings, work, copied music, books bought with our pocket-money. Here we drank their healths, and they drank ours: and the day concluded with a servants' dance, begun before sunset and carried on by moonlight on the lawn in front of the house.[7]

A sadness Georgiana does not dwell on is the death of her little brother Campbell ('Cammy'), who had been so attached to their father that he followed him around everywhere, just like a small dog. But she conjures up the isolation of a girl's life at Renishaw in the 1830s and 1840s:

> When I recall our young days, the extreme ignorance of the world that characterised all our ideas makes me smile. We read a good deal of poetry, of Tennyson, Wordsworth, Byron, Gray and Shelley, and parodied some of their poems in our schoolroom newspaper. But, like other young people of our position whose home was in the country, we lived so simply, read so few novels, heard so little gossip or discussion of other people's affairs, that we lived in an ideal world and could not see life as it really was. There were no scandal-mongering journals such as exist today, newspapers were not considered quite suitable for young ladies, and only the political and historical articles in them were read to us.[8]

Georgiana disliked the impact of industry since her childhood in the 1830s, the 'ugliness that has swallowed up the country' – tall chimneys, monstrous buildings and factories, filthy railway stations and coal mines, all pouring forth black smoke. 'What shall we say, too, of the discordant noises that now assail our ears?' she laments.

> Instead of the gentle rumbling of the distant coach, the patter of trotting horses, and the soft music of the guard's horn as the traveller passed on to some wayside inn trellised with flowers or fruit trees, or to some busy market town, we have the rattle of the train, the snorting of the engine, the hideous screech of the whistle. Truly from many tracts of country the glory of beauty has departed.[9]

Yet she watched with fascination the making of the railway through the park at Renishaw in the mid-1840s, when she was eleven or twelve years old – and the navvies who did the work. 'We used to meet scores of them in all our walks, very fine young men (from Lincolnshire, I believe) and picturesquely dressed in white shirts or smock frocks, and red ties. They drank beer, ate four pounds of meat a day, and fought with their fists.' These navvies were loathed by the locals, and one of them was mysteriously murdered – horribly slashed across the back with a scythe.[10]

Violence was very much a part of rural life in those days. 'People of any rank who *really knew* my father were very much attached to him, and he was very much attached to them,' she told her nephew George Sitwell in 1881. He was distraught when a young gamekeeper was dangerously shot by a poacher. 'The man suffered very much pain, and

I remember my father coming out of the room in the stables where he was lying, with the tears running down his cheeks.'[11]

⁓⁓⁓

Georgiana's paradise eventually came to a sudden end. Osbert Sitwell says that his great-grandfather, 'though only half his father's fortune had come to him, liked to spend as much money',[12] which is unfair. Sir George's problem was bad luck rather than extravagance. In 1840, after years of wrangling in the law courts, he had to pay £40,000 to the crown for the manorial rights of Eckington; while in 1846 he found himself in serious financial trouble when the family solicitor's brother stole £35,000.

Instead of going up to Scotland that year as usual, he took his wife and daughters abroad, hoping to live on £700 a year instead of £12,000. He settled at Wiesbaden, which was the capital of the Duchy of Nassau – an independent state with its own little army of 5,000 troops. They were well received at court, the reigning duke's mother (daughter of the late King of Württemberg) giving them a pleasant welcome. Even so, as Georgiana, pining for Renishaw, tells us, 'a small German Court with its miniature ceremonies – we walked out backwards as to a sovereign – was a very little world to live in'.[13]

Sir George then found himself on the verge of total ruin when the Sheffield Land Bank suddenly failed in 1847, the day after his agent had deposited many thousands of pounds in it for him, having sold land to raise urgently needed cash. Renishaw was boarded up. Most of its pictures, plate, furniture and library were auctioned in 1849. The following year, even its woods were cut down and sold.

At Wiesbaden George was so poor that he could no longer afford a fire in winter, and living there became beyond his means in summer, when prices rose because of the tourist trade. He moved to Nice, but at the end of 1848 went back to England with his wife and daughters. A sketch of him at this period shows a shabby, bewildered wreck of a man who looks twenty years older than his real age.

Together with his family, he went to live near Windsor, then at Bognor, where, having for some time been increasingly frail, he died unexpectedly in March 1853 – to the grief of everyone who knew him.

Kind and well-meaning, Sir George's financial problems were entirely due to circumstances beyond his control. He was interred in Eckington church; during the funeral his ghost, like that of his father, was seen at Renishaw's front door. His widow never returned to the house until her own funeral in 1880, when she was laid beside him.

<hr />

The Sitwells feared, with reason, that Renishaw might be doomed. Their plight was that of landowners all over England who did not possess substantial reserves of cash, since after the recent repeal of the Corn Laws, any income from tenant farms and land values had begun to decline dramatically. Simply trying to keep up the same standard of living could – and did – lead to ruin.

During the winter of 1853, Georgiana, who was not yet married, spent several months at Renishaw with her brother, Reresby Sitwell. He had just recovered from a long fever, supposedly the result of too much walking from stall to stall during the Great Exhibition (of the Works of Industry of All Nations). The only servant in the house, apart from the odd skivvy, was an old Scots housemaid of nearly eighty, Bella Buchanan, who acted as housekeeper. 'Only seven years had passed since my father and mother had taken us abroad: but how different our lives,' wrote Georgiana. 'My dear father was dead. The house had been gutted as if by fire. Now, day and night, the trains could be heard regularly in the distance, as they passed by the edge of the park, and the black plumes of the mines were beginning to sully the air.' She was an accomplished watercolourist, and in a remarkable feat of memory, she carefully sketched the empty rooms as if their vanished furniture and pictures were still in place.

> Trying to recall the aspect of the rooms frequently carried my mind back to the old days, to all those annually recurring months of winter, spring and early summer spent at Renishaw, and I often thought of all the gaieties, as I have described them, in the old house when it was full; the Christmas festivities, with the walls and pillars of the hall festooned and twined with holly or mistletoe, the blazing coal fires so characteristic of the north country, the dancing, the games and music.[14]

The elegiac tone is unmistakable. Georgiana Sitwell believed that her beloved Renishaw was dead and gone for ever.*

---

* In 1856 Georgiana would make a very happy marriage to a prominent Edinburgh lawyer, Archibald Campbell-Swinton of Kimmerghame in Berwickshire, acquiring a fine country house of her own.

Chapter 8

CAMPING IN THE WRECKAGE

At thirty-three years old, Sir Reresby had a daunting inheritance. For once, we can believe Osbert Sitwell unreservedly when he says that shutting up Renishaw and selling off so much of its contents had been a shattering blow to his grandfather.[1]

Reresby was a good-looking young man, to judge from a sketch of him in military uniform. A daguerreotype, probably taken on his honeymoon in 1857, shows a burly, virile figure with a strong face and thick hair who bears a distinct resemblance to his great-grandson (another Reresby). But despite his muscular appearance, he had wrecked his health in the Highlands by too much shooting and stalking, regardless of drenching rain, and by not bothering to eat properly.

⁂

Besides being responsible for his father's debts, Reresby had to provide for his brothers and sisters – and pay his step-grandmother, Mrs Smith-Wright, a jointure of £3,000 a year. After putting Renishaw up for sale in 1854 but failing to find a buyer, in desperation he contemplated pulling down Sitwell Sitwell's additions. He went on living there, in 'bachelor apartments' – the rest of the rooms were locked – and was looked after by old Bella. However, he frequently visited London.

He would be a shadowy figure, were it not for his wife's journals and letters. He had joined the 1st Regiment of Life Guards as a Cornet (subaltern) in March 1840, which was an expensive business. A commission in such a regiment cost £1,260; he also had to buy his uniforms and chargers, entailing an outlay several times his annual pay, and a substantial private income was needed to keep up with brother officers. Possibly because of poor health, in April 1843 Reresby 'sold out' and left the army.

In the same year, his sister Alice became engaged to a fellow cornet of horse – the future Viscount Combermere, who was heir to an estate in Shropshire. (His father, Stapleton Cotton, had been one of Wellington's generals during the Peninsular War.) Almost certainly, the couple were introduced to each other by Reresby. It was the first time a Sitwell had married into the peerage.

Ill-equipped for any other career, Sir Reresby had artistic leanings (he was a friend of John Ruskin) and was a fine watercolourist. Many of his paintings of the Highlands are still displayed at Renishaw, while he was keen enough to take lessons in London from an artist called Thomas Cafe, hiring a model for thirteen sittings. He was also a keen wood-carver, buying tools that would help him while away the time at Renishaw.

Hot-tempered, but capable of strong affection, Reresby was deeply religious. He was a friend and admirer of the great Victorian philanthropist Lord Shaftesbury, whose Low Church faith he shared. In 1857, he was lucky enough to find a soulmate.

⁂

Louisa Lucy, Rereseby's wife, has never received her full due. Although the person who emerges from her daughter Florence's journal and from her grandchildren's autobiographies was in some ways narrow-minded, there were other sides to her, often impressive. Shrewd, determined, imaginative and generous, she needs to be rescued from the caricatures of Osbert and Edith.

A beautiful Anglo-Irish girl, with delicate, aquiline features, fair hair and a speech impediment (she could not pronounce the letter R), Louisa Lucy was nervous but iron-willed. She was born in 1831, one of five daughters of Colonel the Hon. Henry Hely-Hutchinson, who fought at Waterloo and was a brother of the third Earl of Donoughmore. Brought up in considerable luxury at Weston Hall in Northamptonshire (which was her mother's family home) and at her father's London house in Brook Street, when young she enjoyed dinner parties, balls, riding in the park, and the opera. However, her enjoyment was always qualified.

She records in her diary for 25 May 1857:

> went down to Maidenhead to Burnham Beeches, a little crowd of 40 people, the country looked so beautiful and it was the strangest, merriest party I ever knew. I might write a long account of our rustic dinner under the trees and a delicious walk with Mr Drury Wake and Sir Reresby Sitwell, who was very good natured . . . How the time passed with fiddlers, dancing, tea and a gypsy fire and how the flyman [hired carriage driver] got tipsy coming home and ran races in the pouring rain, and how the footman being ditto . . . and how all the young people got into wrong carriages without their chaperones, and how Min [her sister] – wonderfully safe, considering ¼ past 10 . . . I took a great fancy to Lady Wake's sister and her nephew [Reresby Sitwell] seems very nice indeed.

Two days later, 'Minny and I went to have lunch with Lady Wake, and on with their party to the royal academy. We enjoyed it very much and met Sir Reresby Sitwell, who justifies one's first impression certainly.' A week after this, 'Sir R.S. talked to me a little in the evening about Paulina Teby and her earnest life – it seems to me that he is very good and nice himself.' The next day, she visited exhibitions with him. A week later they went riding together, two days running.

Louisa Lucy suffered from a form of neurasthenia far worse than the 'vapours' that afflicted so many Victorian ladies. A psychological disorder whose symptoms included fatigue, anxiety and depression together with high blood pressure and neuralgia, it struck without warning, making social life difficult. She found religion a great help, even if it brought out a puritanical streak. On Wednesday 17 June 1857, she confided to her diary, 'Today I made up my mind that if possible I would leave Town. It seems very weak but I fancy the quantities of society I meet now every day will unfit me for other things.'

Understandably, she was attracted by those who shared her faith, especially someone so personable as her new friend. On 20 June she wrote, 'A pleasant ride in the Park and Sir R.S. told me a great deal about Scotland which I am never likely to see, came home more anxious than ever to leave Town at once.'

A week later, after an evening at the opera, she wrote pensively,

> The music of Don Giovanni was so delicious. I admire the new tenor Giulini very much, and Piccolomini sang like a great thrush, but think – I think – that this must be the last opera for me. I had a strong feeling that I ought not to be there, and there were many things that shocked and offended me. And the ballet! How anyone can like it or look at it I cannot think!

Far from leaving London, on 3 July Louisa Lucy went by steamboat to Richmond in a party that included her admirer, with whom she strolled very slowly up Richmond Hill.

> Sir R.S. talked to me of Renishaw, and then about his 'hasty temper'. 'Do believe it, it is really true, but with God's help I may conquer it yet. Could you take me, faults and all, to be your husband?' As we came home at dusk upon the river, and no one was minding about us, he told me all his plans. 'Rome for the winter and Scotland afterwards, and first of all that wherever we may be we should serve God together all our lives.'

The next day:

> Sir Reresby came about 11 and spoke to Papa, afterwards he was with me till luncheon and left me (I must confess it) rather tired and most sadly frightened, with a diamond ring to keep reminding me it was no dream . . . I believe that to serve God with his whole heart is his first object, may it be mine too, for out of the riches of His mercy, he has given me this priceless affection of my own.

The day after, Reresby went to tell his mother at Huntercombe. He returned with his sister Mary. 'She kissed me with her kind eyes full of tears and said, "Nothing Reresby has ever done has given us half such pleasure."'

The wedding took place on Wednesday 19 August 1857 at the parish church of Weedon Lois near Weston, after which they began their honeymoon at Biddlesden Park, a great Georgian house nearby. From their first meeting at Burnham Beeches at the end of May, it had taken Reresby just five weeks to propose. Despite the whirlwind courtship, the marriage turned out to be an ideal match.

At first, Louisa Lucy was overwhelmed by her malady. 'Oh God help me, I don't know what to do, feeling how grateful I ought to be and am for all that Thou hast given and yet I cannot stop my tears and it must grieve Reresby who is so good to me,' she wrote two days after the wedding. 'In the morning I am better, in the evening it becomes almost intolerable, and I cannot leave him to try and get quieter by myself. He holds me tight in his arms and I hear him praying for me all the time. It must be that I am nervous, not unhappy with Reresby, God knows.'

Renishaw, largely unfurnished and sadly forlorn, terrified her when she saw it in October. The bells of Eckington church were pealing and continued ringing all day, while the couple's dog-cart was escorted up the drive by thirty horsemen from the neighbourhood, wearing white favours and with flowers on their horses' heads. They gave the bride three cheers as they alighted. Then she went 'into the solemn house where I was embraced by the old housemaid Bella, who meant it kindly, no doubt, but it would have been more inspiriting if she had not looked so solemn and not burst into tears.' She cheered up a little at seeing 'Reresby's bachelor rooms . . . so pretty and so droll, and we had a pleasant evening in them'. But she grew frightened by 'the wind howling through the empty passages of this vast house'.

The next morning:

> Reresby tried to show me over it, thereby making me
> sadly confused in my head, and afterwards I tried to

Right: George Sitwell of Renishaw (1657–1723) by Sir Godfrey Kneller. Called 'Mr Justice Sitwell' by his family, he was a Whig who welcomed the 'Glorious Revolution' of 1688.

Left: Francis Sitwell of Renishaw (1682–1753) by Charles Philips, 1742. A confirmed bachelor whose hobby was mathematics, like his father he hated and feared Jacobites.

Above: *The Boy in Pink*, the last Sacheverell, by Verelst, 1726. He drowned in the River Rother when very young and his ghost was supposed to haunt Renishaw – waking pretty girls with a kiss.

Opposite: The Entrance Hall of 1625, where once the entire household ate together. It still has some of the original furniture – supplemented by John Piper's painting.

Opposite: The Great Parlour of 1625, today the Library.

Above and below: The Small Parlour of 1625, today the Ante-Dining Room.

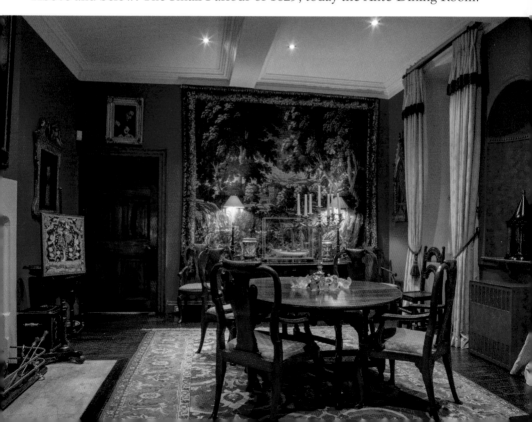

Above: *The Cherry Barrow* by Henry Walton, purchased from him by his friend Francis Hurt Sitwell in 1779.

Above: Francis Hurt Sitwell at right and his brother-in-law Colonel Warneford at left. The boy with the dog is Sitwell Sitwell and the little girl on her mother's lap is Mary Sitwell, later Lady Wake. By the silhouettist Francis Torond, c. 1776.

Above: *A Young Lady and her Brothers* by John Singleton Copley, 1787: Mary Sitwell; Sitwell Sitwell (with whip), later of Renishaw; Frank Sitwell, later of Barmoor Castle, Northumberland; and Hurt Sitwell, later of Ferney Hall, Shropshire.

Left: Sir Sitwell Sitwell (1769–1811), 1st Bt, who hunted down an escaped tiger with his hounds. He transformed Renishaw, adding the great rooms. By Francis Chantrey from a death mask, 1811.

Below: 'The Arch on the Ravine', John Piper's original name for his painting of the folly erected in the park at Renishaw by Sir Sitwell Sitwell in 1805.

Above: Sitwell Sitwell's new dining room, 1795, his first major addition to Renishaw. The apse (for displaying his racing trophies) was inspired by one at Keddleston.

Right: Sir George Sitwell (1797–1853) as a young man, by Octavius Oakley. A keen sportsman, he rented Balmoral for the shooting before the castle was acquired by Queen Victoria.

Left: Sir George in later life, anon. Ruined by an encumbered estate, theft and a bank failure, he shut up Renishaw and sold most of its contents.

Left: Sir Reresby Sitwell (1820–1862). Overwhelmed by financial worries, he tried unsuccessfully to sell Renishaw and then died young of cancer.

Right: Louisa Lucy, Lady Sitwell (1831–1911), Reresby's widow and an unsung heroine, whose financial acumen and determination saved Renishaw.

Above: Sir George Sitwell (1860–1943) by Henry Tonks, 1898. An art collector and a gifted landscape gardener, he created modern Renishaw.

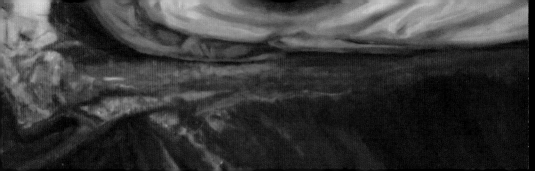

Opposite: Lady Ida Sitwell (1869–1937) aged 19, by Sir William Blake Richmond. Her fecklessness gave her husband a breakdown and earned her a spell in prison, but nonetheless she possessed enormous charm.

Above: The Sitwell Family – Sir George and Lady Ida, Edith, Osbert and Sacheverell – by J. S. Sargent, 1900. The clothes were the artist's suggestion.

Left: Lady Ida in her prime by Bassano, 1904. She was known to give away as many as three of her smartest dresses to friends during her lunch parties.

Below: The last photograph of Sir George, in 1943 at Locarno, Switzerland. He had fallen into the hands of a sinister couple called Woog, who plundered his bank account and were even suspected of murdering him.

explore alone, but could not get it done. Some distant door slammed, or the wind howled like a human voice and back I ran, never stopping till the two boudoir doors were shut behind me.

When she and her husband set off for Rome after little more than a fortnight, from the train window she saw 'the grand old house standing out in full sunshine, looking as if it wondered how it *could* be left, dismantled and deserted'. Despite her fear, Renishaw had already cast its spell over her.

Their lengthy honeymoon in Italy was a great success despite the torrential rain of an Italian winter, the couple's happiness seemingly unmarred by both of them falling ill. Reresby did so more than once – a bad omen. Louisa Lucy spent much of the time sketching (for which she had real talent), as did her husband. Their sketch books survive. 'I am sitting for my picture to Signor Crispini,' she wrote in February 1858. 'He will be clever [if] he makes anything out of my present pale, sickly looking face and it is hard work sitting for him as he can only speak Italian – and we cannot say a word.'

On their return to England they moved into Renishaw. Poor old Bella retired to Scotland, upset by new servants. Children came: Florence Alice in 1859, George one year later, and finally Blanche. The family lived very quietly. Regular attenders at Eckington church, they went in for religious and charitable activities such as 'poor peopling' – which meant visits with medicine and food to the estate's sick or aged labourers and their families – and helping out-of-work miners. The parson was allowed to hold a Sunday school in the ballroom.

Reresby shot a good deal by himself on his own land, over the dogs and along the hedgerows, but gave up hunting as too expensive. His financial problems grew worse than ever. He became wretched at finding himself unable to keep his wife and children in the style he had known as a young man; complete ruin cannot have seemed far away. He could see no possible solution.

Among his burdens was his brother George Frederick, eight years younger, who had also been a soldier – starting as a Cornet in the First Life Guards, but then 'selling out' and transferring into the Shropshire Light Infantry, where he reached the rank of Captain. Penniless and unable to support his spendthrift wife Fanny Fitzroy and three sons, 'Fred' – who lived uncomfortably close, at Leicester – was always begging for money. Even worse, Fred's behaviour had begun to show signs of insanity.

⁕

'No reasonable mind can dispute that he is very ill,' Louisa Lucy wrote of Reresby to one of her sisters, early in the spring of 1862. 'But he is in God's hands and I am full of hope that this new treatment may with His blessing prove successful.' However, the illness was terminal cancer. 'I [had] asked the doctors previously, if they had anything unfavourable to say, to tell me and leave *me* to break it to him, but Dr Bence Jones thought it proper to tell *him* without any preparation . . . that he had an internal tumour for which nothing could be done.' (Henry Bence Jones was one of the most respected physicians of the day, a model for Trollope's Sir Omicron Pie.)

'Dear Alice, you must not fret at not having come directly, indeed I don't think it could have given you any comfort or my darling either, for he was so weak and could hardly say a word,' she wrote to her sister-in-law Alice on 13 April 1862, in the wake of Reresby's death. After he had a violent fit of coughing, 'I insisted upon the doctor staying all night, and did not undress myself, but sat by my darling's side.'

About four o'clock he seemed weaker, and I called the doctor and begged him to tell me truly if those he loved should not be sent for. He still said he would rally soon, but my heart told me otherwise and at six . . . I felt his dear pulse sinking rapidly. Then God helped me to tell him cheerfully that I thought he was going to a better land, where he would be quite happy and not suffer any more . . . I asked him to see how calm I was, rejoicing for his sake at the happiness that would be his so soon, and that he must not mind leaving me and the children, we should all meet again so soon, and he kept looking at me with a happy smile.

Reresby's last words were, 'I don't feel-as-if-I was-going' – and then he died, still with the smile. He was forty-one, and they had been married for less than five years.

'Dear Alice, don't be afraid for me. God will help me, I am *sure* of it.'

Louisa Lucy's slender reserves of strength were exhausted by days and nights of nursing. She collapsed, unable to attend the funeral at Eckington. It was taken by a cousin – Dr Tait, Bishop of London – who wrote to her the next day, telling her how a wreath of late snowdrops and violets had been placed on Reresby's coffin, and how he was laid 'beside his father and brother under the Communion table in the old church'. He added, 'the five really happy years of his life have been those during which he has known you, and it may soothe you to know how much all his friends feel that you were by God's blessing the light of his life.'

Louisa Lucy never forgot her husband. 'I have just been reading through this old journal,' she wrote in her diary in April 1863 – twelve months after he had died.

It seems very strange that I did not write more of our happiness, and the affection we both felt so truly and deeply for each other. Trials deepened and strengthened that every year. My Reresby has left me now, he is gone to his rest, his simple, earnest spirit and loving heart has passed into a higher sphere beyond disappointment or grief to care. My love is still as fresh and as true to him, and I believe his is to me.

Chapter 9

AN UNSUNG HEROINE

Without Louisa Lucy, the Sitwells would have lost Renishaw Hall – but almost immediately she set about saving it for her son, even before she had fully recovered her health.

'I have written to Mrs Beresford-Peirse [to ask] if she would let me stay one night with her at Bedale for I am sure she could give me a good deal of information about my new duties,' Louisa Lucy wrote to her father on 29 July 1862. (Colonel Hely-Hutchinson is unlikely to have been encouraging – after a first visit, he commented, 'By whom, or by how many, Renishaw was built, it is a folly.')[1] Louisa Lucy continued, 'Ask Mama not to be the least afraid about my going back to Renishaw. It must be done some day and now I can really move about, I think I am fit to go.'[2]

Mrs Henry Beresford-Peirse of Bedale Park in Yorkshire was in a similar situation. Recently widowed, with a young son (also heir to a baronetcy), she too was striving on her own to save a great mansion and estate. Whether or not this lady gave good advice, Louisa Lucy got down to work with a will. 'I am expecting Mr White the lawyer to arrive from town tomorrow,' she informed her mother on 18 August. 'I thought it would be better to have a visit from him to set me going in keeping the books etc. I hope it won't crush me altogether but duties must seem very heavy when all the pleasure is gone . . . Tomorrow is our fifth wedding day.'[3]

She was suffering from a bout of her old complaint when little Blanche fell ill. In September 1863, after being invited to spend a holiday with Blanche at Brighton by her mother, Mrs Hely-Hutchinson, she replied,

> It is very good of you to think so much about me, and I wish I could fall in with your plans, for you know how different it would be for me to be amongst you all, but it is a desperate journey from the north of England to the south. I do not think either Blanche or I are capable of it, [and] then the expense would be very great . . . this has been a very expensive year to me.

Alluding to an attempt at restoring her late husband's health, she continues, 'Brighton is full of sad associations for me which perhaps would not help one towards recovery.' She ends, 'I do not expect myself that dear Blanche will recover. In my own mind, I resigned her long ago, but I wish to do the very best for her and not ever to have to reproach myself by dragging her [on] long journeys for my own sake, or taking her inland even, when the doctor thinks she would droop at once.' Blanche died later that year.[4]

In order to live more cheaply Louisa Lucy settled at the Yorkshire seaside resort of Scarborough, where she rented a newly built villa called Sunnyside. She spent only a few months at Renishaw in the summer. This was the first of many economies designed to save the estate. Somehow, she succeeded. 'By no means a rich woman, with little more than her jointure to support her, she possessed a remarkable head for business, and her enterprise and power of organisation enabled her to extract an almost incredible value for every pound spent,' said her grandson Osbert.[5] She may have received a discreet allowance from the Hely-Hutchinsons – her father certainly gave her money from time to time – but it cannot have been very much.

She was given moral support by her son's guardian, Archibald Campbell Tait, the Bishop of London who had buried Reresby and who later became Archbishop of Canterbury in 1868. One of those Scottish relatives whose sojourns at Renishaw had contributed to her father-in-law's ruin, unlike most of them he was grateful and a tower of strength. She was also lucky in having an efficient if temperamental land agent – Peveril Turnbull, who helped to tutor little George – and a capable steward, Reginald Bellyse.

To quote Osbert again: 'by her constant attention and cleverness, she pulled the estate round. She was indeed a woman of remarkable dignity and charm, with latent fires in her, a great personal dignity and an inflexible but softly marked will.'[6] She learned to master her anxiety attacks, although neurasthenia could still prostrate her.

Steel showed in the way she dealt with Uncle Fred, who had become totally unhinged, calling himself 'Duke of Renishaw', not bothering to wash or shave, and running up enormous bills. Lured to Renishaw and certified insane, Captain Sitwell was taken to a lunatic asylum in York, where he spent the rest of his life. The fees of the asylum – one of the best in the country – and an allowance to his family were paid by the estate, which proved cheaper than the former handouts to save him from bankruptcy.[7]

Although she was too shrewd to spoil him, Louisa Lucy's warm affection combined with the absence of a father figure instilled in her son an excessive conviction of his own worth. At the age of four, George informed a stranger on a train, 'I am the youngest baronet in

England.' His later hypochondria owed much to her worries about his health – understandable in view of his father's early death.

⁂

In 1870, when Renishaw's financial situation improved, Louisa Lucy left Sunnyside and bought a property called Wood End on Scarborough's most sought-after street, The Crescent. The big stone house (purchased cheaply from an owner in financial difficulties) had been built in William IV's reign, and had distant views of the North Sea. Her first change was to convert three ground-floor rooms into a single long drawing room whose walls were covered with eighteenth-century Genoese cotton. Later she added a new wing with a vast conservatory, where exotic birds such as cardinals, blue robins, Pekin nightingales and nutmeg finches flew over the heads of the dancers when she gave a ball.

She began collecting furniture, but not the French sort which was then so much in vogue. Her collection included a lovely seventeenth-century silver Augsburg cabinet that she bought in Germany, a fine *cassone*, and four red and gold *seicento* chairs from the Palazzo Buonsignori in Siena. All of these are now at Renishaw.

Louisa Lucy also acquired Hay Brow, a small country house in a pretty setting on the edge of Scalby – four miles outside Scarborough – where she always spent part of the summer. Hay Brow charmed everyone who saw it – especially the garden, with its little lake and rare trees. Inside it was full of flowers, from a hothouse as well as from the garden, in brightly coloured china bowls. Louisa Lucy had engaged a gifted Belgian gardener, Ernest de Taeye – a huge man, described in later years by her granddaughter Edith as looking like 'a dear great lumbering bear had he not been completely bald', who 'spoke of flowers tenderly, as fathers sometimes (I suppose) speak of their children'.[8]

90.

Despite de Taeye's skill, the beauty of the flowers at Louisa Lucy's houses was largely due to her enthusiasm.

She kept what Osbert describes as a 'collection' of cherished old servants. Foremost was Leckley, her personal maid for sixty-three years, who became a gnarled figure with a wise, disagreeable face and keys at her waist. (In her will, Louisa Lucy asked to be buried next to Leckley.) The staff accompanied her when for some years she leased Gosden Lodge near Shalford in Surrey, not far from Guildford. Each spring she and her party travelled by a private train, hired from the Great Northern Railway, which without changing went directly from Scarborough to Shalford via King's Cross, London Bridge and Dorking. The party always included six white Samoyed dogs.

Louisa Lucy also inspired devotion in people other than her staff. At some period during the 1870s, when she was in her early forties, she was visited by the teenage Ethel Smyth – the future suffragette and composer of *March of the Women* – who, years later, wrote an account of their meeting. Always a keen admirer of good looks in her own sex, Ethel recalled, 'I was too infatuated to ask myself whether she was really as beautiful as the vision that haunted me for the next few years; but of one thing I am certain: when Nature set herself to create an ideal Victorian *grande dame* with a pronounced religious bent, she can never have done better!'

Ethel also remembered her wonderful manners. 'You never heard her talking about herself; her conversation always centred on the affairs of the people she was talking to.' She never forgot the impression made on her by 'a most remarkable and lovable woman'.[9]

'Radiance is a better word to match her quality, I think, than beauty, and a certain sad radiance still clung to her,' says Osbert Sitwell, who adds that she possessed a grace of movement he had never seen in another woman of her age. Her houses were brightly decorated, but in the day she dressed in black, and in the evening in dark green or brown or blue velvet. She liked brooches and bracelets, and even when in mourning wore long necklaces of onyx, jet or ivory.[10]

⸙

When George was ten his mother sent him to Dr Chittenden's School, The Grange, at Hoddesdon in Hertfordshire, which in those days was a well-known preparatory school for Eton. (The future Prime Minister Arthur Balfour had been a pupil.) 'A wearisome journey through a flat country to Hoddesdon, George in low spirits all the way,' she recorded in her diary on 6 May 1870. I 'inspected house, gardens, school rooms, play grounds etc. etc.' The next day she wrote, 'Left by an early train. Sad without my boy.'[11]

In the same year that Louisa Lucy purchased Wood End and George Sitwell went off to school, a rich seam of coal was found under the park at Renishaw which revived the family fortunes. Fearing it might run out, she continued her economies and remained at Scarborough. Yet despite the house and the gardens being covered in soot, and the mine at the gates – the rumbling of miners' carts could be heard from the cellars – Renishaw kept its beauty and allure. She still saw it as the jewel of her son's inheritance and spent a few weeks there every summer, making modest attempts at refurbishment.

⸙

Louisa Lucy's was a complex character. For all her economies, she loved travel, and once or twice George complained of being left at Eton for part of the holidays while she was abroad. As has been seen, she dressed elegantly and furnished her houses exquisitely. Yet at the same time, she was a fervent Evangelical Protestant. Surrounded by Low Church clergymen – including the gloriously named Canon Groucher – whom she invited to give sermons and hold prayer meetings, she made Sundays a misery for the less devout, forbidding novels or newspapers.

It is easy to make fun of her charitable works, which Osbert summed up as 'the removal of the inebriate from his drink and the conversion of sirens into Magdalene washerwomen'. Admittedly, they sometimes resembled those of the Ebenezer Temperance Association in *The Pickwick Papers*. 'We are making plans (Mother's idea) for inviting Bar-maids for quiet Sunday afternoons in this garden, where we could read to them, with perhaps a little sacred singing, and get to know and help them,' wrote Florence Sitwell in her journal.

At Scarborough, Louisa Lucy set up the Home of Hope, a hostel for homeless working girls who were given employment in its laundry. Her granddaughter Edith later described them as 'unfortunates' kidnapped off the streets, claiming that on one occasion every single inmate was found to have been made pregnant by a handsome young man who had got into the home disguised as a girl.[12] Yet Louisa Lucy was at least offering her girls a chance to avoid prostitution, which when their bodies grew unsaleable would leave a choice between the workhouse or starving on the streets.

Some of her activities were undeniably practical. Among them was founding and maintaining out of her own pocket a small ear and eye hospital in King Street that later catered for other ailments too – providing the only free hospital in Scarborough – as well as a home for streetwalkers trying to leave their trade, and a club for working women. All were run by properly trained staff. She made a point of having invalid clergy to stay at Wood End or Hay Brow – any ailing curate was sure of a welcome.

She even took care of the town's postmen. At Christmas 1893, they wrote en bloc to thank her, in a naively illuminated address:

> We, the staff employed at the Post Office, Scarborough, venture to approach your Ladyship, to return our grateful thanks for the deep interest you have for a number of years taken in our welfare, and for the many kindnesses you have shown to individual members when on beds of sickness. The presence of your Ladyship at the breakfast you kindly provided for the staff on Christmas morning, and the words of encouragement spoken by you, are not soon to be forgotten. We cannot refrain from referring to the fact that we have received your hospitality on the past twelve Christmas mornings.[13]

Louisa Lucy enjoyed having Archbishop Tait to stay at Renishaw, which he did frequently, his presence proudly reported in the local newspapers. Suffering from a chronically sore throat, the Primate gargled daily during his visits, using vintage port as a prophylactic. In consequence, he drained Renishaw's entire stock of 1815 'Waterloo' port – the best vintage of the century.

Despite her shyness, Florence ('Floss') Sitwell, a year older than George, attended an art school at Scarborough and made cloisonné plates of her own design that sold quite well. The first literary Sitwell, she published two novels in the 1880s that are occasionally reprinted – *Daybreak: A Story for Girls* and *Mistress Patience Summerhayes' Her Diary during the Siege of Scarborough Castle AD 1644–1645*. Even more religious than her mother, in her journal (later to form the second part of *Two Generations*) she recorded the pious life they led together. Osbert says she was trustful and otherworldly, and looked like a saint from a picture by Fra' Angelico. She never married, but her brother saw that she was well provided for, living comfortably in the family's Tudor dower house at Long Itchington near Rugby until her death in 1930.

George always remained fond of his mother and sister, regularly writing to ask Louisa Lucy for advice. They shared many interests – books and furniture, decoration and gardening – while he never forgot how she saved Renishaw. (When he moved in, she made useful suggestions about furnishings and William Morris wallpapers, telling him to install a kitchen range.) Perfectionists, they both possessed the same determination to organise their lives down to the last detail – and the lives of those around them.

When staying at Cannes in the Villa Allegra in May 1881, Louisa Lucy received a letter from George, shortly after he had come into his inheritance. 'Do think finally over the Allegra before leaving it,' he wrote. 'I should be very glad to buy it, leaving you entire control over it, and to settle another hundred a year on you . . . so as to meet the extra expense. I am sure it would be very good for Floss and you, and for me too, to pay you a visit occasionally in the winter.'[14]

Eventually, enfeebled by increasing ill health, Louisa Lucy retired to Bournemouth for the sea air, taking Floss and her beloved staff with her. Her son visited her frequently, and her grandchildren often came to stay. She died at the age of eighty in March 1911 – nearly half a century after her husband's death – and was buried next to Leckley.

George had reason to be grateful to his mother. One could forgive any widow for despairing after an all-but-bankrupt husband's death, while the best-intentioned guardian might well have decided that he had no option other than to insist on the empty house and encumbered estate being sold, if he was to act in his ward's best interests. Strong, shrewd, subtle, Louisa Lucy had laid the foundations for Renishaw's renewal. Above all, she gave her son some of her finer qualities.

Chapter 10

THE GOLDEN YEARS RETURN?

Sir George Reresby Sitwell, fourth baronet of Renishaw, came of age on 27 January 1881. In June, to take advantage of warmer weather, there was a great party in celebration in the grounds of the Hall, attended by all Derbyshire as well as the tenants, the Archbishop of Canterbury's speech congratulating his nephew being reported by *The Times* in full. It looked as if the golden years of Sitwell Sitwell had returned, once again based on solid wealth.

※

Already unmistakably distinguished, George was over six feet tall, slim and well built, with aquiline features, reddish hair and curiously pale blue eyes. He wore a moustache (later a pointed beard) and possessed the art of dressing in such a way that you knew he was well dressed but could not say why. Impeccably mannered, he was at the same time aloof, although he had plenty of charm if needed. Despite his children comparing him to Melone's portrait of Cesare Borgia, he looked exactly what he was – a late Victorian, upper-class Englishman of the 'earnest Eighties', who would not have seemed out of place in one of Anthony Trollope's last novels.

A lady who met him at about this time described George to her husband. 'A curious specimen of highly bred and *educated* young England, twenty, and full of Galton's books on heredity, physiological and psychological questions, old prints, the German school of etchings . . . He told me what he would like best would be to live at Nuremberg and collect old books.'[1] He also told her, 'I often suffer from nerve exhaustion myself, but with me it takes the form of rheumatism in the deltoid muscle, and yields at once to Galvanism.'[2]

Too aware of his gifts, an only son without a father who was idolised by his mother and sister, he had grown up obsessively self-centred. If he had not inherited Louisa Lucy's religion, he possessed her frugality and puritanism, her love of beauty, and much of her kindness. An impish, impenetrably private sense of humour that he never intended anybody else to share was all his own. (His jokes were always with himself.) He was the hardest of all the Sitwells to understand because so complex.

He had fitted in at Eton well enough, contributing a poem, 'Parodies Regained', to the *Eton Chronicle* and playing the Field Game, an uninspiring form of football. For the rest of his life he ordered clothes from the Eton tailor, Tom Brown (if sometimes patronising Henry Poole). He made few friends there, however; and nor did he make any at Oxford, despite his guardian writing seventy letters of introduction. But he joined the Christ Church Shakespeare Society, and at one meeting read from *Macbeth* – the parts of the murderer Lennox and the third witch. He also rowed, hunted a bit and played tennis.

While fond of his mother and sister, he was glad to escape from their stifling piety, and became an atheist. His sceptical attitude towards the next world was confirmed when as an undergraduate he exposed the celebrated medium, Mrs Florence Cook, seizing hold of her during a 'séance' at the British National Association of Spiritualists, an incident reported in the *Daily Telegraph* for 13 January 1880. He was so proud of this feat that he included it in his *Who's Who* entry – 'captured a spirit at the headquarters of the Spiritualists'.

Yet George respected his guardian, staying at Lambeth Palace whenever he visited London until Tait's death in 1882. Just before he came of age, the archbishop sent him a letter of advice (signed 'A. Cantuar') which, despite his lack of religion, he followed in most respects. Throughout his life he gave at least a tenth of his annual income to charity, while he made his mother a generous allowance on top of her jointure of £700, endowed his sister with a decent fortune in case she chose to marry, and contributed handsomely to the family fund for Uncle Fred's maintenance in the asylum until he died in 1884, besides helping Fred's three sons.

He acted on the archbishop's admonition: 'act up consistently in all your tenancy responsibilities both in directly doing what is right to the people on your estates, and also in seeing that as large a number of other people as possible benefit by your good fortune'.[3]

On buying *The Scarborough Post* George briefly turned foreign correspondent, travelling to Moscow in 1883 for Alexander III's coronation at the Kremlin. His patrician appearance, set off by the uniform of a Yorkshire Dragoon (dark blue piped with silver and a plumed steel helmet), gained him a seat in the cathedral – unlike such veteran journalists as George Augustus Sala. He was therefore able to send home an eyewitness account of Metropolitan Leontius crowning the giant Tsar – 'Sasha the Bear' – and his tiny Danish Tsarina.

Rather than the fussy eccentric of Osbert's malicious portrayal, Sir George in his early years was thoroughly conventional, hunting, riding in steeplechases and cycling, playing lawn tennis, golf and cricket. (He was an admirer of Dr Grace.) He installed a golf course which is still in the park, and gave the local cricket club land to use for a pitch. He became a Justice of the Peace, served as High Sheriff and joined the Carlton Club in London. He also enjoyed part-time soldiering in the Yeomanry as a Captain in the Yorkshire Dragoons, attending a cavalry course at Aldershot in 1885.

What he hoped for most was a career in politics. Between 1884 and 1895 he contested the generally Liberal seat of Scarborough as a Conservative in seven elections, winning in 1885, losing the next year and winning again in 1892, when he ousted the Gladstonian Liberal Joshua Rowntree. He was a tireless canvasser, knocking on every voter's door, and a natural orator who was at his best addressing audiences of over a thousand in the days before megaphones. Having sat as an MP during the premierships of Gladstone and Lord Rosebery, asking a few questions in the House but never making a maiden speech, he finally lost the seat in 1895.

Archbishop Tait had told his godson to put aside any income from coal in case the seam ran out, so he invested it in South African mining stock before most financiers saw the potential of its gold and diamonds. He also bought shares at Newcastle in three newly built merchant ships (*Thropton* in 1887, *Scottish Prince* in 1888 and *Asiatic Prince* in 1889), besides buying two small railways. He even acquired shares in Gimbels, the new American department store. Nor did he forget his guardian's advice to make sure accounts were settled twice a year – 'every bill to be examined and paid, and that you always ascertain that you have received more than you have spent . . . guard against excess in any one point of expenditure or any failure in receipts'.

The most looked-up-to figure in Scarborough was the fabulously rich Lord Londesborough, who lived at Londesborough Lodge in The Crescent, a large neoclassical *villeggiatura* that stood next door but one to Wood End. As the town's new MP, Sir George was invited to lunch. Understandably, he was gratified by the summons.

Lord Londesborough possessed a tall, thin, swan-necked daughter of seventeen, Ida Emily Augusta Denison, who looked like a Burne-Jones heroine. Her small and lovely head was adorned by a Grecian nose and huge dark brown eyes, while she carried herself majestically, having been taught deportment by the ballet dancer Marie Taglioni. A complete lack of brains, possibly because of a childhood illness, was disguised by her cheerful, lively manner. Almost illiterate – no governess on earth could have worked the necessary miracle – she was pitifully unworldly, with an allowance of one shilling and sixpence a week pocket money, even if her mother saw that she wore pretty clothes.

In autumn 1886 George proposed to Ida after meeting her twice, at luncheon. He admired not just her beauty but her quarterings, her mother being a daughter of the seventh Duke of Beaufort and thus a Plantagenet through a bastard line. George was marrying up. However, with several daughters to marry off, her parents welcomed the prospect of such a wealthy son-in-law – especially Lady Londesborough, who dreaded being left as a badly-off widow.

Only the Londesborough's medical adviser Dr Dale struck a note of caution, strongly advising that in view of Ida's immaturity the wedding should be postponed for a year or two, but her parents ignored him. As for Ida herself, far from being married against her will, as her daughter Edith claimed, she fancied she was deeply in love. There are some pathetic letters in the archives at Renishaw, childishly expressed and badly spelt, in which Ida tells George how devoted she is to him, promising to be a good wife.

'My own darling, I rejoice to hear of your happiness, though you have taken away poor old mother's breath by talking of being married in a month,' Louisa Lucy wrote to George on 9 October, having received an affectionate letter from Ida. 'I am quite sure that I shall love her, she has a warm heart and a sweet, simple nature.' Canny as always, Louisa Lucy, too, was worried about Ida's childishness, but reassured herself by quoting 'Uncle Richard' as saying, 'I do honour a man who will go into a schoolroom and choose for himself.' She sent Leckley to Renishaw to ensure that everything would be in perfect order for the house's new mistress.[4]

The wedding took place in London at St George's, Hanover Square on 23 November 1886, conducted by Randall Davidson, Dean of Windsor (who was the late Archbishop Tait's son-in-law) and by Lord Londesborough's chaplain, the bride's brother acting as best man. The choir sang 'The voice that breathes o'er Eden'. A lavish collection of presents included costly jewellery for Ida and – because of his interest in history – an ancient teapot, recently dug up at Scarborough Castle, for the bridegroom. The Dean told Louisa Lucy how struck he had been by Ida's beauty and by the couple's 'quiet reverence' during the service. But it was a miserable, foggy day. Immediately after the reception they left for Renishaw and married bliss.

According to one story, during the very first night a tearful bride was found wandering down the drive in her nightgown. She insisted on going home to her mother, who had apparently neglected to tell her about the physical side of marriage. However, Lady Londesborough sent Ida back to her husband at once and they left Renishaw to continue the honeymoon abroad.

When the couple returned to Scarborough at dusk on New Year's Day 1887, the local lifeboat crew drew their carriage from the station to Londesborough Lodge, escorted by 500 cheering townsmen who waved flaming torches. The spectacle was marred by a woman in the crowd dropping dead from fright.

George and his bride settled at Scarborough, which, apart from a sojourn at Renishaw every summer, was to be their home for many years. They rented a number of houses, including Belvoir Lodge, until Louisa Lucy gave them Wood End in 1903. Three children were born: Edith in 1887, Osbert in 1892 and Sacheverell in 1897. Not unsocial, the couple acquired a small circle of Scarborough friends – including George du Maurier, famous for exquisitely drawn cartoons in *Punch*, some of which made flattering use of Sir George and Ida as models.

Yet the 'golden years' were turning into lead.

Chapter 11
A MISERABLE MARRIAGE

Superficially, all seemed well, especially during Sir George's three years as a backbench MP. If he did not achieve very much in his chosen career, he enjoyed the amenities of the House of Commons, the 'best club in London'. Behind the scenes, however, his marriage was going badly wrong, even if Edith exaggerates in saying that her mother found herself in 'a kind of slave bondage to an equally unfortunate and pitiable young man'.[1]

George realised that he had made a disastrous choice. Years later, he wrote of how after they were married, he discovered that Lady Ida (as she became in 1887 when her father was created an earl) did not even know the multiplication tables, and possessed no idea of the value of money.

Her priorities became clothes, jewellery and champagne. When her husband cancelled her orders for cases of champagne, she turned to whisky, and was only saved from destroying herself by his watchful eye. She spent as uncontrollably as she drank. On at least eight occasions he gave her large sums, totalling over £20,000, with which to settle bills. In addition, he later calculated that during the first thirteen years of married life, to fend off writs he had to pay bills for lesser debts at least every three weeks.

For all Ida's faults, her husband was touchingly proud of her beauty. Soon after their marriage, he decided to have her portrait done. Having thought briefly of commissioning Alma-Tadema, he chose Sir William Blake Richmond, who produced an unattractive picture typical of the eighties. Wearing a turquoise blue silk coat, Ida holds a zither, an instrument she had probably never seen; but the face is lovely, such a good likeness that her husband nearly had it cut out and framed. Dissatisfied, he contemplated having her painted by Jacques-Émile Blanche. Finally, he decided on a group portrait of the family by John Singer Sargent, a conversation piece to complement Copley's study of the Sitwell children a century before. It was finished early in 1900.

The £1,500 fee, huge for those days, was in fact a bargain, since Sargent had not yet acquired his full popularity. He makes George strikingly handsome and Edith almost pretty, but does not quite do Ida justice. Some thought he gave the baronet a crooked nose and Edith a straight one, the reverse of real life, because he felt sorry for her.

In his autobiography Osbert belittles the picture, arguing that Sargent could not compete with Copley. He also ridicules his father for wearing riding breeches when he seldom rode.[2] But a newly discovered letter shows it was the painter who insisted on these clothes, not his patron.[3] The group is undoubtedly one of the finest of all Sargent's works.

Early in April 1900, while viewing the portrait at Sargent's studio, Lord Londesborough collapsed from a bout of flu. He then developed pneumonia, which killed him. (Osbert claimed imaginatively that it was the more exotic malady of psittacosis, caught from a parrot.) Writing to his agent and former tutor Peveril Turnbull, Sir George comments that his father-in-law had 'had a remarkably kind and amiable manner and disposition', and that Lady Ida was very upset. He adds that the new earl, her brother William, 'will be what the family call badly off, that is to say he will only have £40,000 a year to begin with and death duties to pay out of that, but eventually there will be £60,000'.[4]

He adds that his wife will now have an income of £600 instead of £300 from the Londesborough estate. 'She really ought to have had this on marriage for though it is possible to dress fashionably on £300, it is certainly not easy for girls who have been been brought up in this way.' As he gave Lady Ida £500 a year, this should have made her self-sufficient, but she was already wildly extravagant. Nor had he reckoned with the dowager.

While not without charm when she deigned to use it, the widowed Lady Londesborough was a thoroughly selfish, ill-tempered woman whom Edith pictured in her prime as 'living in luxury like a gilded and irascible wasp in a fine ripe nectarine'.[5] Now she found, as Osbert put it, 'horses and carriages and grooms and houses and gardens and jewels and plate, and indeed the whole luxurious decoration of life by which she had been so long surrounded snatched away at a single grab'.[6] She turned to moneylenders, who very nearly ruined her. Worse still, instead of helping to control her daughter's spending, she not only encouraged her but tried to use her as a source of income.

In 1905, while Ida was in hospital with appendicitis, the dowager countess made her sign a document demanding a separation from Sir George unless he paid Ida's latest batch of debts and settled a large yearly allowance on her. She signed because her mother told her that her brother Londesborough would have to pay the debts if George refused. Ida then changed her mind.

Desperate for money, the dowager had hoped to use her daughter as a milch calf who would pay her own bills. George recalled bitterly that 'Lady Londesborough's actions nearly killed Lady Ida and prevented me from being able to exercise restraint over her expenditure.'[7]

It was not just extravagance that wrecked the marriage. Ida was incapable of sharing her husband's interests in any way, or of giving him the slightest support. According to her daughter Edith, she lay in bed reading newspapers or trashy novels but could remember nothing of what she read. Otherwise, all she did was play bridge or watch the golfers in the park, or give large luncheon parties without warning her husband. She had constant tantrums, screaming and threatening to throw herself out of the window. And she possessed a wounding tongue.

One reason for her lassitude was chronic ill health. She was consumptive, and nearly died in 1904 after losing a lung. Her tuberculosis made her dangerously vulnerable to any sort of infection and, in the end, was indirectly responsible for her death. Sickness and lack of vitality affected her temperament, contributing to the irrational outbursts of anger. Edith later said that her rages were the only reality in her life. They were increasingly fuelled by heavy drinking.

George, whose own life was meticulously organised, was maddened by the chaos surrounding his wife and goaded by the constant rows; while Ida, gregarious and fascinated by new faces, found his detachment infuriating. While he counted every penny, she loved shopping sprees – even when an old lady, she said she never dared visit Paris for fear she might spend money like a drunken sailor. No more ill-matched couple can be imagined, but divorce would have meant social ostracism. Although Ida did not take lovers, some of his family suspected George of siring one or two red-haired bastards, but there is no evidence.

Something of what he had to put up with can be glimpsed from the story of the Learned Pig ('able to foretell the future') that Ida bought at a Conservative Party bazaar in Scarborough. Although its psychic powers deserted it on its arrival at Renishaw by train, she could not bear to have it killed, instead boarding it out secretly at various farms. When an enormous bill for housing and feeding – and grooming – the animal eventually reached her husband, he immediately ordered it to be destroyed. Any mention of the pig always enraged him.

⚜

Yet Lady Ida possessed a bewitching charm, enlivened by a wonderful sense of fun. If empty-headed, she inspired affection. When young, she was very gay and very generous, says Edith, adding that she had an appealing, childlike quality. Osbert, who adored his mother, writes that her delight in driving through summer woods at night had something of a child's in it, as did her imitations of odd people – she was a gifted mimic – and her enjoyment of ridiculous situations. Children loved her because she treated them as friends, never laughing at anything they said. If a woman friend admired a bracelet or a dress, she immediately gave it to her, sometimes giving away several dresses after lunch. 'Take it, darling.'

Occasionally, she could even be kind about her husband. Warning Osbert not to mention a secret luncheon for sixteen guests because his father made such a foolish fuss about bills, she added, 'But whatever one may say about him, there's no one else like him.'

She, too, had her pet eccentricities, such as a length of hangman's rope twisted round her bedhead for good luck. It was in keeping with her strange, fey nature that she should be unafraid of Renishaw's otherworldly denizens. When little Osbert went into her bedroom in the mornings and asked his mother if she had slept well, she would often answer, 'Oh, fairly well, although the ghosts were about again' – as if they were of no more account than owls or mice.[8]

⚜

109.

In 1901 Sir George suffered a complete collapse in his health, almost certainly because of the tensions within his marriage. There may have been other factors, such as failing to regain the Scarborough seat, but Ida was the catalyst. All that we know about it comes from Osbert's account (in *The Scarlet Tree*) of what he witnessed as a small boy, written four decades later and – as usual – designed to make his father look a fool.

Bewildered by his mysterious and frightening malady, Sir George decided he must give up politics. The doctors could not tell him what was wrong, as it was beyond the period's medical science; each diagnosis disagreed with the next. Hoping a holiday might work a cure, he went to Germany, staying at Nuremberg and then Rothenburg, but he took the cause with him – Lady Ida. For a short time, however, he thought the change of scenery was doing him good.

In May 1901, according to Osbert, his father fell alarmingly ill with what was clearly a nervous breakdown; but in those days doctors scarcely knew the term, let alone what it implied. It prostrated him, and he could not deal with business matters. He became convinced he was a dying man – after all, his father had died at just the same age. Unable to sleep, he tried going to bed in a different house or hotel every night of the week.

Cure after cure was tried, often contradictory: wine or no wine, exercise or no exercise, etc. The illness dragged on for several years, with the patient (the 'dear invalid', as Louisa Lucy called him) showing no improvement. In the end, the local GP ousted the specialists and convincingly advised change. Sir George must travel.

Chapter 12

SIR GEORGE'S ITALIAN CURE

Sir George was cured by reinventing himself as an antiquarian in Italy, where meticulous research into the history and science of designing gardens gave purpose to his travels. He never forgot Archbishop Tait's advice – 'without distinct occupation, no man can be happy'. In finding a new and satisfying one, he became the creator of today's Renishaw. He also acquired another great house, in Tuscany, that gave further scope for his special talents – which had originally stemmed from his fascination with Renishaw.

He had always possessed antiquarian interests, working on medieval family pedigrees with the famous genealogist J. H. Round. His first book, which he printed himself, was *The Barons of Pulford* (1889), a selection of assize rolls and charters. He produced two admirably edited volumes of seventeenth- and eighteenth-century Sitwell letters in 1900–1, with an introduction that shows how much Renishaw meant to him.

'My father died when I was two years old, and at the time I first went to school we used to spend but a few months in the summer at our old house in Derbyshire,' he wrote. 'The library, a gradual growth of three hundred years, and the collection of civil war pamphlets, had been scattered abroad, and little of the original furniture remained except the tapestries, pictures and china, and a few old cabinets of tortoiseshell, rosewood or ebony,' is how he describes the effect on Renishaw of the wreck of his grandfather's affairs.

Of family history absolutely nothing had come down to us but the tradition that our ancestors had lived there since the reign of Elizabeth, and a story concerning the portrait of the 'Boy in red' [sic] (his name was forgotten), who had died by drowning and whose ghost was supposed to haunt the house.

I remember finding, on one of my holiday visits, amongst the old books in the hall, a Greek grammar of the days when Shakespeare was at school, and in it my own name, written by an earlier George Sitwell just three hundred years before.

The lumber room, with its Georgian panelling and arched window looking out upon the staircase, had always excited my curiosity, and being allowed to poke about in it on rainy days, I came upon many strange and dusty relics of the past, the flotsam and jetsam that had stranded there during several generations – old portraits and brocaded dresses, portfolios of eighteenth century prints, the wreck of a machine for perpetual motion upon which someone was supposed to have wasted twenty years of his life, a collection of minerals (two compartments were labelled 'Rubies' and 'Emeralds', but the specimens were not so large as one could have wished), flint lock guns, rapiers and swords, and a spring gun which must have been a real terror to poachers, writing desks with letters and little treasures still stowed in them, and, most precious of all, a few old chests heaped up with manuscripts, parchments and books . . .

Curiosity, and the rather wild hope of hitting upon autographs of Shakespeare or Cromwell, led me to examine these documents, and by the end of my second year at Eton I had unconsciously learned to read them.[1]

This taste for history and antiquities was to be George's salvation.

The first companion of his travels was the doctor who recommended travelling as a cure; but as a general practitioner, he did not have time to accompany George on a regular basis. The doctor's place was taken by the former butler at Wood End, Henry Moat, transformed into a valet and general factotum. Moat and Sir George developed a relationship based on mutual, if far from uncritical, respect.

A huge, purple-faced Yorkshireman from the Scarborough fishing community – who, according to Edith, resembled a benevolent hippopotamus with a voice like a foghorn – the semi-literate Moat was highly intelligent. Amused by his employer's eccentricities, he enjoyed travel abroad, especially in Italy, even learning to speak Italian. Sir George came to depend on Henry, whom he referred to sardonically as 'The Great Man'.

Italy was where Sir George went annually from 1903–15, and again from 1919 until the Second World War – generally in spring, exploring the peninsula from north to south, making notes in his small, neat handwriting. In later years he would take one of his children with him. To some extent, he was inspired by the Italophile writer Vernon Lee, then much in vogue, who was an expert on – among other attractive subjects – the gardens of Renaissance and Baroque Italy. He read her books avidly.

His object was to see as many gardens as possible. Besides albums of photographs, he has left a marvellous record of how he responded to them in his essay 'On the Making of Gardens'. 'These old Italian gardens, with their air of neglect, desolation and solitude, in spite of the melancholy of the weed-grown alleys, the weary drooping of the fern-ringed fountains, the fluteless Pans and headless nymphs and armless Apollos, have a beauty which is indescribable,' he writes. 'In all the world there is no place so full of poetry as that Villa d'Este which formalist and naturalist united to decry . . . Sleep and forgetfulness brood over the garden, and everywhere from sombre alley and moss-grown stair there rises a sweet fragrance of decay.'[2]

Two other great Italian gardens, Villa Lante near Viterbo and Palazzo Giusti at Verona, induced equal rapture. 'The Duke of Lante's garden is of another character, a place not of grandeur or tragedy but of enchanting loveliness, a paradise of gleaming water, gay flowers and golden light.' At Verona, 'when the heavy entrance doors are swung back, an enchanted vista holds the traveller spellbound – the deep, refreshing green of an avenue of cypresses half a millennium old, leading to a precipice crowned by the foliage of a higher garden. For pure sensation there is nothing in Italy equal to this first glimpse through the Giusti gateway.'[3]

He did not place the garden at Caprarola in the first rank, apart from 'the giant guard of sylvan deities, playing, quarrelling, laughing the long centuries away, which rise from the wall of the topmost terrace'. He responded passionately to Villa Torlonia at Frascati, 'a place of mysterious silence, of low-weeping fountains and muffled footfalls; a garden of sleep . . . It is death to sleep in the garden.'

But these were just a handful of the hundreds he inspected. Among others he mentions are the Cicogna garden at Varese, Castello and Villa Gamberaia near Florence, Villa Bernardini in the neighbourhood of Lucca, Bogliaco on Lake Garda, Castello d'Urio and Villa Pliniana on Lake Como, Villa Borghese and Villa Mondragone at Frascati. He speaks warmly of gardens in Italian cities – of the old terrace garden at the castello in Ferrara, the hanging garden at Mantua, the garden attached to the Palazzo Bonin at Vicenza, the gardens raised above street level at Palazzo Durazzo Pallavicini in Genoa, the vistas offered beyond the cortile of Palazzo Raimondi at Cremona.

Writing of the men who created them, he says their first thought was the aesthetic impression made on the individual. 'To them, the garden seemed to be only half the problem, the other half was that blundering, ghost haunted miracle, the human mind . . . It is strange what a sense of power and freedom these mighty outlooks give, lifting the mind high above all the pettiness of life, like a night spent under the stars.'

In garden-making, 'we should abandon the struggle to make Nature beautiful round the house and should rather move the house to where Nature is beautiful. It is only a part of the garden which lies within the boundary walls.' Over and again, he makes the point, 'we must subordinate the house to the landscape, not the landscape to the house'. He would put this into practice at Renishaw. The last, strange words of his book sum up what he hoped to achieve. 'Softly the Triton mourns, as if sobbing below his breath, alone in the moon-enchanted fairyland of a deserted garden.'[4]

In the course of his research Sir George visited all the great cities – Rome, Milan, Venice, Naples and Florence – and countless lesser ones as well. In April 1909, with the sixteen-year-old Osbert, he went up by train from Venice to Conegliano, near Treviso in the north-eastern Veneto, to see some particularly beautiful gardens, which had been so thrillingly described by Miss Lee in one of her books.

In March of the following year Sir George was by himself down at Squillace in Calabria, where the inhabitants' carefree attitude amused him. 'The population is healthy, good looking, as poor as it can possibly be, almost as dirty, and absolutely happy,' he wrote in his notebook. 'Their smiles and happy, merry faces prove that no doubt they prefer freedom to luxury. A Calabrian, I am told, only works till he has gathered together four sous. And then lives like a prince till the money is all spent and he must work again.'[5]

He was unusually adventurous in exploring Puglia, which at that date saw few English visitors. He may have read Augustus Hare's *Cities of Southern Italy and Sicily*, which warned of filthy inns, uncouth natives, savage mosquitoes, danger from brigands and 'the far more serious risk of malaria or typhoid'. Hare did not exaggerate. Vast areas of Puglia were infested by the anopheles mosquito, which killed thousands annually, while most of the scanty water supply was infected – rain sank immediately into the *tufa*, leaving what was in the cisterns for drinking and washing. But George certainly owned a copy of Janet Ross's *Land of Manfred* (a copy is in the library at Renishaw), whose description of the perils faced by visitors to Puglia did not deter him in the slightest.

His travels there have been turned into a ludicrous promenade by Osbert, who in *The Scarlet Tree* claims that Moat recounted how in 1903 his master changed into a white tie and tails before dining at the humblest *trattoria*, besides insisting on being wrapped in a mosquito net every night and having his bed dusted with Keatings flea-powder.

But every valet since Figaro has mocked his master. There was no water to launder white ties, so he cannot have worn one, while mosquito nets and Keatings were indispensable – George records being bitten by fleas eighty times between wrist and elbow during a single night in a Manfredonian hotel. However, there was plenty of clean and comfortable accommodation at Lecce and Bari, both of which he generally used as a base, reaching the interior by train.

As it was, his notebooks show Sir George thoroughly enjoying himself in Puglia, fascinated by its landscape and buildings. He ignored the waterless province's lack of gardens. At Lecce, the beautiful capital of the Salento which he visited in 1903 and again in 1908 – noting how Gregorovius had recently called the city the 'Florence of Rococo Art' – he commented on the 'good Renaissance work in the streets, and later work shading imperceptibly into Rococo'. He was also struck by a 'flower like a water lily' carved on the capitals in several of Lecce's churches.[6]

In April 1909 – accompanied by Professor Bernichi from Naples, the Inspector of Public Monuments for Southern Italy, and by his Pugliese guide Riccio – George went to see Castel del Monte, the mysterious thirteenth-century hilltop castle of Emperor Frederick II.

'The little steam trainway runs through a flat country [of] olive trees, fruit trees or vineyards,' he notes. 'Andria, a white washed town with iron balconies laden with strangely shaped pots of terra cotta and green or orange earthenware, overflowing with stocks, gilly flowers and snapdragons. The streets and market place full of cloaked figures with their cloaks flung round them like a Roman toga and soft, wide-brimmed felt hats. Some of the balconies had in the corner spikes of iron holding nice little green jars, like ginger jars. As we drove towards the castle, the earthen tops [of] walls were covered with flowering weeds, little chrome buttons of the marigold, and now and again a group of the dark blue flowers (like hyacinths). Near the castle, tall yellow flowers like asphodel.' Castel del Monte delighted him, especially a pavement of verde antiqua and bianca e nero.[7]

The next day he went on to Ruvo, where Bernichi had secured an invitation to stay overnight with the bishop. Here he admired the cathedral, one of the finest examples of Puglian Romanesque. A day later he went to Molfetta and Trani by train, exploring both before finally returning to Bari.

Not only was Sir George an avid sightseer, fascinated by architecture as well as gardens, but besides seeking a cure for his mysterious malady, he had two specific purposes. The first was to acquire furniture and pictures that would replace all that had been lost in the great Renishaw sale of half a century before. The other was to make use of his study of Italian gardens for the restoration of those at home. At this date he did not speak Italian, but he found good guides who spoke English.

⚜

'For more than two centuries the gardens of the Italian Renaissance lay under a cloud, exciting, it would seem, little but contempt and disgust in all who viewed them,' George writes, rejoicing in their rediscovery.[8]

He was no less of a pioneer in his taste for the furniture and paintings of the Italian Baroque, although in those days everyone agreed with Benedetto Croce that Baroque was the abomination of painting. 'Old Italian furniture and Italian art objects look exceedingly well – nothing in the world looks better – in company with each other, in spite of a good deal of variety in style and date, with brocade and tapestry on the walls and doorways taken from churches,' he observes in his notebook.[9] Renishaw was to be the beneficiary.

Possessing a good eye and a talent for haggling, George acquired some superb furniture. For example, he records: '3 Jan 1905. Bought of Riccardo Tedeschi, antiquario, S. Eufemia, 25 Verona, two great chairs with the arms of the Doge Morosini, bought at the Morosini Palace at Venice, for the sum of 500 lire [£20], including packing in

118.

strong wooden case. He originally asked 1800 lire. But query was there a doge of that name?'[10]

The arms were in fact those of Doge Marcantonio Giustinian (1684–88), for whom these throne-like chairs had been made by a renowned Venetian wood carver, Andrea Brustolon. Other important items were two huge candlesticks that apparently came from Lucca cathedral. (George had visited Lucca in 1903.) Further pieces included Florentine and Neapolitan cabinets of the late seventeenth century, with inlays in ivory and silver. All of these acquisitions went back to England to refurnish Renishaw.

Decades before Anthony Blunt and Denis Mahon became interested, he collected Baroque paintings, noting on 28 February 1909, 'bought an *Annunciation* guaranteed to be a genuine Francesco Solimena, born in Naples 1657, died 1747, painter and poet'.[11] He particularly admired the fantastic works of Alessandro Magnasco, a Genoese artist from the late Baroque, eventually acquiring three pictures by this artist.

His preference for everything Italian shows in the note he made after visiting what some consider France's greatest garden, at Vaux-le-Vicomte, in May 1909. Not everyone will agree with him: 'A long shadowless garden of Le Nôtre', he comments, unadmiringly. In his opinion, it was a sad example of

> vast resources laid out to little purpose, of dispropor-
> tionate upkeep, of incongruity, the garden being too
> large for the château and unsuited save for a great fête,
> forcing you to walk a great distance in the heat to see
> nothing except an expensive canal. Everywhere marble
> statues, fountains, bronze figurines, bronze and mar-
> ble boxes by the score, but never a trace of fancy or
> invention.

Staying at the Hotel Bedford in Paris, he also visited the house of René Lalique, whom he refers to sardonically as 'the sculptor-gentleman'.[12]

⸻

Sir George had toyed with the idea of building a small palazzo in Sicily, a project he discussed with Sir Edwin Lutyens. However, in November 1909 he joyfully records in his notebook that he has bought half the Tuscan castle of Acciaiuoli or Montegufoni ('hill of the screech owls'). He adds a potted history, with a neat little sketch showing how much it is dominated by its tall campanile. He wrote an excited letter to Osbert, which tells us as much about George Sitwell as it does about Montegufoni.

> You will be interested to hear that I am buying in your name the Castle of Acciaiuoli (pronounced Accheeyawly) between Florence and Siena.[13] The Acciaiuoli were a reigning family in Greece in the thirteenth century, and afterwards great Italian nobles. The castle is split up between many poor families, and has an air of forlorn grandeur. It would probably cost £100,000 to build today.
>
> There is a great tower, a picture-gallery with frescoed portraits of the owners, from a very early period, and a chapel full of relics of the Saints. There are the remains of a charming old terraced garden, not very large, with two or three statues, a pebblework grotto and rows of flowerpots. The great saloon, now divided into several rooms, opens into an interior court where one can take one's meals in hot weather, and here, over two doorways, are inscriptions giving the history of the

house, most of which was rebuilt late in the seventeenth century as a 'house of pleasure'. The owners brought together there some kind of literary academy of writers and artists.

All the rooms in the castle have names, it seems, as the Sala of the Gonfalonieri, the Sala of the Priori – twelve of the Acciaiuoli were Gonfalonieri and twelve, I think Priori – the Chamber of Donna Beatrice, the Cardinal's Chamber, the library, the Museum. There seem to have been bathrooms, and every luxury.

We shall be able to grow our own fruit, wine, oil – even our own champagne! I have actually bought half the Castle for £2,200: the other half belongs to the village usurer, whom we are endeavouring to get out . . . The roof is in splendid order, and the drains can't be wrong, as there aren't any. I shall have to find the money in your name, and I do hope, my dear Osbert, that you will prove worthy of what I am trying to do for you, and will not pursue that miserable career of extravagance and foolishness which has already once ruined the family.[14]

From now on, Renishaw Hall had a rival in Sir George's affections, which he regarded as no less a part of the Sitwells' birthright. This was why he bought it in Osbert's name, to avoid inheritance tax. Although he would have to spend years buying out 150 peasants living in the other half, it was one of the wisest purchases he ever made. Bringing the fifty rooms back to life, finding Baroque paintings and furniture, frescoing walls and recreating the gardens – as well as designing new ones – would reinforce his cure.

Yet George never fully recovered from his breakdown, which had shattered his nerves. For the rest of his life he was tormented by insomnia that made him pace up and down at night, smoking twenty to thirty Egyptian cigarettes each day. A natural introvert, he became a confirmed eccentric, taking refuge in a past he found more congenial than the present.

It was difficult for him to live with others – even with his family, despite his genuine affection for them. His remoteness was increased by his strange, impenetrable sense of humour. Nobody could tell when his remarks were designed to tease, or whether or not he was laughing at them.

However, his basic kindliness is well attested. When he died, Jack Proctor, who had first worked for him in 1903 as a secretary, wrote 'Sir George was always very kind to me . . . I was his guest on many occasions and he was always such a generous host.' Another secretary, George Airey, recalled 'his very many kindly acts to other people'.[15] Young people loved him. 'He was kind, very, when I was a child, and I remember that always,' said a cousin, Veronica Gilliat.

For all his handicaps, Sir George Sitwell was still capable of some remarkable achievements.

Chapter 13

A NEW RENISHAW

Despite spending so much time in Italy, Sir George had scarcely been idle in England. He continued to be a part-time soldier, commanding the Second Volunteers, Prince of Wales Yorkshire Regiment, from 1904 until 1908, when he retired as an honorary Colonel. Admittedly, this involved little more than a fortnight's army camp in the summer during which, in uniform and mounted on a charger, he reviewed his troops and watched them drill or perform simple manoeuvres.

Where he achieved most was in his writing and at Renishaw. He had already written one or two books, which he had himself printed at his own press in Scarborough, notably *Letters of the Sitwells and the Sacheverells*. According to his son, his literary output also included such titles as *Lepers' Squints*, *The History of the Fork*, *Domestic Manners in Sheffield in the Year 1250*, *Marriage Chests of the Middle Ages* and *The History of the Cold*. No copies survive, which is scarcely surprising as they never existed outside Osbert's imagination – he took every opportunity to make his father look a fool.

When his major Italian expeditions came to an end after the purchase of Montegufoni, George wrote a book about what he had seen. In September 1909 John Murray published *On the Making of Gardens: Being a Study of Old Italian Gardens, of the Nature of Beauty, and the Principles Involved in Garden Design*, by George Reresby Sitwell. Sadly, this little volume, less than ninety pages long, did not cause the sensation for which he had hoped, although it was admired by experts.

Arguing that his father was obsessed by the Mediterranean view that gardens were meant as places of rest and peace rather than for displays of blossoms, Osbert later claimed he knew nothing about flowers and did not even like them, believing they must not attract attention by hue or scent but 'form vague pointilist masses of colour that could never detract from the view'.[1] This was simply not true, as can be seen from Sir George's unequivocal statement that 'It was a new revelation of beauty to the present writer when in 1882 he saw at Wortley a bed filled with single dahlias and herbaceous flowers.' (Wortley Hall near Sheffield, then the seat of the Earls of Wharncliffe, is still famous for gardens which include an immensely long and beautiful herbaceous flower-bed.)

While damning the book's lush style as a Victorian period-piece from the days of Walter Pater – 'couched in phrases often of stilted beauty', etc. – Osbert grudgingly conceded that the principles it defined were invaluable ('so my gardening friends, whose judgement I trust, tell me') in the practical design of gardens, in the counterpoint of light and shade, and in the correct use of water as a device for variation.[2]

The Story of an Old Garden, written by Sir George in 1921 but never printed, tells us how in the 1880s he had excavated the foundations of the formal garden destroyed by his great-grandfather. From surveys and rentals, he found that it dated from before 1594 and had been remade when the house was built. A decade later, some boxes of old legal papers were sent to him. 'My feelings may be imagined when I opened out a large plan upon parchment of the year 1766, showing the various gardens in detail.'[3]

He then added a restored version of the original gardens to the overall scheme that he had designed and laid out in 1886–9. This was essentially a symmetrical scheme. The best way of appreciating it is to stand in the centre of the Middle Lawn's steps with the Hall behind you, from where you can see that the gardens are merely a foreground to the view of the natural boundaries beyond – which is why he placed the statues looking away from the house, to draw the eye outward. The flowers on the borders were limited to pink, blue or mauve, giving a sense of peace that did not distract one's eye from the symmetry.

From 1899 to 1904, Renishaw had been leased to a rich Sheffield businessman. When Sir George regained possession, he set about transforming the gardens in the light of what he had seen abroad. This was when he added the statues and marble fountains he had bought in Italy. Among the statues were two by Tiepolo's friend Caligari, placed at the south end of the 'Middle Lawn'. One is Diana, with a little hound, and the other is Neptune, who 'has risen from his watery realms and is drying his backside with a stone bath towel' (this description of Neptune can only have come from Sir George's grandson, Reresby).[4] He also added two carefully sited lakes, which were dug by unemployed fishermen whom he hired at Scarborough.

While working on the gardens, Sir George had consulted an expert on the subject living nearby: Francis Inigo Thomas, whose mother was Louisa Lucy's sister. Thomas had illustrated Blomfield's *The Formal Garden in England* (1892) and designed some famous gardens, including one at Sandringham. He sent plans that incorporated his ideas. In addition, George was in close touch with the renowned Gertrude Jekyll, besides seeking the advice of her professional partner Edwin Lutyens – the pair were famous for their new 'natural' style of gardening, which combined shrubs and herbaceous borders while making full use of the architectural background. Yet what was done at

Renishaw was essentially George's own creation, as can be shown from *The History of an Old Garden*.

Even while living in Tuscany between the wars, he returned almost annually to make further improvements, his last addition being the fish pond in 1936, although this was not to be completed for over three decades. Renishaw suited perfectly his axiom that a house must be subordinated to its garden. The grim northern aspect of the Hall, with its bleak grey walls above flat, flowerless turf, hid what lay beyond, so that after walking through to the other side of the house the visitor was spellbound by the unexpected, enchanting vistas to the south.

At the same time, Sir George renewed Renishaw's interior, creating a new stairwell with a (modern) 'Jacobean'-style staircase of natural oak which was later stained black by Osbert. He also employed Lutyens to redesign the billiard room as another fine drawing room that linked the Great Drawing Room with the ballroom. It was given a coved ceiling, windows on to the park, a French window into the garden and two black columns flanking the ballroom door.

Lutyens also refurbished the ballroom, which now housed many of his employer's recently acquired paintings and furniture (notably the enormous Brustolon chairs). Sir George even suggested that he might redecorate a room in the 'Aubrey Beardsley style', but did not ask him to take the idea any further.[5] While he enjoyed Beardsley's drawings, it may well have been a joke – Lutyens never realised that his host enjoyed teasing him.

When Edwin Lutyens first came to Renishaw in September 1908, he reported to his wife that besides helping to restore the gardens and the work inside the hall, 'Sir George wants me to build a little water palace, one room on the lake, which would be a delightful thing.' This suggestion, too, may have been a joke. Lutyens was on firmer ground, however, in observing that his new employer 'affects all things Italian'. Presumably he was referring to his unfashionable taste for the Baroque.[6]

Sir George never ceased to improve Renishaw, placing a particularly fine Neapolitan cabinet in the dining room. However, in 1911, because it was costing him £500 a year in insurance fees, he sold one of the house's great treasures – Perugino's *Three Maries* – to John Pierpont Morgan for £30,000.[7]

He worried about every aspect of decoration, down to the last detail. In June 1905 his agent received a letter from him listing which rooms were to be repainted and repapered and how, and which pictures were to be cleaned, varnished or rehung. A French window must be made for the ballroom, opening onto the lawn, so it could be used as a drawing room. 'Take down all curtains and put up again in a month's time,' ordered the letter. 'Syringe poison into all the worm-holes in the furniture' – the furniture being the old oak chairs from seventeenth-century Renishaw.

Lady Ida never commented on what her husband was achieving inside the house or in the gardens. She spent as much time as possible on a chair in the Gothic porch on the north side, proclaiming her disinterest. However, she presided graciously enough over his entertaining. George could well afford this, since his changes at Renishaw and Montegufoni were all paid for by money he made on the Stock Exchange.

Far from unsocial, he gave annual parties at the Hall for the Doncaster races in September, although racing bored him. These parties were always on an extravagant scale, with chefs and extra footmen being engaged and German bands hired (housed in the Sitwell Arms) while new linen and delicacies were purchased, with the family's silver plate brought in from the vaults of the local bank. He often entertained as many as thirty houseguests.

He also went regularly to dinner parties in London. On 2 June 1910 he recorded in his notebook,

> The Williamsons had at dinner Prince Frederick (of Prussia), Mrs George Cornwallis-West – formerly Lady Randolph Churchill – Lord Hothfield, Sir Robert and Lady R. Manners, Sir Trevor (he collects old Japanese lacquer) and Lawrence and their daughter, Sir Hugh Lane, Mr Creighton, Mr Pierpont Morgan the great collector, Ida, Edith and I.

Lawrence was president of the Royal Horticultural Society, and Lane (who went down with the *Lusitania*) was a lover of Impressionist art, his collection becoming the nucleus of the Hugh Lane Gallery in Dublin.

Characteristically, in the entry for the dinner party, Sir George also notes, 'Lutyens writes that for flat stone borders to flowerbeds he never puts less than 15 inches.'[8] – for his mind always remained fixed on Renishaw. Osbert Sitwell says dismissively that his father 'abolished small hills, created lakes, and particularly liked to alter the levels at which full-grown trees were standing'.[9] In reality, inspired by what he had seen in Italy, he had accomplished something breathtakingly original, transporting the Mediterranean to Derbyshire.

In doing so, he showed that he was one of the finest landscape gardeners of his age. Osbert claimed mockingly that his father told him he wanted to go down in history as 'the great Sir George'; but that is what he was. He received little recognition in his lifetime, from his children or from anyone else. One day, however, a grandson would understand his vision for Renishaw Hall, and would see that it came true.

Chapter 14

RENISHAW CHILDREN

ost literary-minded people who hear the name Sitwell think
of Edith, Osbert and Sacheverell. Although most of their
childhood was passed at Scarborough, where they were born, the
family having moved back into Wood End, the three spent several
months every summer at Renishaw. Despite grumbles about their
parents, all recalled their time there as magical. On a window in
the old night nursery, the first room they knew, had been cut with
a diamond the words, '*Charmes des yeux, Renishaw 1825*', which was
justified by the view.

⁓

Renishaw meant most to Osbert, who, born in 1892, was aware from
an early age that the house and the estate were going to be his. He
said that as a very little child he was frightened at night by 'this large,
rambling old house, haunted and haunting', lit only by candlelight. Yet
'my home always meant Renishaw', he recalled, while admitting that
most of his childhood had been spent in Scarborough or London on
visits to his grandparents or away at school.

He lyrically described summers at Renishaw as a small boy. When
he arrived, he would run through the hall to the low half-door on
the other side, over which came through the open window 'the over-
whelming and, as it seemed, living scent of stock and clove, carnation

131.

and tobacco-plant on a foundation of sun-warmed box hedges'. He never forgot the joy with which he arrived, nor his sorrow at leaving.

Although scarcely a countryman – he neither farmed, hunted nor shot – he developed a deep sympathy with the surrounding country, responding to its sombre charm. He liked to think that his forebears who built up the estate had bequeathed 'something still very real and active in my nature; this love seemed to me so much older than myself and so much part of me'.[1] One day, he would find an artist who shared his vision and painted both house and countryside for him,

In particular, Osbert loved what he termed the 'impalpable essence' of the house, 'laden with the dying memories of three centuries, pervading the mind like a scent faintly detected, the smell of woodsmoke for example'.[2] Despite being an agnostic, he believed in ghosts, joining the Ghost Club – dedicated to investigating the paranormal. In an early poem called 'Night' (one of the best he ever wrote), he conveys the eeriness that he sometimes felt at Renishaw:

> A door that opens slightly, not enough;
> The rustling sigh of silk along a floor;
> The knowledge of being watched by one long dead;
> By something that is outside Nature's pale;
> The unheard sounds that haunt an ancient house;
> The feel of one who listens in the dark,
> Listens to that which happened long ago . . .[3]

Five years older, Edith responded in much the same way to the atmosphere, and seems to have had Renishaw in mind in one of her own early poems, 'The Sleeping Beauty'.

In *Taken Care Of*, written just before she died, she tells of her child-ish fondness for a beautiful peacock in the gardens there, 'Peaky', who seemed to return her affection, every morning running to be fed by her, until the day came when he was given a peahen for a mate and abandoned poor Edith. She consoled herself with a puffin who had a wooden leg, and a baby owl who snored to lure mice within range.[4]

Renishaw left no less impression on Sacheverell, even though he would acquire a fine old house of his own. In *All Summer in a Day*, he writes of an idyllic childhood there, and only the happiest memories can have inspired such nostalgic poems as 'The Renishaw Woods' or 'The Lime Avenue' (in *The Cyder Feast* of 1927).

Yet 'Sachie' had sinister memories too. He recalled the ballroom and the Great Drawing Room when he was a child as 'terrifying to be alone in, or even to walk through by oneself', and that being asked to fetch something left in the red dining room was 'an excursion fraught with horror' – the portraits on its walls turned their heads, following him with their eyes.[5]

When young, by his own admission, Osbert loved his father; he was grateful for advice on overcoming a terror of Hell (which did not exist for Sir George), or getting on with other boys at Eton. But during his late teens they fell out. Part of the reason was Sir George's nagging fear that his son might grow up to be a spendthrift, warning him of the dangers of extravagance which had proved disastrous for the fam-ily in the past.

Yet Sir George had more influence on his eldest son's develop-ment than Osbert liked to admit. Few fathers can have presented a ten-year-old boy with a tiny edition of Pope's *Rape of the Lock*, illustrated by Beardsley, as he did; when Osbert grew older he advised him to read Ruskin, and Darwin's *Origin of Species*. Above all, he taught him to love Italy, taking him to Venice – which for the rest of his life remained his favourite city – and to Rome, Florence and Naples, as well as instilling an enthusiasm for the Mezzogiorno.

⬥

Always a strong character – she aimed a blow from her pram at the actress Mrs Patrick Campbell for calling her a 'baby' – Edith later claimed to have detested her parents from an early age. However, her letters give the impression that she was fond of both into her teens. Yet she certainly had reason to dislike them, having been rejected from the start as an ugly little female oddity instead of the darling boy for whom they hoped, and made more miserable still by Osbert's arrival.

Embarrassed by having produced such a 'fright', Lady Ida was often harsh with Edith, who in old age claimed bitterly that her mother had bullied her throughout her childhood because she embodied an unhappy marriage. 'You'd better run, Miss Edith,' she recalled Moat warning. 'Her ladyship is in one of her states and looking for you.'

Her abnormally long, attenuated limbs seemed dangerously weak, which worried her father. (She may have suffered from Marfan Syndrome, a malady that affects the connective tissues.) She hated George for sending her to a quack specialist who made her wear steel braces to strengthen spine and ankles, and a brace to straighten her crooked nose. She called the apparatus her 'Bastille', never forgetting the pain and humiliation. Yet this was the best, most expensive treatment available – she could scarcely complain of neglect.

In all her writings she says nothing of Sir George shaping her mind, save for his disapproval of her fondness for Swinburne. But her finest

134.

biographer, Victoria Glendinning, believes that little as Edith cared to admit it, she derived from George 'much of his liking for strange information and the habit of books'.[6] It is probable that he taught her to enjoy Alexander Pope's verse, since she recalls learning by heart *The Rape of the Lock* before she was thirteen – in her bedroom, by candle-light – and *The Rape* was one of his favourite poems.

Only from Osbert and Edith do we have accounts of Sir George's shortcomings. Despite Sachie's closeness to his siblings, he had nothing but good to say about their father, although fully aware of his eccentricity. He was especially grateful for being taken to Italy in the Easter holidays – by the time he was nine he had seen not only Rome, Florence and Venice, but Lucca and Bologna. 'Even when I was really young', he recalls, 'my father was always talking to me about the paintings and the buildings he had seen, particularly in southern Italy.'[7]

As for his mother, Sachie loved her unreservedly. In *Splendours and Miseries* (1943), the chapter 'Songs my mother taught me' is a paean of gratitude. 'Her character, when I first remember her, was a compound of natural high spirits and a sort of palace-bred or aristocratic helplessness.' He adds, 'There was always something tragic in her appearance, which I felt deeply as a child, in spite of her gaiety and powers of mimicry.'[8]

Even so, Lady Ida all too frequently lost her temper, and while Sir George was the main target, she savaged the children as well. (As late as the 1930s, watching two Guatemalan volcanoes, Osbert joked that it reminded him of life with his parents.) But Sachie, the youngest, suffered least.

Nevertheless, Ida fascinated and charmed all her children with her beauty and sense of fun. When very small, she took them to make butter in the dairy at the home farm, to fish for pike in Foxton Dam or to hear an old farmer's ancient wife sing part of the Hallelujah Chorus in a cracked voice – their naive pleasure causing her much secret amusement. When they were older, discovering that her Swiss maid Frieda knew how to yodel, she persuaded the girl to give a performance for them in her bedroom, although the bashful Frieda would only do so from behind a Japanese screen.

In July 1907 she arranged for someone else to present her daughter at court – a bit overdue, since Edith was already twenty and girls typically came out at eighteen. Besides inheriting Sir Sitwell Sitwell's great beak of a nose, Edith had grown to be six feet tall, which accentuated her 'freakish' looks. It looks as if Ida did not wish to be seen with such an unsightly child, whom in her superstitious way she regarded as a changeling. In a long white gown and elbow-length kid gloves, ostrich feathers in her hair, and looking more of a 'fright' than ever, poor Edith nervously made her curtsy at Buckingham Palace to Edward VII and Queen Alexandra.

Lady Ida was always trying to outwit the husband she saw as a penny-pinching tyrant. She took advantage of his absence in Italy to order enormous quantities of champagne and give lavish parties, or to go on manic shopping sprees in London, as well as acquiring a taste for gambling. Understandably, she resented being put on a tight rein when he came home and, naively cunning, tried to turn her children against him. Edith recalls her confiding, 'with a far-away, idealist look in her eyes, "What I would *really* like, would be to get your father put away in a lunatic asylum."'[9] She also told them that a baronet was 'the lowest thing on God's earth'.

Edwin Lutyens' account of staying at Renishaw for the first time, in September 1908, portrays the family as perfectly normal – despite his being put in the Duke's Room, which he felt sure was haunted. 'Sir George Sitwell is very courteous, very civil . . . Lady Ida is a darling.' He noticed the house was full of pictures, 'some quite, some very good'.[10] He sent off a telegram for colours and materials to redecorate the ballroom, which proved a big success.

The only thing Lutyens thought odd about his stay was being taken by cab to see Hardwick and Haddon Hall. 'They have no horses or motors here, but hire taxis from Sheffield.' Learning that the great architect was in the neighbourhood, the new Duchess of Devonshire, who happened to be at Hardwick, sent a message to say how delighted she would be to meet him. Having made the vast old house habitable by putting in hot pipes, she wanted free advice on decoration. Afterwards, 'Sir George said he had never seen anybody pick a man's brains so completely.'

During further visits to Renishaw, Lutyens modified his opinion. He found Sir George an unusually demanding employer, who actually dared to improve on his plans or even to reject them and was 'rather sticky about the garden'. He also realised that while the beautiful Lady Ida might be 'a darling', her behaviour could be horribly embarrassing when she'd had too much to drink.

Impudently, young Osbert asked him if any of his twelve brothers and sisters shared his talent. He never forgot Lutyens' reply, which was that none of them did, and that he attributed his gifts to a childhood illness that had stopped him playing games and made him use his eyes instead of his feet.

Osbert was miserable at his preparatory school, Ludgrove, where at first he tried to find relief by malingering. He called it 'Bloodsworth', claiming he had been sent there because the headmaster was 'the most famous dribbler in England'. (Osbert did not care for football.) His salvation was an Italian holiday each spring. In 1908 his father was delighted to find how much he enjoyed Rome. 'No amount of travelling or sight-seeing tires him and he always sleeps and eats well,' his father wrote proudly to Ida on 30 April after showing him the city. 'He is such a dear boy, altogether.'[11]

'I liked Eton,' Osbert wrote sardonically in his memoirs, 'except in the following respects: for work and games, for boys and masters . . . It was extraordinary how delightful, easy, cheerful, the school looked [in the summer holidays], without masters, matrons or pupils.'[12] A heavy, moon-faced boy, lumpish yet nervous, who mumbled and had atrocious handwriting (which he never tried to improve), his work was invariably third-rate and he avoided all sporting activities like the plague. His favourite relaxation was arranging flowers at the local florist's shop.

All he learned was to read voraciously – novels, verse and plays – a habit he retained for the rest of his life. This was why he claimed to have been 'educated in the holidays from Eton'. He also developed a malicious sense of humour, and the knack of becoming the life and soul of a party. What he would never admit was that during the holidays his father's influence gave him an intellectual curiosity and, in consequence, a remarkable openness to new ideas.

Osbert conjures up how Renishaw felt in those days, especially when he was alone there with his father in October or November:

> Then, with so few people in the house, we lived for the most part in the Carolean core of it, and everything as a result looked as strange to us as if we inhabited a

different mansion in a different world. But even though we used only the Little Parlour and the Great Parlour, abandoning the large eighteenth-century apartments, nevertheless you could feel the vastness of the stretch of rooms that lay there beyond, on each side, empty . . .

But were they empty, for at moments during the evenings as we sat by the fire, so many creakings and rustlings made themselves heard, so many of those inexplicable sounds of an ancient dwelling place, that it appeared as though there were more ghosts than human beings in rooms and corridors? One would say to oneself that it must be the wind: but I still do not believe that it was. Phantoms, when one is young, no more prevent sleep than do the hooting of engines or other modern noise – but those we heard were ancient, issued from some cave in time where they had hidden and to which they returned, or so it seemed to me.[13]

⁂

While Edith gained much from the beauty around her at Renishaw, she found the atmosphere stifling. When not lugged off by her parents to Scarborough, London or abroad, she had to stay in Derbyshire, but not without a hint of rebellion. (Taken to the races to mark her coming of age, she sat with her back to the course.) Looks like hers meant that she did not have any male admirers, and she was unattracted by her own sex. Very lonely, she devoured a vast amount of English verse, especially Swinburne, to whom her governess introduced her.

In 1909, in another act of defiance, Edith ran away from her grandmother's house at Bournemouth and went with a maid to the Isle of Wight. There, at Bonchurch, she laid a wreath of flowers and libations of milk and honey on the grave of her hero Swinburne, who had just died. But she returned immediately to her grandmother's, meekly accepting a scolding.

Yet Edith had an audience, of sorts. In her melodious voice she was always reading selections of her favourite verse to her brothers, who believed she was a genius, revelling in her wild humour. She was also encouraged by her former governess, Helen Rootham, who had been engaged in 1903 and had stayed on as a companion. Helen was liked by nearly everyone (although not by little Sacheverell, who loathed her); even Osbert admired the way she played the piano. She has been described, perhaps a little too imaginatively, as 'a cross between Miss Havisham and one of Bernard Shaw's "new women"'.

Plain and lonely herself, Helen grew very fond of the clever, sensitive girl whose odd looks deprived her of friends. She did her best to develop Edith's talents, making her play Chopin and Brahms, teaching her to appreciate Ravel and Debussy and to read Baudelaire, Verlaine and Rimbaud (whose verse Helen had translated). They went to Berlin and Paris together, visiting art galleries, going to concerts.

Besides being an excellent musician, Helen was a gifted linguist who spoke Russian and Serbo-Croat. Although a Catholic, she was fascinated by Madame Blavatsky's occultism and the writings of the Orthodox seer Vladimir Solovyov (a friend of Dostoyevsky, who used him as a model for Alyosha in *The Brothers Karamazov*). Helen also took an interest in alarming aspects of the spirit world.

'I saw a ghost when I was young,' Edith told Elizabeth Salter years later. 'It was a face in a golden helmet on the Roman road that runs through Renishaw.'[14] No doubt, she saw it with Helen's enthusiastic encouragement.

Deciding that Edith had heard a phantom walking in the 'ghost passage', Helen went through the house at night with her, reciting the Catholic prayers for the dead. They heard footsteps overhead, then coming down stairs, with 'a horrible suggestion of the very soul of evil', after which a shapeless black mist floated past. That night it visited Helen, but was driven off by her prayers. Edith said the ghost was never seen or heard again. The story sounds as if Helen's obsession with the occult had a lot to do with the phenomenon.[15]

Sacheverell profited more from Eton than Osbert, developing highly individual tastes. He was encouraged by an imaginative tutor, Tuppy Headlam, to use the school library and read what he pleased. Among the books he borrowed were Ernest Fenollosa's *Epochs of Chinese and Japanese Art*, just after its publication in 1912, while he devoured William Beckford and Gustave Flaubert. The son of a man who admired the new as well as the old, Sachie was at the same time fascinated by what was most up to date in art and literature. At sixteen he began a correspondence with Filippo Marinetti, impressed by his *Futurist Manifesto*. He also took Wyndham Lewis's Vorticist magazine, *Blast*.

He responded far more than his siblings to his father's influence and to what had been created at Renishaw. This was where he learned that the art of past ages is always worth re-examining. When he grew up, he was one of the first to sing the praises of Francesco Solimena and, with Osbert, founded a Magnasco Society. Pictures by these two Baroque masters hanging on the walls at home must have been the earliest examples of their work he ever saw, since even in Italy few galleries would have bothered to display them – they were considered vulgar beyond words.

These years at Renishaw shaped all three children's development, as it was here that their father kept his most treasured possessions – and he obviously spoke to Osbert and Edith just as he did to Sacheverell. What he said played a crucial role in forming their taste. Sadly, his daughter could never forgive him for seeing her as the ugly duckling that she was, while for a different reason Osbert, too, would grow to hate him. Sachie was very much the exception.

Chapter 15

LEAVING THE NEST

After such a dismal career at Eton, there seemed little point in sending Osbert up to Oxford, although he would have liked to go. His father hoped a spell in the army might instil self-discipline, so he was sent to a crammer to prepare for the Sandhurst entrance examination. When he failed it twice, Sir George obtained a commission for him as a second lieutenant in the yeomanry, from which he was immediately seconded to the 11th Hussars, a crack cavalry regiment – known as the 'Cherry Pickers', on account of their crimson breeches. They were garrisoned at Aldershot, where Osbert spent six months in 1911.

Osbert's career as a Hussar was a black comedy, shudderingly recalled in *Great Morning*. At dawn, every day except Sunday, NCOs made him undergo the inane routine of sabre drill (four cuts with a cavalry sabre, over and over again) and to ride bareback without a saddle, facing his mount's tail – forced to remount every time he fell off, which he did all too often since his 'singularly vicious and oafish horse' threw him regularly. 'I abominated [horses], and the brutes, with that animal instinct of theirs, knew of my loathing and returned it a thousand fold.'[1] Nor did he think much of the full-dress uniform with its yellow frogs and plumed fur busby – a 'pseudo-Hungarian affair'.

Having failed to learn to shoot properly with a twelve-bore at home – 'I was a profoundly, almost an inspired bad shot' – he was no less useless with a cavalry carbine. Since the main amusements of his dashing brother officers, who had names like 'Pongo' or 'Snorter', were hunting and shooting, these deficiencies did not endear him. In turn, they taught him to 'plumb the depths of the real and active hatred that the stupid in England . . . cherish towards beauty in every form'.

London was only a short rail journey from Aldershot, however, so occasionally he could run up by train and visit theatres or art galleries. He never forgot the night he first saw the Ballets Russes perform Stravinsky's *Firebird*, when Tamara Karsavina was dancing. It was one of the great formative experiences of his life. 'Now I knew where I stood,' he wrote thirty-five years later. 'I would be, for so long as I lived, on the side of the arts . . . I would support the artist in every controversy, on every occasion.'[2]

<hr />

Osbert's time in the cavalry coincided with being dragged into the whirlpool of his mother's financial problems. Her husband had been bailing her out for years, but by 1911 she had amassed debts of over £2,000, after promising him she would keep within her income of over £1,000. In desperation, Lady Ida asked her son for advice. He told her to go to somebody who had been recommended by Willie Martin, a fellow pupil at his crammer's.

This was an elderly Anglo-American gentleman, a charming old Harrovian with literary pretensions called Julian Osgood Field, who lived at the Grosvenor Hotel. Invited to stay at Renishaw, Mr Field made an excellent impression on his hostess, gaining her complete confidence. In reality, he was an undischarged bankrupt who had been to prison for forgery, a professional swindler and blackmailer.

After persuading her to sign two bills for £6,000 in the name of a Miss Frances Dobbs – a rich old lady from Streatham who had fallen into the clutches of one of his shady friends – Field had them discounted by a moneylender named Owles. He then involved her in further transactions so that by the end of the following year she owed more than £11,000, but had received less than £600. Ida was reduced to such straits that she was forced to sell her jewellery and borrow from the servants, at one point owing £125 to the butler Moat.

When Lady Ida complained to Field about receiving such paltry sums, he cowed her by threatening to tell her husband, after which he bullied her into trying to find other victims to underwrite the sums she owed. In a letter to him, she wrote that when her son joined the 11th Hussars, 'there must be some boy he can get hold of'. Eager to help his mother, Osbert persuaded the aforementioned Willie Martin, now a subaltern in the Rifle Brigade, to guarantee a bill. Ida herself wheedled a young Yorkshireman called John Philip Wilson into borrowing money from Field. Inevitably, Martin found himself pestered for money, and threatened to tell his colonel.

Eventually Sir George discovered what was happening. He discreetly settled the debts of Martin and Wilson, with those of his wife, except for the £6,000 owed to the moneylender Owles. He knew Field had broken the law by pretending to Owles that Miss Dobbs had agreed to extend her bill, and thought Field would have no option other than to pay Owles the £6,000. He did not realise that Field was penniless.

For a time Lady Ida was banished from Renishaw, to live at Wood End by herself. From there, she bombarded her husband almost every day with harrowing letters in which she begged to come home. She also wrote to her son, imploring him to intercede.

The situation was too much for Osbert, who had a nervous collapse and was given a long period of leave by the regiment. He spent it in Florence, regaining his equilibrium. His father then arranged for him to transfer as a subaltern into the Grenadier Guards, which he joined late in December 1912.

⚜

Osbert found a Grenadier's life less demanding than a cavalryman's. Morning parades were at 10.00 a.m., after which the day was free for officers, unless on ceremonial duty at St James's Palace, Buckingham Palace, the Tower or the Bank of England. They had three months' leave, the only proper soldiering being a few weeks on manoeuvres in the summer. Even so, when the old Chelsea Barracks was pulled down, Osbert recalled bugles summoning him to 'one unpleasant task or another'. He spent his free time at the theatre, the opera, the ballet or art galleries and read voraciously – not only modern writers such as H. G. Wells or Arnold Bennett, but Strindberg and Samuel Butler, the last two becoming favourite authors.

As a young Guards officer who could amuse and knew how to flatter, he was sought after by London hostesses, whom he later recalled as the '*vieillesse dorée*', receiving invitations to dinners and balls in palatial houses. Six foot three and beautifully dressed, if far from handsome he looked distinguished, with a profile that had become became positively Hanoverian – not unlike George III on a coin.

He went regularly to parties given by the prime minister's wife, Margot Asquith; at Grosvenor Street by Mrs George Keppel (the late King Edward's mistress); and by his aunt Londesborough. The ones he liked best were Lady Cunard's in Cavendish Square, because the other guests were so interesting – here he met Delius and George Moore, besides flirting with his hostess's 'nymphomaniac' daughter Nancy. At a Cavendish Square dinner he sat next to the eighteen-year-old Lady Diana Manners, who was astonished when the foppish 'guardee' asked her, 'What do you really think of Stravinsky?'

146.

The ponderous youth who had been such a clumsy failure as a caval-ryman acquired confidence and poise, though he perhaps dressed a little too elegantly – his concern with making the right impression hinted at a certain insecurity. He loved dancing, and made a number of girl friends, including Lady Diana. However, when Mrs Keppel's daughter Violet proposed to him (on the rebound, after her adored Vita Sackville-West married Harold Nicolson) he bolted out of the house, pretending he had an urgent appointment. Yet he says that he went everywhere with an eighteen-year-old girl whom he does not name – 'to her, companion of my youth, I owe an inestimable amount of happiness and sorrow, of joy and regret'. If this is true, it was a purely platonic romance.[3]

For the moment, Osbert was on good enough terms with his father to ask him to dinner at the Marlborough Club in Pall Mall, which he had just joined, and then to the Hippodrome theatre. He soon overspent his allowance of £700 a year, however. 'One had to spend money,' he wrote. 'To this pursuit I brought the zest and sureness of touch inher-ited from my ancestors.'[4] In consequence, within a few weeks of joining his new regiment he had run up debts – not large ones, but well beyond his capacity to pay. He had to ask his father to settle them, sending a letter of apology in his childish handwriting.

As someone who put his trust in double-entry book-keeping and had been driven to the brink of insanity by his wife's extravagance, Sir George was appalled, bombarding his son with stern letters. Early in 1913 he reminded Osbert of how his grandfather Lord Londesborough had nearly ruined himself, implying that he might take after him.

When Osbert declined to give a detailed estimate of every expense for the next year (including what he would spend on cigarettes), his father reacted angrily. 'If I had no previous experience [meaning Lady

Ida] I would not feel it so much,' he wrote. 'But I am sick and sore to the soul from 26 years of the same experience, and I recognise in this the same ideas, part of the same cycle. If I could have felt you were in your heart sorry and would be more careful in the future, I would have paid.'

Osbert had refused to keep his yearly expenditure within his allowance of £700. 'You would not give up your servants, would not promise not to book theatre tickets, not to smoke less expensive cigarettes,' went on Sir George. 'And you seemed to be under the impression that the money to pay the old bills was falling from the sky . . . This difference between us has been growing like an evil tree until it has now led to a break of the old relations.'

'Loyalty to your regiment will oblige you to dress well,' admitted the volunteer colonel. Yet 'there should be some feeling of shame, not only on spending on clothes, cigarettes, etc., much more than I do, but at having to be self-indulgent at all.' (This is the puritan voice of Louisa Lucy.) 'You should be self-denying in small things, must realise that you must make some return to the world, must work and take trouble without grumbling, must not complain about boredom when you have a single dull day. Then I shall be able to feel real respect for your character.'[5]

An (unjustified) suspicion that his soldier son wore lace pyjamas did not help matters. By the summer of 1914, Sir George felt he had had enough. One morning Osbert received a letter from his father ordering him to leave the Grenadiers, place himself on the Reserve, and return to Renishaw. A job was waiting for him in the office of the Town Clerk of Scarborough, where he would find fewer opportunities for extravagance. He had to obey or starve.

In 1913, a poem by Edith called 'Drowned Suns' appeared in the *Daily Mirror*. It was her first published verse. Delighted at being paid two sovereigns, she began to nurse the wild hope that she might have a career as a poet, encouraged by the paper publishing further poems.

By now Lady Ida had returned from exile at Wood End, and was drinking more than ever. Her noisy rows with Sir George became intolerable. Edith complained bitterly that her mother, incoherent from whisky (and something very like paranoia), was declaring frantically that 'only middle class people look down on her'.[6] Nothing could possibly have been worse than the atmosphere at Renishaw.

Although penniless (apart from a legacy of £100 a year) and despite her mother's hysterical protests, Edith decided to leave Derbyshire, accompanied by Helen Rootham. In May 1914 Edith pawned a little diamond brooch, after which the pair pooled their scanty funds and took a train to London, where they found refuge at Miss Fussell's boarding house for ladies in Bayswater. Sir George paid the rent.

Soon they moved to Pembridge Mansions, a grim red-brick block in nearby Moscow Road, into a sparsely furnished top-floor flat up four flights of stone stairs (there was no lift). They kept body and soul together on buns, packets of soup and tins of beans. Again, Edith's father paid the rent, but little else. For a time, she worked as a clerk in the Chelsea Pension Office, earning 25 shillings a week. Despite her poverty, she began to give literary tea parties. Yet she never uprooted herself from Renishaw altogether, returning there every summer.

Sir George's parsimony must be seen in the light of an obsessive insecurity. He could not forget his grandfather's ruin, how debt had helped to destroy his father – financial worries had overshadowed his early childhood. Moreover, not just his wife but her whole family were pathological spendthrifts.

Having inherited a rent roll of £100,000 a year together with investments worth two million, his father-in-law Lord Londesborough had squandered huge sums on chorus girls, theatrical ventures, racehorses and yachts; and despite a lavish marriage settlement, his widow went to moneylenders. Ida's equally self-indulgent brother kept a private fire-engine at hand so that he could rush to conflagrations, fire stations being paid to alert him.

Understandably, George feared his children might have inherited extravagance from one side or the other, putting everything that he had restored and created at Renishaw at risk. He was shaken to the core by Osbert's jokes about money, such as, 'Look after the pounds and the pennies will take care of themselves.'

Yet something more than Sir George's anger at his son's extravagance must have made Osbert hate his parent so bitterly; something that was never put on paper. Sachie, too, depended for money on his father, who gave him far less, but he did not react like Osbert. The most plausible explanation (and it is only a guess) is that Sir George suspected early on that his eldest son was homosexual, and would never produce an heir to carry on the Sitwell line – a crushing blow to a man who set such store by primogeniture. Although his affection for his son never wavered, he could well have voiced these suspicions in a way that proved traumatic for Osbert, who may not yet have accepted his homosexuality.

Chapter 16

THE GREAT WAR, AND LADY IDA'S ORDEAL

At 8 a.m. on 16 December 1914, Scarborough was awoken by enemy shells, fired by three German battleships so close inshore that the inhabitants could see the sailors who were working the guns. The shelling went on for nearly an hour. Scarborough Castle, the Grand Hotel, three churches and numerous houses were badly damaged, while eighteen townspeople were killed or mortally wounded and many more seriously hurt. Panic-stricken men, women and children ran into the surrounding countryside.

Sir George was at Wood End, which was damaged by shrapnel during the bombardment (Osbert says his father insisted that the Germans shelled Scarborough because they knew he was there). He took shelter in the cellar while, true to form, Lady Ida stayed resolutely in bed. After this Sir George decided that he and his wife should live as far away from the sea as possible, which meant Renishaw, where they spent the rest of the war – their longest period of unbroken residence.

Osbert had been only too glad to be recalled to the Colours by the Grenadiers on the day before war was declared. It meant an escape from the ghastly life that his father had been planning for him at

Scarborough Town Hall. He ordered his 'soldier-servant' Robins to pack his evening clothes, which would of course be needed when the British occupied Berlin; but instead of going to France with the British Expeditionary Force, he fell ill and was left to guard the Docks, missing the Mons Campaign.

Having recovered, he received his marching orders two days after the Scarborough bombardment. 'My darling Boy,' wrote his mother, 'I miss you too dreadfully, it is all too awful – Darling, I could not stand seeing you leave . . . if ever I have been hard or cruel or unkind, please forgive me and realise I adore you and if it was in my power I would do anything in the world for you.'[1]

He went into the line near Fleurbaix just before Christmas, shortly after his battalion had been given a severe mauling. He recalls how shaken he was by 'the first sight of the flying fountains of dead earth, the broken trees and mud, and at the first sounds, growing ever more ominous as one drew nearer to the bumping and metallic roaring which resembled a clash of comets . . .'.[2] The routine was four days in the trenches, then out for four days' rest before going in again. Sir George sent him antiseptic soap, waterproof boots and tins of Keating's flea-powder – 'tell me what you want, just as a schoolboy does, and I'll see to it'.

In March 1915, Osbert was recalled to London in case he should be needed as a witness at his mother's trial. In November the previous year, her suit against Field had been heard in the King's Bench Division. Field, stated Lady Ida's lawyers, had defrauded her of £7,775. Anxious to conceal he was an undischarged bankrupt, he offered no defence. Judgement and costs were awarded to the plaintiff after a short hearing; but it was a Pyrrhic victory, as Field was penniless and could not pay.

Worse still, the heirs of the moneylender Owles (who by then had died) wanted to be repaid his £6,000. But Sir George remained fully convinced that there was no need to settle. When a prosecution for fraud was brought against Field and Lady Ida early in 1915, instead of paying the money – which he could easily have afforded – Sir George and his lawyers made the mistake of thinking his wife could not possibly be found guilty; it was not as if she had been signing cheques in someone else's name. They were unaware of the letters that she had written to Field.

The trial took place at the Old Bailey in March. In his statement to the court, George revealed the strain his marriage had put on him. 'She was seventeen years old when I married her,' he said. 'It was clear that her education had been neglected, but I thought her mind and character would develop if taken out of those surroundings. Ever since the time of her marriage she has been quite unable to appreciate the value of money. She has never understood business matters and she has never been able to appreciate the liabilities into which she has from time to time become involved.'[3] He described how often he paid her debts, after she had promised she would never ask him again.

Medical evidence was produced to show the defendant was not responsible. Dr Salter, who had attended Lady Ida for twenty years, described her as suffering from nervous problems, including insomnia, loss of memory and even an inability to walk – in 1911 she had been confined to her room for three months. Any calculation of figures was beyond her, he insisted, her mental development having been 'arrested by serious illness in childhood'. Dr Vernon Jones, who had also treated her for twenty years, stated that Lady Ida's capacity for understanding business matters was nil and that she was 'incapable of acting alone in any important matters . . . an easy prey to anyone who advised her or sought to guide her actions'.[4]

What Sir George had not taken into account was Mr Justice Darling, who had little sympathy with the rich while less privileged people were suffering from wartime privations and the daily shock of casualty lists. He turned against Lady Ida after her letter asking Osbert to find 'some boy' to guarantee her loans was read out in court – on the face of it, a damning piece of evidence – and refused to take into account the doctors' testimony.

On 13 March he ensured, with a summing-up overstating the case against her, that she was found guilty of conspiracy to defraud. He then sentenced her to three months' imprisonment in Holloway. She had been condemned as an accessory for aiding and abetting Field, without any allowance for circumstances.

Despite his age, Julian Osgood Field got eighteen months' hard labour, served at Wormwood Scrubs. He never recovered, dying alone in a room in the slums of Kilburn in 1925 and leaving just over £13.0s.0d. – as Osbert, always a good hater, gloatingly records in an appendix to *Great Morning*.

A horrified George sent a twenty-eight-page document to the Home Secretary, arguing that a miscarriage of justice had taken place.

> The truth is that Lady Ida has no knowledge of the world, no education, no knowledge of affairs. It is a poor maimed brain . . . incapable of acting alone. Lady Ida's power of resistance and independent action may be judged from the fact that in the first of these transactions she was dragged, feebly protesting, to Leslie, the moneylender whom she knew had half ruined her mother eight years before. Everyone who knows Lady Ida knows that under pressure she will plead guilty to mistakes and faults she has not committed.[5]

But there was no mercy, and Ida's experiences in Holloway cannot have been all that different from those of Oscar Wilde in Reading Gaol, even if she was treated with a certain degree of respect. Yet she was tougher than Wilde. When a local doctor's wife proposed calling on her, Lady Ida refused to see the woman, saying that she was someone whom she would never have received at Renishaw and did not see why she should do so at Holloway. She also declined the Archbishop of Canterbury's offer to visit her, as it might embarrass both of them.

'Mother came out yesterday and I went to see her at Aunt Millie's,' Edith reported to Sachie on 19 May, Lady Ida having been released early. 'She seems absolutely unchanged; rather nervous, it is true, but she actually made jokes about the life in there.'[6] Lady Ida went straight home to Renishaw to recuperate. Lying in the next bedroom to her daughter, she called out during the night, 'Edith, have you ever been happy?' When Edith said, 'Yes, haven't you?', her mother replied, 'Never *bird*-happy, but I have three very nice children.'[7] After that, relations were better between them.

Sachie was sent home from Eton by an understanding housemaster. He never forgot his mother's 'calm and dignity during, and after, the extraordinary and unlikely tragedy that befell her'.[8] Nearly sixty years later, he wrote of 'a terrible time in our family . . . which was to tie the three of us together, two brothers and sister, in our determination to live, and leave a mark of some sort or kind'.[9] This was the period when he wrote his first poems.

Sir George's failure to save their mother from going to prison intensified Osbert's hatred. Not only was he horrified by Lady Ida's imprisonment, but he sympathised with her extravagance, which he had inherited, if not to the same manic extent. By now, he was quarrelling more than ever about money with his father, who increasingly feared his son and heir might already be far along the road to inevitable ruin.

⸙

Osbert went back to the trenches, this time with the Grenadiers' second battalion, with whom he served for nearly a year. Rats and mud were ubiquitous, the water came up to his knees and he lived on hot rum to ward off the cold. Sleep was impossible – once, after being pulled out of the trenches, he slept for an unbroken eighteen hours – and he developed a horror of moonlight after seeing a young soldier shot in No Man's Land.

The boredom was as bad as the menace. He said that in 'these coffin like ditches where death brooded in the air' one day was as sad, cold and hopeless as the next. He developed 'a sort of careless courage', but it dismayed him whenever he heard a brother officer who felt the same way remark, 'The Boches won't get me now! I've been out here too long.' He noticed that men who said this were dead within a few days, even hours. The one thing that saved him from going mad was reading – Dickens, Shakespeare and Dostoyevsky.[10] Like more than a few others, he would later claim that the war had been his university.

In autumn 1915 he was in a reserve battalion at the Loos offensive, during which the British used gas for the first time. Shortly after occupying a German trench he saw really savage hand-to-hand fighting at bayonet point when the enemy counter-attacked. Still only twenty-three, he was promoted to captain. His platoon remembered him as brave and efficient, and were grateful for the trouble he took to see they had decent rations – and for buying them a Christmas dinner out of his own pocket.

In January he wrote his first poem, 'Babel'. (The original, written in the trenches, survives at Renishaw.) It was not a very good poem, but it gave him a sense of having found a purpose for his life – if he lived. He spent the rest of the war turning himself into a poet.

Despite casualties all round him, with guardsmen – some of them school friends – pulped into bleeding fragments, hung out to die a lingering death on the barbed wire or maimed for life, Captain Sitwell bore a charmed existence. But in April 1916 he cut his finger, and the ubiquitous mud ensured blood poisoning. After several weeks in a hospital behind the lines he was shipped home, still seriously ill, to convalesce at Renishaw, where a qualified nurse was engaged to look after him – 'which aroused the strongest feelings of competition in my father'.[11]

George, too old to fight, was serving his country in a different way. From 1916, damage done by German submarines to British shipping meant food was in short supply and had to be rationed. Farmers were paid subsidies to grow crops or produce meat on a bigger scale, so Sir George put 2,000 acres under the plough, supplying bumper yields of potatoes. His son sneered at the sight of his father driving round the estate in a dog cart with his agent; yet not only was Sir George's produce useful but, because of the subsidies, it brought in a lot of money.

⸺⸻⸺

Although Osbert rejoined his regiment, he never served in France again despite repeated requests to do so. This was either because the medics diagnosed a weak heart, or because Lady Ida's scandal had given his senior officers the impression that he lacked the 'moral fibre' to command troops in action. In any case, he was thoroughly disillusioned with the war.

He followed Siegfried Sassoon's example in writing anti-war poems that appeared in the *Nation*. His disillusionment was expressed in his 'World-Hymn to Moloch' of 1917:

157.

In spite of all we've offered up
Must we drink and drain the cup?[12]

When a former foreign secretary, Lord Lansdowne, provoked outrage by sending a letter to the *Daily Telegraph* urging the Allies to stop fighting and negotiate, Osbert wrote (from the Guards' Club) to congratulate him. He also admired Sassoon's public protest against a war that had turned into one of 'aggression and conquest'.[13]

Meanwhile, Sacheverell joined the Grenadiers straight out of Eton. Diana Manners never forgot meeting him just after he did so, 'a tall innocent boy in uniform – looking to my older, pitying eyes too tender and frail and quite unfit for the fearful trenches of Flanders'.[14] However, bouts of severe ill health kept him away from the Front, in a training battalion at Aldershot. He spent much of the time with Osbert in London, where they leased a house at Swan Walk, Chelsea (paid for by Sir George), giving parties for their new intellectual friends and going to avant-garde art exhibitions and the ballet.

Sometimes the brothers went home to Renishaw – as did Edith, with whom they kept close contact. In 1916 she and Osbert published a slim volume of verse, only twenty-eight pages, which they called *Twentieth Century Harlequinade* – from a poem by Osbert. Both brothers contributed to the six anthologies of verse, *Wheels*, that Edith brought out between 1916 and 1921. Other contributors included Aldous Huxley and, less impressively, Nancy Cunard and Iris Tree. The slim volumes attracted attention, and helped the three Sitwells to acquire a place among the period's avant-garde poets.

Edith was definitely the leader, however, publishing *Clowns' Houses* and *The Wooden Pegasus*, and by 1920 she had become fairly well known. She also produced an elegant little book in prose, *Children's Tales from the Russian Ballet*. She was trying to write verse in a new way, using simple, almost nursery-rhyme language combined with the imagery of French symbolism, looking for assonances and dissonances. The result was undeniably original.

Osbert and Edith also devoted a lot of time to what would today be called networking, cultivating anyone prominent in literature or art. Among the writers were a subaltern in the Manchesters, Wilfred Owen (who was killed just a week before the Armistice); Siegfried Sassoon; Lytton Strachey; Robert Graves; Aldous Huxley; and the 'Super-Tramp', W. H. Davies – who, rather surprisingly, became a great friend of Osbert. As for artists, Osbert had dinner with Augustus John and Wyndham Lewis at the Eiffel Tower restaurant in Fitzrovia, while Edith met Nina Hamnett, who took her to see Walter Sickert.

Others included Oscar Wilde's friend Robbie Ross, and Sir Edmund Gosse, a highly influential critic who had 'discovered' Rupert Brooke. (On first seeing Gosse, Huxley described him as 'the bloodiest little old man I have ever seen'.) Osbert invited Gosse to dine at St James's Palace when he was Captain of the Guard. Another whom he wined and dined was the immensely successful novelist Arnold Bennett, who helped him become literary editor (with Herbert Read) of a quarterly, *Art and Letters*, although this ceased publication after barely a year.

Osbert failed to make much impression on Bernard Shaw or H. G. Wells, however, despite entertaining them lavishly. Others, too, had reservations. Referring to *Wheels*, in a letter to his brother of August 1917, Aldous Huxley sneered unpleasantly that 'the folk who run it are a family called Sitwell alias Shufflebottom . . . I like Edith, but Ozzy and Sachy are still rather too large to swallow. Their great object is to REBEL.'[15] Huxley would come round, but only for a time. Even so, when the twenty-year-old Sacheverell published his first slim volume of verse, *The People's Palace*, the following year, Huxley – perhaps with tongue in cheek – called him *'le Rimbaud de nos jours'*.

⚜

On Armistice night 1918 the Sitwell brothers gave a small dinner party at Swan Walk for the great Russian impresario Sergei Diaghilev, who bemusedly asked Osbert, 'Qu'est que c'est, cette Aldershot? C'est une femme?' when Sacheverell ran off to catch the last train. They had invited Diaghilev without having any idea that Germany was on the verge of collapse – even in November, many thought the war would continue for another two years.

The evening that they spent entertaining Diaghilev asserted their determination to be in the avant-garde, now that the Great War was over. 'It's quite evident, if you read the family letters, that we've been working up to something for a long time, for well over a century,' Sir George had told Osbert.[16] That 'something' was about to happen.

Chapter 17

'SITWELLIANISM'

Osbert mourned for dead friends such as Ivo Charteris and Bimbo Wyndham Tennant, and for countless other companions of his generation. Among the few to survive was the future Field-Marshal Alexander. Ironically, in 1919 Osbert was almost killed by the Spanish flu, which permanently impaired his health.

He had matured into a strange mixture of eccentricity and arrogance, of frivolity and pomposity, of kindness and malice. He hoped to make his mark as a distinguished writer, unable to accept that he lacked the talent. However, he was better equipped to achieve his other goal – of becoming a patron of the arts.

Although by instinct a man of the right, the war had turned Osbert into a pacifist. In the election of November 1918 he stood unsuccessfully for Parliament at Scarborough and Whitby as an Asquithian Liberal, hoping to find a platform from which to express his views. He also developed an intense dislike for Winston Churchill after learning how he had told Sassoon that war was man's natural occupation.

British troops were being sent to aid the Whites against the Reds in Russia, so Osbert sent an angry piece of doggerel, 'The Winstonburg Line', to the socialist *Daily Herald*, ridiculing a politician whom he saw as a warmonger. It included the lines: 'Only three years ago/I was allowed to waste a million lives in Gallipoli'. Communist sympathisers distributed the poem at pro-Bolshevik rallies, although the last thing that Renishaw's heir hoped to see was a Red revolution in his own country.

What really interested him was art and literature, not politics. With his siblings, he was determined to make the most of them in the exciting new world after the war.

Sacheverell had gone up to Balliol College in 1919, but Oxford, full of ex-servicemen reading for degrees to help them earn their living, did not yet enjoy the sparkling society of Evelyn Waugh's period. Dons were unsympathetic, and his tutor sneered that his essays read like a Ouida romance. Sachie, who spent more time in London, made few friends there – two exceptions were a very young William Walton (still only sixteen) and the eccentric novelist Ronald Firbank, the genius of whose novels he at once appreciated. Sachie soon went down of his own accord, without a degree.

During 1919 the Sitwell brothers put on an exhibition of modern French art at Heal's in the Tottenham Court Road. It was really an exhibition of the cosmopolitan School of Paris. Among the painters represented were Derain, Dufy, Matisse, Modigliani, Picasso, Soutine and Vlaminck. Since at that date only a tiny minority of English art-lovers appreciated them, this was a great achievement, and Arnold Bennett gave the Sitwells the praise they thoroughly deserved. Most reviewers damned the exhibition, however, Osbert incurring more odium for his association with it than for attacking Churchill.

They also persuaded their father to commission the neoclassicist Gino Severini to fresco a room at Montegufoni. Sadly, despite Sachie's fervent advocacy, Sir George did so in preference to Picasso, whom he thought too expensive. No less unfortunately, he declined to lend his sons the money to buy the entire contents of the recently deceased Modigliani's studio.

In 1920, after recovering from his Spanish flu, Osbert rushed over to Italy with Sacheverell. Recalling their father's stories, they set out to discover the Mezzogiorno. What they saw at Lecce in Puglia (in those days visited by few tourists), and at the remote Carthusian monastery at Padula in the Cilento, deepened the taste for the Baroque that George had given them. (In 1975 Sacheverell told me how, when they arrived at Lecce, the city fathers insisted on paying their hotel bill because they looked so distinguished.) In Sachie's opinion, there were more beautiful buildings at Lecce than at any place he ever saw save Venice. They inspired him to write what he considered to be his best book, *Southern Baroque Art*.

However, the two established their headquarters on the other side of the peninsula, at Amalfi, in a Capuchin friary that had been turned into a hotel. They returned here again and again, finding it a good place in which to work. Ironically, it was also among Sir George's favourite hotels.

On the way home they called on the Futurist poet Gabriele D'Annunzio, one of Sachie's great heroes, in Fiume, where he was briefly dictator of the little independent state. They hoped to persuade him to write a preface to a new edition of Rabelais that Picasso was illustrating. D'Annunzio was not interested, and would only talk about greyhounds or complain of his boredom. Neither brother spoke enough Italian to understand much of what he was saying.

In late 1919 the Sitwell brothers' London base became a small house in Carlyle Square, between the King's Road and the Fulham Road in Chelsea, which in those days was still a slightly seedy area. (Edith declined to join them, refusing to leave Helen Rootham.) The 'amusing' decor included conch-shaped dining chairs from Naples, stuffed birds, and a bowl of press-cuttings about themselves. There were some good pictures, ancient and modern. The pair were looked after by a devoted housekeeper, Mrs Powell, who had been in service at Castle Howard.

Here, eager to find allies, they entertained the literati with excellent dinners. Hyper-sensitive to criticism, they refused to tolerate anyone who questioned their obvious brilliance. Anyone suspected of doing so was immediately dropped from the guest list.

In 1923, assisted by her brothers, Edith gave a recitation of her verse at the Aeolian Hall, chanting through a 'sengerphone' to music by William Walton. *Façade* was when the wider public became aware of 'the Trio', even if many people in the Aeolian Hall thought it 'nonsense' and there was heckling. (One old lady attacked Edith with an umbrella.) Nasty reviews appeared in the press. But others, including Lytton Strachey, applauded. Harold Acton, who brought with him a twenty-year-old Evelyn Waugh, hoped Edith would give more recitations like this. The not-so-young novelist Ada Leverson gasped, 'Wasn't it wonderful?'[1] Arnold Bennett also enjoyed the evening.

Predictably, the Trio reacted with fury when later that year Noël Coward's revue *London Calling* featured a skit in which the comedienne Maisie Gay played the poetess 'Hernia Whittlebot'. A squat, goggle-eyed, froglike creature who wore a dress of draped sacking and Bacchanalian clumps of grapes for earrings, flanked by her brothers 'Gob' and 'Sago', she howled nonsense verse through a trumpet.

The 'poem' that drew the heartiest guffaws among philistines in the audience was 'Poor Shakespeare', whose opening lines made crude references to the wind coming from 'a goat's behind'.[2]

For some time after, Coward continued to mock 'the Swiss Family Whittlebot', who, he sneered, were 'two wiseacres and a cow'. He made particular fun of Edith, publishing two slim volumes of nonsense poems attributed to Hernia Whittlebot. It was decades before they forgave him.

⁕

Yet this sort of ridicule was useful publicity, of a sort. The fact that Coward took the trouble to single out the Trio for mockery in his revue (which ran at the Duke of York's Theatre for over a year) shows just how much they had become a feature of the London scene.

Another performance of *Façade* in 1926 at the Chenil Galleries in Chelsea was received with acclaim by nearly all the music critics, notably the great Ernest Newman of the *Sunday Times*. The Sitwells had survived the mockery and triumphed in the end.

All three understood public relations. The young Cecil Beaton – who had himself introduced to Edith in the same year, hoping that the Trio might further his career – was particularly useful. His photographs, especially those of Edith (one in a coffin horrified Lady Ida), were a great help in promoting their image, and in return they recommended him to their friends. They also persuaded Duckworth to publish his first book, *The Book of Beauty*.

Beaton genuinely admired them, and not only because he was a social mountaineer. 'With their aristocratic looks, dignified manner, and air of lofty disdain, they seemed to me to be above criticism,' he wrote in his diary for 1928. He added, 'A whole new world of sensibility opened to me while sitting in candlelight around the marble dining table in Osbert's house in Chelsea.'[3]

In contrast, Bloomsbury rejected Beaton. When he wrote to ask Virginia Woolf if he might photograph her, she declined – unpleasantly dismissing him in a letter to Vita Sackville-West as 'a mere catamite'. Her refusal strengthened Beaton's commitment to the Sitwells.[4]

In 1924 Sachie published *Southern Baroque Art: A Study of Painting, Architecture and Music in Italy and Spain of the Seventeenth and Eighteenth Centuries*, which created a sensation. Many aesthetes found it shocking – the Baroque had been despised since the eighteenth century – but others were enchanted.

Today it seems very old-fashioned, with no awareness whatever of the geometry and mathematics behind Baroque architecture and an embarrassing inability to see that the florid buildings of Lecce cannot rival those of Rome or Naples. In the view of one modern authority, it was 'a sort of conjuring trick of a book, in that it managed to communicate a modish enthusiasm for Baroque art without actually discussing it in visual terms'.[5]

Even so, it provided an introduction and a gazetteer to a neglected style. It was undeniably readable, full of exotic detail and good stories then little-known – for example, the Cypriot origins of El Greco, or how Carlo Gesualdo, composer of exquisite madrigals, had murdered his wife and her lover. As Kenneth Clark put it, 'The music of Scarlatti, the singing of Farinelli, the *Commedia dell' Arte*, all these were part of the Sitwellian revolution.'[6]

Southern Baroque Art explains why contemporaries held Sachie in such esteem. Fifty years later, John Piper referred to it as 'the most wonderful book . . . a completely revolutionary approach to architecture, which seemed to be the reverse of all I'd been taught by my elders and betters'.[7] Undoubtedly, it enhanced the Trio's reputation. Clearly there was more to them than megaphones.

Sachie's elegant if oddly impersonal 'autobiographical fantasia', *All Summer in a Day*, was also well received when it appeared in 1926. Writing in the New York *Herald Tribune*, Rebecca West (a passionate admirer of *Façade*) thought it 'in many respects a delightful book'. She added, 'neither the importance of the Sitwells as a group nor of Mr Sacheverell Sitwell can well be exaggerated'.[8]

In 1926, too, he wrote a ballet plot for Diaghilev, *The Triumph of Neptune*, with Lord Berners supplying the music and George Balanchine the choreography. His plot was a 'harlequinade scenario' of twelve tableaux whose design was inspired by 'penny-plain and tuppence-coloured' prints from the early nineteenth century – the story being how the sailor Tom Tug, changed into a fairy prince, marries the sea god's daughter. It was performed by the Ballets Russes at the Lyceum in December.

He carried on breaking new ground with books such as *German Baroque Art* (1927) and *The Gothick North* (1929). Like *Southern Baroque Art*, these owed a lot to what his father had told him as a boy. At the same time he was regularly publishing verse, including *The Cyder Feast*, with its poem on the Renishaw woods. Yet, while firmly believing that the art of every past age deserves revisiting, he was genuinely thrilled by Modigliani, Picasso and Matisse.

⁕

Edith's poetry was being published to acclaim. It included the volumes *The Sleeping Beauty* in 1924, *Troy Park* in 1925 and *Gold Coast Customs* – one of her most important works – in 1929. Apart from

Eliot, no Bloomsbury, let alone Georgian, could rival her and she was taken very seriously indeed. After reading *Gold Coast Customs*, W. B. Yeats commented that 'something absent from all literature for a generation was back again, and in a form rare in the literature of all generations, passion ennobled by intensity, by endurance, by wisdom'.[9]

She enjoyed playing to the gallery. All three of the Trio secured entries in *Who's Who* fairly early in their careers, an indication of the impact they had made. Edith's entry tells us archly how 'in early life [she] took an intense dislike to simplicity, Morris-dancing, a sense of humour, and every kind of sport except reviewer-baiting; and has continued these distastes ever since'.

⌘

If not in the same class as his siblings, Osbert strove manfully to keep up, churning out verse, essays and short stories, and even a single embarrassingly bad play, *All at Sea*, which he wrote with Sacheverell. Yet while his 1919 book of verse *Argonaut and Juggernaut* was mocked by traditionalists, it turned him into a poet who interested avant-garde critics. *Discursions on Travel, Art and Life* (1925) was also taken seriously – Frank Megroz thought it 'entrancing'.

His first novel, *Before the Bombardment* (1926), was a satirical recreation of the upper-middle-class life in Scarborough that had been ended by German shells. Although there was not much of a plot, the critic James Agate ranked it among the twenty best novels to appear since Dickens' time, while it became a favourite of George Orwell.

In Anthony Powell's view, the weakness of all Osbert's novels and stories was that while full of good ideas, he simply could not write well enough. Powell believed his real role was as a leader of literary fashion, a writer of lively letters to the newspapers, someone who kept the arts before the public eye – 'by no means a useless function'.[10] Even so, *Before the Bombardment* is still readable.

Osbert banged the Baroque drum with enthusiasm, and not only in his *Discursions*. As a committee member of the Burlington Fine Arts Club, he wrote an introduction to the catalogue for its 1925 exhibition, *Seventeenth Century Italian Art*, in which he extolled artists such as Caravaggio, Carlo Dolci, Domenichino, Artemisia Gentileschi and Strozzi – all disdained by the pundits. Most of the pictures shown were loaned by great English country houses, including Renishaw, and Osbert helped to track them down.

At Oxford, Sachie had 'discovered' the composer William Walton, who became almost an adopted brother. (Constant Lambert put about a rumour of William being Sir George's son by that great composer Dame Ethel Smyth.) When Walton went down without a degree in 1920 Sachie and Osbert invited him to live in the attic at Swan Walk, and then at Carlyle Square, where he stayed for fifteen years. They paid for lessons from leading musicians such as Busoni and Ansermet, gave him clothing and pocket money, and took him to Renishaw and on their travels. They also contributed to his work; in 1929 Osbert selected and supplied the words for his immensely successful oratorio, *Belshazzar's Feast*.

Walton did not always make a good first impression – 'rather like a maggot, but I believe he has more character than appears', observed the novelist Edith Olivier.[11] Disappointingly, he produced comparatively little music during his time with the Sitwells. Eventually his enormously rich mistress, Alice, Viscountess Wimborne, who was twenty years older but still beautiful, gave 'Willie' a flat and persuaded him to leave the Sitwells.

Sheltering and supporting Walton was a remarkable gesture on their part. While it included an element of posturing, it was nonetheless a piece of patronage in the grand style. It also gave Osbert the idea for encouraging other gifted acquaintances, if in a less demanding way.

⸺⸻⸺

The only entertainment Edith could offer in her shabby flat was mugs of tea and buns. Yet during the twenties every English writer of note went at least once up the stone stairs to her Saturday tea parties, filling the tiny drawing room to capacity. When she gave a party for her American poet friend Gertrude Stein, even Virginia Woolf accepted an invitation.

'We were at a party of Edith Sitwell's last night,' Mrs Woolf reported to her sister Vanessa. 'It was in honour of Miss Gertrude Stein who was throned on a broken settee (all Edith's furniture is derelict, to make up for which she is stuck about with jewels like a drowned mermaiden).'[12] Among other guests were Siegfried Sassoon and E. M. Forster. The refreshments consisted of bowls of cherries and jugs of barley water.

Edith dressed in an eye-catching style of her own invention, in brightly coloured pre-Raphaelite robes, with tall hats and bizarre jewellery. Huge rings of amber or ivory, of jet or aquamarine, were a speciality, as she was very proud of her hands. The effect was not always quite what she intended, however. In 1923 she was mobbed outside a music hall, mistaken for the comedienne Nellie Wallace in costume – and Nellie's most popular role was the Widow Twankey.

Yet women can see a beauty in one of their own sex that is imperceptible to men. Some female observers discerned a strange allure in

Edith. Writing to Vita Sackville-West, Virginia Woolf compared her to 'a clean hare's bone that one finds on a moor with emeralds stuck about it'.[13] Perhaps Virginia was trying to make Vita jealous, but she also told her sister Vanessa that she found Edith very beautiful. Curiously, save for Wyndham Lewis (while painting her portrait), the only men who ever thought her beautiful were homosexual, such as Cecil Beaton or her platonic love, Pavel Tchelitchew.

Not only had Edith become one of the sights of literary London, but she possessed real influence in the literary world. So did her two brothers. After *Façade*, the Sitwells held an acknowledged position throughout the 1920s as trailblazers in the worlds of modern art and modern letters. Sir Edmund Gosse called them a 'delightful but deleterious trio', claiming in 1927 that the modern writers who interested the young most were the Sitwells, James Joyce, T. S. Eliot and Siegfried Sassoon – in that order.

During the same year a literary critic, Rodolphe Mégroz, devoted a whole volume to them, *The Three Sitwells*.[14] 'Sitwellianism', he stated solemnly, is 'a freak product of centuries of bucolic culture and continuously augmented tradition such as only the English county family can boast today, married to the evanescent spirit of futurism.' Even if few people were able to swallow such nonsense, there were plenty who saw the Trio as an interesting phenomenon.

They had enemies, however, and not just Noël Coward. Wyndham Lewis suddenly turned against them, while the verse of all three was savaged by the poet and journalist Geoffrey Grigson. More seriously, in 1932 a Cambridge don, F. R. Leavis (in *New Bearings in English Poetry*) sneered, 'The Sitwells belong to the history of publicity rather than literature.' Leavis was an influential academic who carried much greater weight than Coward, Wyndham Lewis or Grigson, and his gibe did them lasting damage. But he missed the point.

'The great thing about the Sitwells was that they believed, however idiosyncratically, that the arts were to be enjoyed,' wrote Anthony Powell, more perceptively, 'not doled out like medicine.'[15] Cyril Connolly agreed. They were the 'natural allies of Cocteau and the École de Paris, dandies, irreproachably dressed and fed, who indicated to young men just down from Oxford and even Cambridge that it was possible to reconcile art and fashion'.[16]

Yet the Sitwells were far more than fashionable dilettantes with a following restricted to the 'Bright Young Things'. Even if it should not be exaggerated, their influence was much stronger than either Powell or Connolly, let alone Leavis, realised. While their writing (Edith's verse occasionally excepted) was not of the first quality, they undoubtedly made a modest but lasting impact on the arts and really did help to shape taste.

They were convinced that the art of every age is worth investigating, and their interest in Baroque and Rococo paved the way for a more serious re-evaluation by Anthony Blunt and Denis Mahon, while they encouraged a new appreciation of Strawberry Hill Gothic. They also helped to create a whimsical, nostalgic mood which influenced Rex Whistler's painting and Cecil Beaton's photography and designs for the stage as well as a decorative style that Osbert Lancaster called 'Curzon Street Baroque'. The mood was reflected as late as the 1960s in Lancaster's own murals and stage sets.

The Trio lived as much for the extreme avant-garde as they did for the neglected past, with their admiration for the Paris School, affection for Futurism, Dadaism and Surrealism, and worship of Picasso and Cubism. (Osbert had his head portrayed by Frank Dobson, who in those days was still influenced by Futurism and one of the most interesting sculptors in England.) Their love of the Romantic tradition in painting looked forward to the English neo-Romantics of the mid twentieth century, in particular to John Piper.

All this was too much for Bloomsbury.

Chapter 18

RIVALRY WITH BLOOMSBURY

Inevitably, the Sitwells clashed with the Bloomsbury Group, who then dominated London's literary and artistic scene. To put it mildly, their tastes were not the same. As the Trio saw it, the Bloomsburies were both iconoclastic and dogmatic, innovative yet limited.

Another divisive factor was class. Philip Ziegler, author of the definitive biography of Osbert Sitwell, writes of him as being torn between pride of birth and belief in the artist's superiority.[1] This verdict, which is also true of his siblings, cannot be bettered. During the 1920s the patrician element in the image that they cultivated – elegant and haughty, with a great country house in the background – dazzled many. However, it rankled with the Bloomsburies, including Virginia Woolf, who felt that literati had no business to be 'aristocrats'.

'It is a period that is now thought to have roared with routs of ladies in low brimmed hats lurching out of the Eiffel Tower restaurant supporting their bearded Priapus; but its products were for the most part dismal and puritanical' is how Kenneth Clark recalled the twenties. 'In painting the dull purples and browns of Bloomsbury applied to a street-scene or still-life; in poetry the Georgians . . . It was a world in which fantasy, richness and elaboration were completely excluded. Into this world of virtuous fowls, laying their identical eggs, there strayed three golden pheasants – the Sitwells.'[2]

At first, the Trio courted the Bloomsburies, who were not unfriendly. Osbert and Sachie were impressed by what Roger Fry and Clive Bell had written on Impressionism, which encouraged them to go to Paris and find pictures for their 1919 exhibition. However, they soon developed reservations.

They rejected Roger Fry's pseudo-classicism and Clive Bell's 'Significant Form'. In contrast, they admired the Vorticists (who in 1914 had rebelled against Bloomsbury's adulation of the French Impressionists above all other painters), and they even contemplated mounting a Vorticist exhibition in Paris, despite the movement having petered out during the war.

Another reason for the parting of ways was the Bloomsbury Group's sheer drabness. Looking back from the 1970s, Cyril Connolly wrote that the Sitwells had not merely combined art with dandyism, the only valid alternative to Bloomsbury,[3] but tried to build their own group. What made friction inevitable was that the Bloomsburies were no less self-obsessed, if smug rather than haughty. Nevertheless, Osbert and his siblings stayed on outwardly friendly terms with the leaders – the Woolfs, Lytton Strachey and Roger Fry – whom they referred to in private as the 'Junta'.

There were no open hostilities and the Junta were invited to dine, but it was an uneasy relationship. Ziegler imagines the atmosphere at these dinner parties as resembling that in Glencoe between MacDonalds and Campbells, just before the massacre.[4] The Junta did not think much of Osbert's or Sachie's verse, if one or two felt a reluctant admiration for Edith's. Nor, except for Roger Fry, did they like Baroque art. Even Fry was astounded by Osbert's enthusiasm for C. R. W. Nevinson, whose work he himself dismissed out of hand.

The cold perfectionism of Cambridge University, which had formed the minds of more than a few Bloomsburies, was incomprehensible to the Trio. And while the immaculately tailored Osbert made fun of the flaming red ties and shaggy tweed suits affected by male Bloomsburies ('woven from the manes of Shetland ponies'), the Bloomsburies claimed to despise Sitwell 'dandyism'. Yet the Trio's patrician background secretly impressed the Junta, even if they did not care to say so. One need only contrast Charleston, the Sussex farmhouse that epitomised the good life for Bloomsburies, with Renishaw to see why. But sometimes they admitted in their diaries what they thought in private.

<hr />

After their first meeting in May 1925 at his house in Carlyle Square, Virginia Woolf (always a crashing snob) wrote, 'Osbert is at heart an English squire, a collector, but of Bristol glass, old-fashioned plates, Victorian cases of humming birds, & not of foxes brushes & deers horns.' She added, 'And I liked him too.' But in March 1926 she grumbled, 'They're aristocrats, I say, thinking criticism upstart impertinence on the part of flunkeys.' She also remarked that he had a 'very sensual, royal Guelf face'. Later she sneered that in Osbert's prose 'the rhododendrons grow to such a height', while she described his collected poems as 'all foliage and no filberts'.[5]

For his part, Osbert thought Virginia something of a joke, claiming that she and E. M. Forster must be the natural children of a secret love affair between George Eliot and Ruskin. At one of his Carlyle Square dinner parties Virginia said she knew 'Captain Sitwell' said horrible things about her, which was all too true, although he blandly denied it. Just before her arrival, he had told guests she would come wrapped in an old lace curtain from a Notting Hill boarding house that smelt of mothballs – probably a not entirely unfair description of the impression made by Mrs Woolf's wardrobe.

Nonetheless, he quite liked her. 'Her beauty was certainly impersonal, but it was in no way cold, and her talk was full of ineffable fun and lightness of play and warmth.'[6] If there was a streak of malice in her, he adds, there was also unusual gentleness and kindness. Yet despite expressing admiration for her prose, not a single copy of any of her books was in his library at Renishaw.

Even so, there was friendship between them – of a sort. In 1940 Osbert published *Two Generations*, his great-aunt Georgiana's memoir of Renishaw with his aunt Floss's journal. (Printing these had been the idea of his father, who edited them, but insisted that Osbert should take the credit.) Virginia wrote to him to say how much she enjoyed it, saying somewhat surprisingly that she had liked Florence more than Georgiana had.[7]

Vanessa Bell also wrote to Osbert in April the following year, in reply to what had clearly been a moving letter of sympathy from him after Virginia's suicide. Vanessa then recalls a recent letter from him about a dinner party where she and Osbert had been guests.[8] There is no hint of enmity.

A Bloomsbury for whom Osbert had nothing but praise was T. S. Eliot, whose poetry he described as an enormous source of pleasure and excitement. He was fascinated by the American with the strange, bony features. Such unqualified admiration was all the more remarkable in view of Eliot's contempt for Osbert's own verse, which he openly dismissed as third-rate, and his declining an invitation to Renishaw.

Osbert was not so complimentary about other Bloomsburies. After Lytton Strachey was safely dead he wrote that he had looked like a pelican, or a satyr-like Father Time. (Yet, when writing of Sir George,

Above: Two of Sir George's Italian statues, Amazon and Warrior, at the entrance to the Wilderness at Renishaw.

Above: *The Sitwell Family at Renishaw*, in August 1930. The three year old Reresby was already devoted to his grandfather. Photo by Cecil Beaton. (Courtesy of Sotheby's.)

Above: *Edith Sitwell* by Rex Whistler, 1929. This is among Whistler's best portraits and possibly the most successful of Edith, who is sitting in one of the Brustolon chairs acquired by her father.

Left: Sir Osbert Sitwell (1892–1969), by Frank Dobson, 1923, which T. E. Lawrence so much admired that he bought a cast and later left it to the Tate Gallery.

Right: Osbert's 'Hanoverian' profile when he was in his prime, a photograph that helps to explain why Virginia Woolf thought he had 'a very sensual royal Guelf face'.

Opposite: Salvator Rosa's *Belisarius in Disgrace*, the finest picture at Renishaw, purchased by Osbert in 1946.

Top: The North Front at Renishaw Hall, by John Piper. Osbert assembled the largest collection of Pipers in private hands and it is still at Renishaw.

Middle: The Dining Room alcove at Renishaw by John Piper, a rare interior by the artist.

Bottom: The Ball Room wing at Renishaw by John Piper.

Opposite: Another view of the North Front at Renishaw Hall by John Piper.

Left: Reresby Sitwell in 1966, the year after he had taken over Renishaw. He is holding a copy of *Mount Athos*, the book that he wrote with John Julius Norwich and A. Costa.

Opposite: The Temple in the Wilderness at Renishaw.

Right: Reresby Sitwell (1927–2009) at Renishaw in the late eighties. Photo by Nuala Allason.

Above: Penelope Sitwell, by Molly Bishop.

Opposite: The Great Drawing Room at Renishaw, reconfigured and redecorated by Reresby and Penelope Sitwell.

Opposite: Another view of the Great Drawing Room.

Above: The Ballroom at Renishaw, reconfigured and redecorated by Reresby and Penelope.

Above: The entrance hall from the staircase at Renishaw.

Opposite: The south front of Renishaw from the gardens.

Above: Alexandra Sitwell and her husband Rick Hayward.

Osbert may have well been influenced by Strachey's iconoclasm in *Eminent Victorians*.) He also made fun of Roger Fry, apostle of Cézanne and Van Gogh and pioneer of 'avant-garde painting', claiming that Fry had once been a fervent admirer of Alma-Tadema and that Fry's own early pictures were inferior versions of Alma-Tadema's work. There could be no crueller insult, but Fry, too, was dead when Osbert made it.

At the end of the war and just after, he was close to Aldous Huxley – on the fringes of Bloomsbury – but in 1921, Huxley gave a character in *Crome Yellow* traits that were recognisably those attributed to Sir George by his son. Worse still, he caricatured Osbert himself in a short story ('The Tillotson Banquet') as Lord Badgery, a rich, pacifist peer with pig's eyes, thick lips and a 'Hanoverian nose', who revelled in malice and every two minutes changed any topic he was discussing. It ended their friendship.

Looking back, Edith – an equally good hater, and vicious when she thought other writers failed to admire her work – savaged 'this world of superior intellect' whose inhabitants seemed 'inexplicably intertwined'. 'The trouble was,' she told her friend Elizabeth Salter, 'the Bloomsbury group civilised all their instincts away.'[9] She enjoyed Gertrude Stein's gibe that Bloomsbury society was like the Young Men's Christian Society with Christ omitted, observing that some male followers looked as if they were foetuses waiting to be born.

She tells us she knew Lytton Strachey only slightly and did not care for his work, saying that he saw the people about whom he was writing in profile, never full face. She also referred to his 'nibbling, rat-like little books', although she owed a good deal to his style in her own prose histories.[10] When his letters to Virginia Woolf were published, they made Edith 'blush all over' with their feminine mannerisms and name-dropping, while his long 'gardener's beard' reminded her of a comic demon in a Russian ballet. Nor did she like the way he snubbed people. Fortunately, she did not know that Strachey had said her nose resembled an anteater's and called her poetry absurd.

However, Edith was fond of Roger Fry, who painted her portrait several times. Fry's hopeless impracticality made her laugh, while she admired his gift for making and keeping friends. She also liked Aldous Huxley and his first wife Maria, of whom she saw a lot during the twenties. Huxley she regarded as one of the most accomplished talkers she had ever met, revelling in his monologues on the love life of the octopus with 'so many arms to enfold the beloved', or on that of melons – no melon, apparently, was safe from the advances of another melon. She considered T. S. Eliot, a loyal friend, to be one of the greatest poets of the last hundred and fifty years.

As for Bloomsbury's female followers, Edith thought they had faces like felt hats that had been sat on. She sneered at their writing about women whose sole interest, in her view, was their sex and promiscuity. Virginia Woolf was an exception. Edith praises her 'moonlit transparent beauty', her large, thoughtful eyes, and tells us she found her company delightful because her conversation, always straight to the point, was so stimulating. Yet if she liked some of Virginia's novels, she considered Huxley a better writer.

<hr/>

Sacheverell, the shyest Sitwell, mixed very little with Bloomsburies, who seldom refer to him in their letters or diaries – they may have been taken aback by his erudition. If he sometimes met them at his brother's dinner parties, we do not know how he reacted. The exception is Lytton Strachey, whom in after years he recalled as having 'something unpleasant to say about every contemporary in turn'. In Sachie's opinion, 'The whole of life and of intellectual experience was for Strachey one long and high pitched giggle.'[11]

Where Sitwells and Bloomsburies agreed was in loathing the 'Philistines of England', by which they meant the middle classes who failed to welcome modern art and literature – in fact, most of the educated public. They identified the core of their enemy as a group of poets, the 'Georgians', who had been publishing anthologies since 1912. Some were very good, as both Sitwells and Bloomsburies admitted, such as Graves, Sassoon or D. H. Lawrence; but others, like Alfred Noyes, were undeniably third-rate.

The Georgians' leader was J. C. Squire, editor of a monthly, *The London Mercury*, that published their verse. Hearty and right-wing, he embodied everything the Sitwells and Bloomsburies disliked, including 'a predilection for sheep'. Virginia Woolf thought he was 'more repulsive than words can express', while Lytton Strachey called him a little worm. But for ordinary mortals the boozy, chuckling umpire of the immortal village cricket match in A. G. Macdonell's *England, Their England* was more congenial than his opponents. ('I am not so think as you drunk I am' is Squire's best-known utterance.)

For all his drinking, Jack Squire was formidable. He disapproved of the Sitwells from the start, savaging *Wheels* and in 1919 dismissing Osbert's *Argonaut and Juggernaut* as the work of an 'ordinary immature writer of verses'. Osbert never forgave him. Later, Edith can have been no less unamused by a ballad he contributed to *Punch*: 'I once saw Edith Sitwell buying Fish'. One of many qualities Osbert disliked about Squire and his 'Squirearchy' was their cult of the countryside, and he sneered at them as 'lark-lovers'. But in terms of public esteem,

Squire – an immensely popular figure who was knighted in 1933 – was the winner.

An even more ferocious foe was Wyndham Lewis, novelist, painter and founder of the Vorticist movement. What antagonised this poverty-stricken arch-Bohemian of the hard right was the combination of private incomes, left-wing politics and smug superiority that in his eyes characterised not only Sitwells, but Bloomsburies as well. In his long, rambling satirical novel of 1930, *The Apes of God*, he attacked both, Virginia Woolf being wounded to the heart by a wickedly funny parody of her stream-of-consciousness novel *Mrs Dalloway*.

It was the Sitwells who suffered most, however, caricatured as the 'Finnian Shaws', a clan of rich mountebanks, defined as 'God's own Peterpaniest family . . . a sort of ill-acted Commedia dell'Arte . . . a middle aged youth movement'. Osbert received the closest attention as 'Lord Osmund Finnian Shaw', who was 'more or less male' while credited with the 'goat-like profile of Edward the Peace Maker'.[12] Yet Wyndham Lewis had been an ally of the Trio – contributing to *Wheels*, painting Edith and staying at Renishaw (losing his only shirt collar during the visit). Unique in being a man who found Edith physically attractive, his defection may have been due to her rebuffing him when he made a pass.[13]

Osbert's revenge was a campaign of teasing that drove Lewis, someone so paranoiac that he always carried a revolver, nearly insane. His most successful ploy was sending a letter, supposedly from the organiser of an exhibition of Jewish art, to the rabidly anti-Semitic Lewis, asking him to contribute a picture. The result was an appalling row with the Jewish artists that almost ended in bloodshed.

Chapter 19

RENISHAW AS PATRONAGE

Bloomsbury could not compete with the Sitwells where patronage was concerned. Its sole largesse was a job in the Woolfs' tiny publishing firm, working their hand-operated press (a privilege available only to one or two acolytes), or a weekend in a country cottage. In contrast, a horde of writers could be invited to stay at Renishaw Hall, whose splendours would not soon be forgotten.

'A sister and two brothers, each of them tall and fair, talk and laugh with each one in the formal Renishaw gardens,' was a recollection of a visit there during the early twenties that the literary critic Raymond Mortimer prized for half a century. He also recalled the sad appearance of their once beautiful mother, and the courtesy of their formidable father, 'pondering further, more extravagant landscapings'.[1] Many other 'men of letters' shared similar memories. However, soon afterwards Osbert was left as the sole patron when his brother and sister began to go their own ways, staying away from Derbyshire.

In 1925 Sir George handed Renishaw over to Osbert – surprisingly, in view of his son's attitude to money. Osbert thought that extravagance was part of the 'artistic temperament' and made people tolerant and generous, while in emulating his mother he was avenging himself for what he saw as his father's cruel treatment of her.

During the previous year, however, Sir George had been shocked by the election of Britain's first Labour government, and he did not want his son to pay death duties that might wipe out the estate. He also wished to remove Lady Ida from a country where her reputation had become a little rusty after her stay in Holloway. Above all, he hoped to do for Montegufoni what he had done for Renishaw.

In the event, he and his increasingly frail wife would find there something approaching the happiness that had so far eluded them. He enjoyed bringing the castello and its gardens back to life. Ida, on the other hand, liked the climate and the English society at nearby Florence, which included such friends of many years as old Mrs Keppel and Arthur Acton (Harold's father), who never objected to paying for her huge whiskies at the Gran Caffè Doney.

Despite calling Sir George 'the best father in England', Osbert's gratitude quickly evaporated; although for years Sir George always offered to help if he needed money, besides making him an allowance of an extra £1,000 a year, and more than once he paid off his debts. He even helped him buy some Romney drawings, with a cheque for £500. As for meddling, in 1929 his father wrote to say that he had made (and paid for) alterations to the gardens 'at your desire . . . because it was an old promise to you to complete the garden'.[2]

Yet Osbert never ceased to tell his friends that he was a victim of his parent's parsimony and constant interference. He genuinely seems to have believed this himself, his secret hatred growing by the day. He disliked and discouraged his father's presence at Renishaw.

'I have spent a month in the summer with you about once in two years,' Sir George eventually complained. 'I have never entered the house except with your permission, verbal if you were in England, written by letter if you were abroad. On these occasions I have not slept in the house, but have put up either at the Sitwell Arms, or if I have business elsewhere at Sheffield and have motored over. You have allowed me to use a bedroom for writing letters, and to have some of my meals here.' He adds, 'These visits have been in winter when the house is unwarmed and unlighted.'[3]

In the same year that Renishaw was handed over, Sachie married a girl from Canada, Georgia Doble, who flatteringly claimed to have read *Southern Baroque Art*. Reporting the wedding, a Canadian newspaper gave details of the Sitwell family that entranced Edith. 'The witty and beautiful daughter of the Earl of Londesborough . . . from whom her children inherit their brains, has been the sensation of London more than once,' she quoted with wild glee in a letter to the happy couple. 'She is a most keen ornithologist and her collection of birds' eggs is one of the most famous in Europe.'[4]

Osbert was not so cheerful. The marriage meant that his adored brother ceased to live at Carlyle Square or at Renishaw. For the first time other than the months with the 11th Hussars, he knew loneliness. Perhaps for the first time, too, he admitted to himself what his father may have already told him – that he was homosexual.

He would eventually find happiness with David Horner, a handsome, auburn-haired young man, well-born, clever and amusing, with beautiful manners, who was unaffectionately christened 'Blossom' by Edith, a name adopted by the rest of the family. They discovered that he was greedy, vain, arrogant and compulsively malicious, even if Osbert turned a blind eye to these little failings. However, the partnership did not materialise until 1929.

Sacheverell and his wife came to Renishaw less and less after his father gave them the Hely-Hutchinsons' Weston Hall, which he had recently inherited. ('I don't propose to do much here,' said Sir George, always the landscape gardener. 'Just a sheet of water and a line of stat-ues.') Incapable of earning a living, Sachie depended for money on his father and then on his brother – who remained fond of him, but developed a strong distaste for his quarrelsome, mischief-making wife.

Sachie's biographer, Sarah Bradford, describes Georgia as 'highly sexed, materialistic, ruthless and socially ambitious. Behind her elegant back, Osbert called her "Juggins".'5 The fact that she was notoriously unfaithful – for a time she was Oswald Mosley's main mistress – did not endear her to her brother-in-law, whose dislike grew steadily as the years went by.

From 1921, even before he gained possession of Renishaw, Osbert had been inviting the creative to stay, rather as Ottoline Morrell did at Garsington, but with more discrimination. (The Sitwells did not admire Lady Ottoline, nor her excessively open door.) During their vis-its, a slightly bewildered Sir George and Lady Ida mingled with them.

Despite Sachie's 'desertion', Osbert went on supporting Willie Walton, although sometimes Willie's weakness for women caused trouble. One admirer, scheming to ensnare him, told Lady Ida that he had forced himself on her with what might be serious consequences. If only it had proved to be true, commented Edith, the lady in ques-tion, who was no longer young, 'would have left Abraham's Sarah at the starting post'.6

In 1924, Peter Quennell found a 'strange Peacockian household' at Renishaw. Fellow guests included Walton, Helen Rootham, a Georgian poet named Wilfred Childe and 'the charming old eccentric' Ada Leverson, who had once been Oscar Wilde's 'Sphinx'.

He gives us a pathetic glimpse of Lady Ida, who rose late before putting on a black silk dress and a black silk toque, after which she would totter gently into view, supporting her steps with a small cane. She seemed very old, although only in her mid-fifties. 'Ain't it amusin', Henry', she asked Moat at luncheon, showing him a caricature of Sir George dressed as a scoutmaster. 'Very amusing, I am sure, milady,' he replied with an unappreciative growl.

Outside, beyond the statues guarding the house, stretched a broad industrial valley, and after dark Quennell could see red light from the pit-heads shining through the leaves of the trees planted to screen them. 'Yet there was a sad magnificence about Renishaw that is reflected by the Sitwells' prose and verse,' he thought. 'Few writers have owed so much to the surroundings of their childhood.' However, even Quennell's not very marked sense of decorum was shocked by Osbert's behaviour. Whenever Sir George spoke, his son would make loud popping noises with a finger in his mouth, as if opening a champagne bottle.[7]

⁕

'Blighted skies and blasted trees and blackened exhaustion' was how Renishaw Hall seemed to the lugubrious Siegfried Sassoon, who decided the lake was too shallow for suicide. He detected 'wicked influences'. As for the Trio, they were 'Regency relics'.[8]

In contrast, the painter Rex Whistler (of whose work Osbert was a keen supporter) loved it, returning again and again. So did Whistler's mother figure, Edith Olivier, who thought their host reincarnated Horace Walpole. 'A vast pile of a house – 18th century windows and battlemented' was how it seemed to her. 'Filled with pictures and tapestries – and lovely beds. Mine is a marvel with great red plumes at the corners of the canopy – rising from vases elaborately painted in green, grey and blue.' The other guests were Edith Sitwell and Sachie (with Georgia), Walton and Lord Berners. In the morning Edith read Miss

Olivier her poem 'Gold Coast Customs', its bleaker verses reducing both to tears.

Edith Olivier was thrilled by the way the oil lamps lit up the tap-estries, creating a 'feeling of mystery and madness'. She adds, 'They say the house is haunted but the ghosts are the living people. Every evening Lord Berners and Willy Walton play violent impromptu duets on the piano – in order to drive Sir George to bed. When they succeed, we sit round and Osbert tells many amusing and cruel stories about people he dislikes.'[9]

***

Neither Beverley Nichols nor Anthony Powell cared for Sir George. 'When he came in to luncheon he glared at me as though I were an intruder and when Osbert introduced me he merely sniffed and went away to sit by himself in a corner,' Nichols wailed in *The Sweet and Twenties*. 'He suddenly looked at me and said, "I never know anybody in this house."'[10] But not everyone took to Beverley Nichols.

Powell's antipathy may have been due to embarrassment at his own gauche manners. Strolling with Walton on the lawn before luncheon, they ran into Sir George. 'I have just been reading about medieval painted chambers,' he told them. 'Strange, very strange, rather horrible at times.' As Powell admits, Walton and he guffawed by way of reply. 'Sir George showed no sign of irritation, simply walking away.'[11]

Most visitors admired their host's father, however. Harold Acton thought he looked like a Van Dyck portrait, while Quennell describes him as 'tall, noble-looking . . . always ceremonious and gravely courte-ous'. The romantic Edith Olivier called him 'a shadowy man, exquisite and cruel and sinister and blade-like'. In contrast, Evelyn Waugh did not find him in the least frightening, let alone sinister, but 'very gentle'.

Some sensed his kindness, which took a practical form – Siegfried Sassoon managed to borrow £100 from him, as did Rex Whistler, who sent a touching letter of thanks.

Osbert never ceased baiting his father, whom he invariably referred to as 'Ginger' behind his back, because of his red beard. However, Sir George never lost his dignity, always 'playing a straight bat'. At one Renishaw dinner party in the twenties, after alerting the other guests, Osbert persuaded his friend Lady Aberconway to ask his father loudly, 'Is there much incest in Derbyshire?' 'I regret to say there is,' he answered, unruffled. 'Generally in isolated farmhouses.'[12]

There was plenty of luxury, with superlative food (a chef was hired from the Ritz Hotel in London), while the cellar – chosen by Osbert – was excellent. Vintage champagne flowed. He always breakfasted on melon or pineapple, which were expensive delicacies in the days before refrigeration and never served to guests. Beverley Nichols went into ecstasies over the perfumed log fires, the scent of Parma violets everywhere.

Ninety years ago luxury and comfort were not quite the same thing as they are today. When Lutyens – by then Sir Edwin, designer of the Cenotaph – came again in 1928, he grumbled at his bath, the only one in the house, being on the floor above and the WC on the floor below, while 'there was no po in my bedroom'. (He found Sir George suave, smiling and fussy, Lady Ida gaunt and unhappy, and Osbert looking more than ever like George IV.)[13] Even so, during winter Renishaw was warmer than most houses, thanks to an abundant supply of logs and servants.

The atmosphere was not only luxurious, but relaxed. Peter Quennell recalled with amusement Moat's outrage at male guests bathing naked in the lake,[14] while there was a good deal of horseplay, including apple-pie beds. There were also charades.

When Edith was old and bedridden, the ballet dancer Robert Helpmann told her a story that gives some idea of Renishaw's ambience at the height of Osbert's pre-war regime. Having invited Somerset Maugham to stay, Osbert asked the party to wear fancy dress on the first evening of the great novelist's visit, but then changed his mind. He forgot to tell Helpmann, who swept down the stairs dressed as Queen Alexandra only to find all the other men in dinner jackets. Maugham showed no hint of surprise when he shook hands with him.[15]

No one fell quite so desperately in love with Renishaw as did Evelyn Waugh. Gradually it cast its spell over him, in the end more completely than Madresfield (the model for *Brideshead Revisited*). Renishaw was his earliest experience of country house life, before he knew Madresfield.

He first came in August 1930 when he was twenty-seven, finding the entire Sitwell family in residence, plus William Walton and Arthur Waley (famed for his translations of Chinese verse). 'Very dark hall', is how he recalled his arrival. 'Many other rooms of great beauty, fine tapestry and Italian furniture.' He noticed that the lake was black with coal dust and that pit-heads, slag-heaps and factory chimneys could be seen from the gardens.

Never, apparently, having been in a house with footmen before, Waugh was taken aback by the staff's 'feudal familiarity'. He noted down with amazement the response of a 'footman' (probably one of the butlers, Robins or Moat) to Edith's asking one of her brothers to go in her place when Lady Ida summoned her. 'Well, come on,' said the man. 'One of you's got to go.'[16]

Among Osbert's more attractive qualities was kindness to servants.

He inspired lasting devotion in his housekeeper at Carlyle Square, Mrs Powell. Robins, who had been his batman in the 11th Hussars, became Renishaw's butler, remaining until retirement in 1952 with a generous pension and cottage in the park. When he burned a big hole in a valuable carpet and expected the sack, Osbert told him, 'After we've been together for so many years, you can't imagine that it will make any difference?'[17]

A would-be guest who found the Sitwells away when he called at Renishaw was D. H. Lawrence. After meeting Osbert and Edith in Italy, he had been taken over Montegufoni by Sir George: according to Lady Ida, if shown some treasure during the tour, Mrs Lawrence – 'an enormous German' – would stare at her host, lean against a gilded bed and breathe heavily.

Later, a suspicion that Mr Lawrence had given Osbert's characteristics to the cuckolded Sir Clifford in *Lady Chatterley's Lover* infuriated Edith. She never forgave Lawrence, saying that he looked like a garden gnome. As their nephew Reresby realised much later, however, the real model for Clifford Chatterley must have been Joseph Arkwright of Sutton Scarsdale – near Renishaw and not far from Lawrence's birthplace, Eastwood – who broke his spine in a riding accident and then acquired a young bride.

Even so, Sir Clifford does sound uncannily like Osbert. 'Just a little bit frightened of middle and lower class humanity', but rebelling against his own class, he wrote stories about people he had known, 'clever, rather spiteful . . . The observation was extraordinary and peculiar.' He was 'morbidly sensitive' about these stories, wanting everybody to think them good. Nevertheless, Osbert was magnanimous enough to describe Lawrence as a genius.

Some of Renishaw's guests got more than they expected. Against his host's advice, one of them visited a rarely-used bedroom in the 'ghost wing' at midnight. He emerged half an hour later, dazed and needing brandy. 'I know it sounds ridiculous,' he told Osbert when he pulled himself together. 'But I felt that I was drowning, that I was wretched beyond words, and that my face was covered with some hanging wet stuff.' What made this so odd was that he had never heard the story of the Boy in Pink.[18]

Chapter 20

MARKING TIME IN
THE THIRTIES

During the 1930s, many lost interest in the Sitwells. They were ageing, while no longer acting as a Trio had diminished their image. Better writers were emerging – Joyce, Waugh, Greene, Powell, Auden – even if Eliot and Woolf stayed on their pedestals. Nor did a patrician background keep quite so much glamour in the era of the Slump and the Jarrow Hunger March.

Among the reasons why Sitwellianism waned was that Edith had stopped producing poetry and gone to live in Paris, where she wrote prose to earn money. Her one novel, *I Live Under a Black Sun*, was a failure despite kind words from Evelyn Waugh, but her other books, such as the delightful *English Eccentrics*, were very good indeed. None, however, made the same impact as her verse. She was also distracted by the painter Pavel Tchelitchew, the love of her life and one reason why she went to Paris, in an unhappy platonic romance that dragged on for a quarter of a century.

Yet another cause was the Trio's disinterest in politics. Marxism and the redistribution of wealth failed to attract them. If repelled by Nazism, they did not object to Mussolini, who preserved 'the social order' and Montegufoni. They refused to take sides during the Spanish Civil War, which Osbert regarded as 'a horrible and incredible gladiatorial combat', although they were relieved by Franco's victory.

This was an unusual position for English intellectuals in the late thirties when so many saw hope in Communism.

━━━

Osbert nonetheless remained a significant figure in the literary world. According to Anthony Powell, this was because he was essentially 'a personal appearance artist'. It also owed a lot to his kindness to young writers, whom he encouraged and helped with small gifts of money.

Powell does not mention how Osbert intervened for him with his employers, Duckworth in Henrietta Street, who published Osbert's books. A copy of Powell's first novel, *Afternoon Men*, at Renishaw is inscribed 'For Osbert Sitwell (cher maître). In admiration, and because he has always done his best to protect me from the ungovernable tantrums of my employers, from Tony Powell, May 28th 1931'. *From a View to a Death*, published two years later, has written on the flyleaf, 'For Osbert, the Hero of Henrietta Street'.

Moreover, Osbert corresponded with countless writers, established and aspiring. He also went on going to literary parties in London, including those of Bloomsbury. And he continued to entertain intellectual friends at Renishaw. At the same time, he enjoyed his role as squire, reviving rent dinners for his tenant farmers. Twice a year they trooped into the dining room, handed a cheque to the agent and then sat down to a hearty meal with their landlord.

Eager for Renishaw to have a role in public life, in 1931 Osbert joined Oswald Mosley's New Party, allowing it to hold a rally in the grounds that was attended by thousands. Yet, while he strongly approved of Mosley's determination to avoid another war, he declined to become a member of the British Union of Fascists.

━━━

During the thirties, the 'Gingers' came even less to Derbyshire. They were enjoying life at Montegufoni too much. However, a photograph taken at Renishaw by Beaton in summer 1930 shows the entire family, with the Judocus de Vos tapestries as background. Sir George looks as distinguished as ever, while Lady Ida, in a cloche hat and sitting on one of the throne-like Brustolon chairs, still shows traces of beauty. Sachie's nervous little three-year-old son Reresby perches between the old couple, whom he much preferred to his difficult, self-obsessed parents.

There was increasing friction between Osbert and his own father. Besides his luxurious regime at Renishaw, Osbert spent heavily on his London establishment and lived well beyond his means, running up a huge overdraft at Coutts. After years of warning him that he was risking bankruptcy and might end by having to sell Renishaw, in 1933 his father threatened to go to law in an attempt to curb his expenditure.

Osbert's response was to tell everybody that he was being cruelly persecuted by an unnatural parent. Visiting him in August, Edith Olivier wrote of the house being haunted by 'the nightmare hatred of Sir George for his whole family . . . He moves about like a Poisoner's Ghost with his thin cruel smile' (clearly Osbert's description).[1] Luckily, the spendthrift's finances suddenly improved when more money started coming in from the estate – thanks to the work of a dedicated land agent – and he began to make a better income from journalism.

As Osbert was never going to produce an heir, George placed all his hopes on Reresby. 'Life begins again with the grandchildren,' he wrote at about this time.[2] The little boy was already promising. 'What a charm the child has!' wrote Cecil Beaton after meeting him at Montegufoni in 1933, 'with an extraordinary mind and with the fantasy of the rest of the family'.[3]

Making Reresby the ultimate beneficiary of his will, his grandfather kept in touch with him as he grew older through letters accompanied by small cheques. The correspondence was often about sea monsters, for which his grandson had a passion. In November 1936 he wrote from Montegufoni:

> Our golden wedding passed very happily, but it would have been happier still if you had been with us. We had all the school-children of the neighbouring villages at the castle and gave them cups of whipped cream, which they prefer to tea or coffee, cakes, and little bags of sweetmeats . . . The monster world has been quiet lately. But some fishermen on the river Po at Mantua, which you will remember is West of Venice, got the fright of their lives, owing to some creature more like a huge animal than a fish climbing on to the bank near them. They did not give a more complete description, as they ran away as fast as they could . . . I enclose an illustration of the carcase of a sea-monster which was washed up on the shore of Morocco. It had choked to death, owing to having swallowed a large net full of fish and possibly the fishermen as well. Sea-monsters should eat slowly and avoid taking too big mouthfuls.[4]

The next year, 1937, Lady Ida fell ill with pneumonia. In July – inevitably, given she had only one lung – she was brought home to England to die. 'Today my darling Ida died,' her husband wrote in his notebook. He cried all day and was too upset to go to the funeral. Despite all the misery she had caused him, and although her inability to share his interests had made him very lonely, he had never thrown off her spell. He explained in his notebook, 'It was the child in Ida one loved, but often she was a very naughty child.'[5]

He wrote to Reresby, 'I feel lost without your Grannie, but we must try and bear up, as she would have wished. It will be a great comfort having you with me.'[6] Until he left Italy, he continued to give annual tea parties on her birthday for the children at Montegufoni.

Fearing that his father's loneliness might end in an unsuitable attachment (and a new will), Osbert engaged a male private secretary for him. This was Francis Bamford, formerly the Duke of Wellington's librarian at Stratfield Saye, who, it was hoped, would get on with Sir George because he too liked history and genealogy. He was told by Osbert to 'take Mother's place'. Despite thinking his new employer looked like Don Quixote and was equally eccentric, Bamford found him very good company – 'amusing, with a puckish sense of humour, and . . . a fund of recondite information'.[7]

The Trio's biographers all refer to Sir George as if by now his brain had atrophied, yet it remained as active as ever, and he was working on a history of the Sitwell family, although he would never finish it. However, *Idle Fancies in Prose and Verse*, eight short poems with a preface and a postscript, appeared in 1938 in an edition of fifty copies. Admitting that his poems are old-fashioned, in a style 'after Tennyson', he says there is 'little in them except the expression of the grudge against Time, which anyone who has been moved too quickly into his 79th year may feel'.

Apart from a nod of approval in the preface to Sacheverell's book on German Rococo, he does not mention the Trio. While his poems are forgettable if charming, the postscript is impressive, especially when he reflects on time and space after a careful reading of Einstein's Theory of Relativity and Hermann Minkowski's refor-mulation. (It is unlikely that any of the Trio read, let alone under-stood, Einstein.)

He also says he has changed his attitude to religion. 'We cannot exclude the possibility of control or influence by a higher power,' he writes. 'Some definite code of ethics is required, and beyond reason-able doubt Christian ethics are the happiest and the best . . . The Communion service, as anyone may observe in Catholic as well as Protestant countries, is an aid to right living.' This sworn enemy of spiritualists admits, too, that after all there may perhaps be 'real ghosts'.[8]

Not even a secretary so understanding as Bamford could fill the void that Ida herself had never filled. At the end of October 1939 Sir George wrote to Osbert, 'I have been very much alone all my life as your mother could not be and did not try to be a companion, and I am satisfied to die alone when the time comes.'[9]

He continued his correspondence with Reresby, now twelve, writ-ing to him the next month that he really must work harder if he wanted to pass well into Eton. He added wistfully,

> I spent three weeks at Venice at the Hotel Luna, a few
> yards from St Mark's Square, and often thought of the
> happy times we had together there, five years ago . . .
> All the stucco figures in the grotto *[at Montegufoni]* were
> restored during the summer, as well as the painted vault
> and most of the water jets, but the marble pavement will
> have to wait for better times. I spend alternate weeks
> at the Castle and at the Hotel Grande Bretagne *[in
> Florence]*, where they give me a bedroom looking out
> on to the Ponte Vecchio.[10]

He also went on worrying about his elder son's extravagance, and Renishaw's future.

Meanwhile, Osbert's social life soared to giddy heights. He was introduced to the Duchess of York by Sir Philip Sassoon (for whom he had fagged at Eton), and his catty stories delighted her – 'I can tell you, we used to laugh our heads off,' she recalled sixty years later.[11]

Then in 1936 he endeared himself not only to the duchess, but to the entire Royal Family by defending Edward VIII in his poem 'Rat Week', fiercely denouncing those who wanted him to abdicate. When the duchess became Queen, Osbert was soon invited to stay at Balmoral, besides being given a seat in Westminster Abbey for King George VI's Coronation in 1937. He had become a part-time courtier.

Two years later, the Second World War broke out.

Chapter 21

RENISHAW AND
THE SECOND WORLD WAR

Prudently, Osbert spent the entire war at Renishaw Hall, rarely visiting London even after the Blitz was over. He made it his self-appointed mission to keep the arts alive, giving the occasional party for writers and artists and asking some of them to stay. He also encouraged those whom he felt were suffering from poverty or isolation, sending money and letters of encouragement.

Another consequence of the war was the return of Edith, who in autumn 1940 came back to Renishaw and made it her home for the next twenty years. Her dislike of Osbert's 'friend' David Horner smouldered as intensely as ever, but conflict was averted by his joining the RAF in August. The last person left who still remembers Edith and Osbert together at Renishaw, their niece by marriage Penelope Sitwell, says that brother and sister made a splendidly impressive couple.

A committed pacifist who could never forget the horror he had seen in the trenches, Osbert was shocked by Britain joining the Second World War, despite his loathing for Hitler. He still regarded Winston Churchill as a bombastic adventurer, the man responsible for the disaster at Gallipoli.[1] He even felt some sympathy for Oswald Mosley as the one politician who openly opposed the war, if for the wrong reasons. Quite apart from his pacifism, Osbert believed that Germany and Russia were bound to fight each other to the death and there was no point in wasting British blood and treasure. Luckily, he possessed enough sense of self-preservation not to air these views.

The war had forced Edith to leave Paris, where, apart from summer visits to Renishaw, she had been living since 1932 in the rue Saint-Dominique, a run-down street in what was then a seedy area. Above a bistro and opposite a coal merchant, her flat was even worse than Pembridge Mansions, without a lavatory or running water. She had gone there to be near Tchelitchew and to nurse Helen Rootham, who had been struck down by an agonising, inoperable spinal cancer. (Some of Helen's medical expenses were paid by Sir George.) By now Helen had died, and Edith was only too relieved to join Osbert at Renishaw.

Now that she had come home, like her mother she spent most of her time in bed, insisting on a blazing log fire in her bedroom even during the summer months, until wartime conditions made logs hard to come by. However, she always came down for dinner. She was busy enough, working on new poems with books spread all over the bed, or knitting shapeless socks for the Forces. Curiously, unless it was raining heavily, again just as Lady Ida had done, in the evenings brother and sister liked to sit together in the porch on the north side where the house seems dullest and darkest, instead of in the exquisite gardens to the south.

The only child of a multi-millionaire shipowner, Bryher Ellerman, best known as an historical novelist, arrived from Portugal in autumn 1940. Osbert joked that the tough little lesbian must have come on a German invasion barge. When she first saw the house after walking up from the station, 'The range of windows reminded me of those old

Italian palaces that are a town in themselves and the formal garden was still a blaze of summer flowers.' (On her next visit, the flower beds were growing vegetables.)

At dinner she found herself next to the novelist Charles Morgan, who was pessimistic about how long the war would last and what it might do to civilisation. The next day, once the other visitors had left, Edith 'read me poems, sitting outside on the terrace in the pale, October sunshine', recalled Bryher. 'It was indescribably peaceful to sit listening to the poems with the sweep of the gardens in front of us and the feeling that behind the poetry there could be something indestructible in the mind.'[2]

Yet Edith thought their world might not survive, even if the Nazis were beaten. 'Ours was a world of shadows, and of unmistakable shadows, although the passing sound of that far off music among the ruins was for ever with us', she tells us, in a Chekhovian passage. She hints at a fear that they would be the last Sitwells to live at Renishaw – there might be a revolution after the war.[3] Both she and her brother believed they were living at the end of an age.

Despite these forebodings, the pair produced their most important work during this time. The end of Osbert's demanding social life in London enabled him to write the mammoth autobiography he had long been planning. This was also the period when Edith wrote her best poems.

<hr />

Food rationing made little impact on the Sitwells, since they ate illegally killed pork from the farms, pheasant, partridge or hare (out of season as well as in) and rabbit untainted by myxomatosis. Anthony Powell describes a shopping expedition to Sheffield when, wearing a high cylindrical hat 'between an archimandrite's and that of a Tartar horseman', Edith even managed to buy an entire salmon, which was sent home by train in time for dinner.

Life at Renishaw was under constant threat, however. A dozen evacuees had arrived from the London slums at the same moment as Edith – two mothers with children, all of them dirty 'fried fish shop types', who mercifully preferred to move out into cottages on the estate. A few officers were billeted for brief periods. There was also a possibility of requisition by a government department, but the pampered civil servants could not face the cold and lack of electric light.

The house was kept in working order by Robins – despite his age and bad temper, and aided by his wife Susan, the housekeeper – but only just. Staff were almost impossible to find, as they were serving in the Forces or employed in factories. A fourteen-year-old maid who seemed to be possessed by a poltergeist left broken china in Edith's fried whiting and shards of broken glass near Osbert's gouty foot, and was finally sacked when her face broke out in a disgusting rash.

Because of coal-rationing (an irony in a house built on top of coal), only wood was available for heating, and when this became rationed too, the sole warmth in winter – apart from one or two bedrooms which had scanty log fires for part of the night – was in the tiny ante-dining-room. 'We sit in it too, now,' grumbled Osbert in a letter to David Horner. 'It's squalid and middle class and I hate it, but it's better than being cold.'[4] Yet he gave a new overcoat to a gamekeeper who was fire-watching. As in peacetime, the drawing rooms were lit by Aladdin paraffin-lamps and bedrooms by candles in white enamel candle-sticks.

Although no bombs fell on Renishaw, from autumn 1940 onwards they heard German planes passing overhead at night to bomb Sheffield, eight miles away; then distant explosions, with flames lighting the sky.

By November, refugees were being rehoused at Eckington. The following month Sheffield suffered two particularly severe air raids that killed over 600 people – seventy died when a hotel received a direct hit. There were more raids during the weeks that followed. Going into Sheffield shortly after a raid, Edith was moved by the shop assistants' courage. In April 1941 she learned that in London a land-mine had obliterated Pembridge Mansions, killing everyone who lived there.

'How simple-minded of the Germans to imagine that we British could be cowed by the destruction of our ancient monuments!' Osbert joked. He was referring to the Baedeker Blitz that had begun with the obliteration of Coventry. 'As though any havoc of the German bombs could possibly equal the things we have done ourselves!'[5]

Newly discovered letters reveal that Osbert wrote regularly to members of the Renishaw staff serving with the Forces, letters in which he showed much kindness and understanding. (After all, he knew what war meant.) Among them were Cooper the chauffeur and Shafto the gardener. He also sent letters of sympathy to villagers whose sons had been killed. As has been seen, another kind letter went to Vanessa Bell after her sister Virginia Woolf drowned herself.

Writers continued to stay at Renishaw. Besides Bryher and Powell they included Evelyn Waugh, Arthur Waley, Lord Berners, John and Rosamond Lehmann, and also L. P. Hartley, who became his close friend and trustee. (A copy of *Eustace and Hilda* in the library is inscribed 'For my dear ward, Osbert, with love from a faithful & vigilant trustee, Leslie.') A member of the family always remained puzzled by the friendship since, with the best will in the world, she had found Hartley 'a fat and boring little man'. His homosexuality may perhaps explain why Osbert liked him, not to mention his unremitting flattery.

As a lover of Brighton, Osbert had been delighted by the publication of John Piper's *Brighton Aquatints* in 1939. He commented in *The Listener* that they made 'a charming book, beautifully produced, and Mr Piper has called the tune to exactly the right note . . . He shows a rare aptitude for the rendering of architectural surfaces and manages to convey atmosphere with the strictest economy of means.' Deciding that Piper was the ideal man to illustrate his autobiography, Osbert then wrote to him, inviting him to paint Renishaw.

'I am delighted with the idea of painting Renishaw Hall and of staying there with you,' Piper replied in April 1940. 'Its beauties look very great from the postcards you send, and I look forward with enthusiasm to seeing it and you.'[6] It was two years before the project finally got under way, but in May 1942 they agreed on a price suggested by the artist – '£1 per inch measured the longest way.'

Piper's first visit was in June. He was given David Horner's bedroom, which he occupied on all subsequent visits – much to Blossom's resentment – and he enjoyed Edith's company when she came down in the evenings and put Debussy records on the gramophone, though he was alarmed by her consumption of neat gin. He left in an ecstasy. 'I got home, with my head full of black-trunked trees, scythed grass, the tumbled beauty of Renishaw Park, Bolsover in the mist, and Sutton Scarsdale in drizzle and Barlborough in fitful sun', he told Osbert in a thank-you letter.[7]

Osbert's commission of Piper echoed Sir George's choice of Sargent. In 1945 Osbert claimed, with justice, in a preface to an exhibition of his work at the Leicester Galleries that in Renishaw,

> Mr Piper has found a territory peculiarly suited to his
> sombre and fiery genius . . . His landscapes are imbued
> with the very spirit of a countryside that knows no rest

from work, and that throbs with a strange dual life; for, under the age-old surface processes of farming, forestry and the like, runs the cramped subterranean existence of mines. Here in this hilly land of slagheaps and chimneys is a vividness not to be found in tamer districts of the South.[8]

Renishaw possesses over seventy paintings and drawings by John Piper, the largest collection of works by any leading British artist of the twentieth century in private hands. When you step into the hall you see an oil of Venetian scenes over the fireplace, while on the side walls are *Derbyshire Domains*, with views of Renishaw and the ruins of Bolsover Castle. The 'smoke' room next door contains further Pipers. There are others throughout the house – even a tiny stained-glass window.

Piper fell totally under Renishaw's spell, like so many before and after him. Proposing himself for another stay in June 1943, he wrote, 'it feels like arranging to come home again'.[9] He grew devoted to Osbert, as can be seen from over thirty letters to his host. In 1951, asking him to be his son's godfather, he ended 'I long to see you', while during the 1960s he referred to him as 'the most generous person I've ever known'.[10] It has to be said that John Piper gave a great deal in return.

In February 1941 the Trio were once more in the headlines, with a libel action at a time when it still looked as if Britain was going to lose the war. (Germany had not yet turned on the Soviet Union, nor had Japan bombed Pearl Harbor.) Reviewing *Edith Sitwell's Anthology*, the *Reynolds News* described the three as 'literary curiosities of the 1920s', sneering that their prominence in those days had been due to self-advertisement, but 'now oblivion has claimed them'. They sued the paper, pointing out that they had published many books in recent years, and won £350 each in damages as well as costs.

They deserved to win. A year later Edith published a collection of her latest verse, *Street Songs*, which received enthusiastic reviews and became a triumphant success. Here at last was the breakthrough for which she had always hoped. The book contained one of her finest poems, 'Still Falls the Rain', a meditation on the bombing of London during the Blitz that she compared to the crucifixion of Christ. There could have been no better proof that the Sitwells were far from out of date.

In April 1943, in a further demonstration that the Sitwells were still relevant, Edith and Osbert organised a poetry reading in the Aeolian Hall. The poets they chose included T. S. Eliot, Edmund Blunden, John Masefield, Walter de la Mare and Lady Gerald 'Dotty' Wellesley (soon to be Duchess of Wellington), among others.

The reading, attended by the Queen with Princess Elizabeth and Princess Margaret Rose (who sat in the front row) went off well. Edith declaimed her 'Anne Boleyn's Song'. The only shadow was cast by Dotty Wellesley, who, very drunk, attacked Harold Nicolson with her umbrella under the impression that he was Osbert, using frightful language about the Queen and Edith. Reresby Sitwell, fifteen at the time, remembered the fracas as one of the funniest things he had ever seen, saying that it sent the young princesses into fits of laughter.[11]

Despite the war, Sir George stayed on in Italy until 1942 when, says his grandson, 'lack of his favourite food, roast chicken'[12] drove him to take refuge in Switzerland, in a hotel at Locarno where he grew a beard like that of an Old Testament Prophet. His children learned with horror of his plan to marry a German nurse and settle

£500 a year on her. Then he fell into the hands of a Swiss man named Woog whose English wife came from a family George knew in Derbyshire, and after engineering the German nurse's expulsion from Switzerland, the couple plundered his bank account. When he died in July 1943, Osbert believed the Woogs had murdered him. The war made it impossible to investigate, but with hindsight, it looks as if he died a natural death.

Although he was a strange, badly damaged man, George Sitwell had been infinitely kinder and more human than any of his offspring, as well as far more intelligent. As will be seen, his elder son's revenge would turn him into a genuinely tragic figure.

During recent months Osbert and Edith had resembled Aesop's fox waiting for the crow to drop the piece of cheese, so they were horrified by their father's will, which left them less than they expected and made Reresby the ultimate beneficiary. Osbert got nothing, as he had already been given Renishaw and Montegufoni, while Edith received a mere £1,000. They were otherwise unmoved by his passing. Only Sachie mourned him. Even so, there was a decorous memorial service at Eckington.

***

Among Osbert's guests at Renishaw during the war was the actor Alec Guinness, who came for a weekend in 1941, bringing his wife and baby. During dinner, Robins announced that 'Young Master Guinness' was yelling his head off upstairs. 'I expect the baboon has just looked in and frightened him,' said Edith playfully. 'And suddenly in that extraordinary house with its oil lamps and creaking stairs and miles of corridors and haunted rooms, one really could imagine that there might be a baboon or two roaming around,' commented Guinness.[13]

A pre-war guest who might have been expected to come and stay regularly was Rex Whistler, but he was serving with the Welsh Guards. Osbert was deeply upset by news of his death in action in France, shortly after D-Day. Besides providing dust jackets for the entire Trio, Whistler had designed Osbert's bookplate (showing the author, quill in hand, on a Baroque staircase) and also a letter heading, an exquisite little drawing of Renishaw Hall that remains in use today.

The most appreciative guest during these beleaguered years was undoubtedly Evelyn Waugh, who saw the house as a last bastion of patrician civilisation. Yet even at Renishaw, the 'war effort' lurked menacingly in the background. A dedication to Osbert, scrawled in a first edition of *Put Out More Flags* which is still in the library, reads, 'Don't go down the mine, Daddy'. This was a cruel reference by Waugh to Osbert's nagging fear that the local authorities at Sheffield might arrange for him to be conscripted as a 'Bevin Boy' – a coal miner.

Posted to the War Intelligence Centre at Matlock in Derbyshire in June 1942, Waugh took the opportunity to visit Osbert and Edith. In his thank-you letter [c. 22 June 1942], he rejoiced at not finding Nissen huts in the garden or evacuees on the stairs, and said that Lord Woolton would disapprove of life at Renishaw. (Minister of Food, Woolton had introduced ration books, dried eggs, Snoek fish and the ghastly Woolton Pie.)[14] Waugh told his wife, 'Renishaw is just as you saw it. Shabbier outside with the lawns long & the hedges ragged so that you might think the house deserted till you come inside . . . Banks of potted plants & bowls of roses: piles of new & old books & delicious cooking.'[15]

Waugh visited Renishaw again that summer, and wrote again [c. 14 July 1942] from Smedley's Hydro (famous for health-giving mineral water) to thank Osbert for his stay, during which the pair had indulged their taste for Baroque art and good wine. 'Vincenzo Re and Léoville-Poyferré' Waugh recalled happily. (Vincenzo Re had been an eighteenth-century designer of stage scenery for the Teatro di San Carlo, and Osbert possessed handsome engravings of some of his sets; Léoville-Poyferré is a prized second-growth claret.) 'What could have been more delightful or more different from Smedley's Hydro?'[16]

He kept in touch with Osbert for the rest of the war. In 1943 he wrote to condole on Sir George's death, commenting that he liked the way the obituary in *The Times* referred to his attempts to recreate a view of Derbyshire life in the thirteenth century.

In August 1944, writing from Croatia to thank Osbert for a letter that congratulated him on surviving a near-fatal air crash, Waugh says he has heard that Montegufoni has survived in reasonably good condition. He adds that he has given instructions for an advance copy of *Brideshead Revisited* to be sent to Renishaw.

From White's, in April 1945, Waugh thanked Osbert for the first volume of the English edition of *Left Hand, Right Hand!* 'It is stimulating to find a writer nowadays with the power and hope to plan a work on a large scale and the grace and detachment to carry it through.' However, he did not like the illustrations which he called, 'Mr Piper's sketches'. He thought that perhaps they had suffered in reproduction.[17]

Brideshead Revisited was published to acclaim in May 1945. Osbert would have been superhuman not to feel a twinge of envy; but it was more than a twinge. 'Jealous, doesn't like talking about it,' was how Waugh's loyal friend Nancy Mitford described his reaction.[18] Osbert told Horner that, 'with all my great admiration and warm friendship for Evelyn, I think it is a bad book. It reveals unpleasant snobbishness in the author.'[19] Yet he never openly criticised *Brideshead* or any other novels by Waugh.

For his part, showing rare self-control, Waugh never expressed reservations about the autobiography's later volumes, even pretending to qualify his dislike of Piper's illustrations. Nevertheless, despite all the compliments he paid Osbert, privately he did not think much of his literary gifts. 'Well, he was as bad at painting as Osbert is at writing,' he told Nancy Mitford in 1945 when discussing Benvenuto Cellini. 'For Christ's sake, don't repeat that comparison *to anyone*.'[20] But he was sincere in praising Osbert's patronage of letters.

Because it was valued by both men, their friendship survived the war, which was a remarkable achievement for two such difficult personalities. What held them together was Renishaw.

On her final wartime visit, Bryher found it sad that 'I should never see Renishaw again in quite the same way. It was already drawing back into some private enchantment of its own.' She thought it unfair that Osbert and Edith should receive so little credit for all they had done. 'A few intimate friends apart, nobody thanked them when the war was over.'[21] However, in 1947 Cyril Connolly wrote in *Horizon* that they had not only produced their best work during these years, but found time to be of immense help to other writers.[22]

Chapter 22

THE SITWELL RENAISSANCE

Habitual pessimists, Osbert and Edith feared some sort of Bolshevik upheaval would engulf Britain when hostilities ended, with a police state run by very unsympathetic people indeed. They thought there was going to be no place for Sitwells. However, the Attlee Terror proved comparatively mild, and within a few years it was followed by an attempt to bring back the pre-war world. There would, after all, be plenty of room for Sitwells – and Renishaw.

Admittedly, the new Socialist Britain was miserable for the upper classes. London had become a slum where malarial mosquitoes bred in bomb-site pools; a city of wrecked buildings, with stucco peeling off the façades of Belgravia. Exhortations to eat in the 'British Restaurants' (corrugated iron huts kept on from wartime) heightened the gloom, as did the prospect of the 'Festival of Britain'. Taxation was punitive, food and clothing still rationed, and there were financial restrictions on travel abroad. The future seemed bleak for houses such as Renishaw.

Like Evelyn Waugh, Osbert developed a loathing for the 'Common Man'. His version of Hooper, Waugh's philistine subaltern in *Brideshead Revisited*, was Demos, who personified the drab new age. In a 'secular oratorio' called *Demos the Emperor*, in which Demos fights Autork, a figure who is either Hitler or Stalin, for world domination, Demos declares, 'I am the Mass Mind of Red Bungalows . . . .'.[1]

'It's icy here, and I'm getting elderly,' Osbert moaned to his friend Christabel Aberconway on Boxing Day 1945.

> What we all need is what we want – and how to get it.
> I want, this house, electric light and heating instituted,
> works of art, champagne, caviare (I'll let the foie gras
> go), mangoes, peaches, Southern climate, and masses
> of money as well as fame. Not much to ask. And, of
> course, no gout.[2]

He feared the Labour government might take Renishaw away from him, as they had Wentworth Woodhouse from the Fitzwilliam family.

Yet despite intimations of ruin, he remained as generous as ever, helping such needy writers as Edith's boozy young protégé Dylan Thomas, whom even she admitted looked like a youthful Silenus painted by Rubens. In August 1946 the bard wrote to thank 'My dear Osbert' for cash that enabled him to go to Ireland (and get beastly drunk). 'Your book I am reading slow as a snail because I do not want that journey or that world to end; and the money you sent me from the kindness of your heart made me proud and happy.'

'It was all Christmases and birthdays the morning of getting it,' Thomas wrote again at the end of November 1946 after receiving another handout.

> It was new shoes and sweaters for the [water] voley river
> cold, and school bills paid with a flourish, and some
> Algerian [wine], and books I've wanted for months, and
> a heater for our hutch, and more things and more, and
> such happiness to think that you were thinking of us

and could spare, in this taxed dark, such a very marvellous gift.[3]

In the event, apart from electricity and a cure for his 'gout', the modest
needs Osbert had listed in his Boxing Day letter to Lady Aberconway
were to be satisfied. Ironically, the provider was the Labour government, who ended his money worries by nationalising coal mines. On
the advice of his shrewd agent Maynard Hollingworth he used the
compensation to buy farmland, which then soared in value.

Even Montegufoni survived relatively unscathed, as Osbert found
on a brief visit in summer 1946. It had been used by Mussolini's
government as a repository for the greatest paintings in the Pitti and
Uffizi galleries (by Botticelli, Cimabue, Ghirlandaio, Giotto, Duccio,
Uccello). Castello and pictures survived occupation by first German
and then Indian troops. Their salvation was largely due to Guido, an
unpleasant but faithful servant from a nearby village. The following
year Osbert brought John Piper to paint the castello, with the usual
happy results.

The years at Renishaw during and after the war were Osbert's most
fruitful period. His first volume of autobiography was published in
1945; the last would appear in 1950. Although full of good stories
narrated with feline wit, and containing fascinating reminiscences
of aristocratic society and the great hostesses of London during the
Edwardian twilight, it does not really work as biography, because its
pathologically secretive author reveals so little of himself. He conceals
his homosexuality, never mentioning Horner, and ends when he is only
thirty. Nonetheless, for a time the book was an enormous success.

'These five volumes have given him a secure place in English literature,' wrote Waugh in 1952 in the *Sunday Times*, calling them 'a masterpiece'. He claimed the Sitwells had 'taught the grandees to enjoy their possessions while they still had them', although comparatively few 'grandees' can ever have met Osbert, Edith or Sachie, read their books or visited Renishaw. However, another novelist, Elizabeth Bowen, was justified in observing that Osbert 'anatomised' his age and society. He had done so by using Renishaw as an ivory tower.

Even George Orwell, scarcely an admirer of the patrician way of life, praised the autobiography, which, says Philip Ziegler, was 'to be found in virtually every English house which bought books with any regularity; matching in popularity the Bible and Shakespeare, the histories of Arthur Bryant and the novels of Evelyn Waugh'.[4] It sold well in America too, spreading Renishaw's fame across the Atlantic. One reason for its success in England was nostalgia for the past, fuelled by the petty social controls and boredom of Attlee's Austerity Britain – the period's most popular film was *Kind Hearts and Coronets*. Renishaw became the emblem of a lost age.

⁂

Sir George, who appeared in every volume, had (as L. P. Hartley put it) been turned into a 'comic character as unforgettable as Don Quixote or the White Knight'. Some of the stories about him, such as his invention of a musical toothbrush and a miniature revolver for shooting wasps, are among the most enjoyable things in the book; but they belong to fiction, or are wildly exaggerated. Even Hartley, clever observer that he was, failed to realise that the portrayal was a lie. It was Osbert's final, venomous settling of accounts.

Much of the lie can be detected in the detail. For example, Osbert says that the 'bevy' (his name for father's female admirers) included a Miss Fingelstone, 'very strict and old fashioned in her ideas', who lived in Venice, supporting herself by introducing well-heeled tourists to antique dealers and writing books on Venetian history. Among 'the better-known titles were – and still are', claims Osbert, '*Byron – or Love on the Lido!*, *Round the Convents with Casanova* and *Amblings with Aretino*'. However, a strict, old-fashioned lady is unlikely to have read the works of Venice's two greatest pornographers.

What Osbert says about his father is often very amusing, but nearly always untrue or exaggerated. Often the portrait is almost flattering, then followed by story after story of ludicrous behaviour that builds up relentlessly the impression of a bumbling, egotistical buffoon. None of Sir George's achievements are mentioned, let alone leaving the family finances in a condition that enabled the Sitwells to go on living at Renishaw.

Sacheverell was horrified. 'It is most painful to realise your hatred for your father,' he wrote after reading the first volume. 'It is, I know, useless, to try and persuade you that, in his heart, he was in his queer way devoted to you.'[5] In 1973, when Osbert and Edith were dead, he stressed how much he owed to George 'for his intelligence and for his interesting mind, which have been cruelly derided, with no one to speak up for him and protect his memory'.[6] He came to Renishaw even less, staying at Weston, where he pursued his fascination with the exotic and macabre in such strange books as *Splendours and Miseries*.

Reresby, too, rejected the 'sometimes unfair as well as cruel assessment' of 'a benevolent and understanding grandfather'.[7] Throughout his life, he cherished the letters that Sir George had written to him when he was a small boy.

Osbert's revenge had buried the real George Sitwell in a merciless, long-drawn-out caricature that constitutes the most savage parricide in

English literature. Ironically, he himself was far more impractical and self-indulgent than his fictional portrait of his father.

Even so, he shared Sir George's passion for Renishaw, adding further treasures. He recovered the original crescent-shaped table for the dining room apse – slightly shortened, it was otherwise intact – and, besides such eccentric objects as Robin Hood's putative bow and an outsize Regency bookcase that covered an entire wall, he bought two genuinely important pieces of Baroque art. One was Salvator Rosa's magnificently sombre *Belisarius in Disgrace* in 1946 (in a frame designed by William Kent), which now hangs at the end of the ballroom and is the finest picture in the house, not excepting the Copley or the Sargent. The other was Tiepolo's *Rinaldo and Armida*.

He purchased Henry Walton's *The Three Young Surgeons* (from a descendant of one of the surgeons) as a pair for Walton's *Cherry Barrow*. He also bought a large number of twentieth-century drawings and paintings, mainly from the Leicester Galleries. The artists included Picasso, Augustus John, Henri Gaudier-Brzeska, Paul Nash, Gino Severini, Rex Whistler, Pavel Tchelitchew, Wyndham Lewis, William Roberts, Thérèse Lessore, Ethelbert White and C. R. W. Nevinson.

<hr />

Osbert's success gave a boost to Edith, who had arguably been the most popular poet of the war years – Cyril Connolly declaring that her verse possessed the purest poetical content of any modern poet, not excepting Yeats, Eliot or Auden. The two older Sitwells became national figures, Edith being made a Dame of the British Empire in 1954 and Osbert a Companion of Honour four years later. *Life* magazine called them 'England's most celebrated literary family'.

Seen as equals in achievement, Osbert and Edith toured the United States together, arriving in New York at the end of October 1948 to stay at the St Regis Hotel. Both lectured as far afield as Buffalo, spending Christmas in Boston, fêted and lionised, before sailing home in March. They had made a considerable impression on the Americans, even if one journalist thought they seemed 'as remote from the Century of the Common Man as the Aztecs'.[8]

Also in New York, Waugh was green with envy, writing to Nancy Mitford that Osbert and Edith are known as 'The Fabulous Sitwells' and having 'one hell of a time'. He says Osbert has let his hair grow so long that he looks like Einstein. Asking them if Sachie was there too, he was told blandly, 'Alas, Sachie is serving as High Sheriff of his County and therefore unable to leave the United Kingdom'. (Because it meant bringing Georgia too, Osbert had refused to pay the fare for his cash-strapped brother, who was furious at being left behind.) In another letter, Waugh denies he is jealous of Osbert, saying no sane man can envy his 'ostentatious progress' through the USA, and claiming implausibly that it has increased his sales by only eighteen copies.[9]

The visit's outstanding event was a party in Manhattan given by a legendary bookstore, the Gotham Book Mart, for the Sitwells to meet American writers. The most famous of these were the poet Marianne Moore and two young men, novelist Gore Vidal and playwright Tennessee Williams. Others included William Rose Benet, Elizabeth Bishop, Richard Eberhart, Charles Henri Ford, Horace Gregory, Randall Jarrell, Delmore Schwartz and José Garcia Villa. Two English poets were there, too, Auden and Spender.

'The group photograph has something of Aquinas's Vision of the Heavenly Host, with poetry's angels and archangels grouped around their virgin queen', comments the Trio's biographer, John Pearson.[10]

The pair returned in summer 1950 to lecture as far afield as Austin, Texas and Columbus, Ohio. They went back again early in 1951, visiting Hollywood, where Edith gave readings from Shakespeare

– flatteringly, during the sleep-walking scene from Macbeth a spectator had to be carried out of the hall screaming and frothing at the mouth.

She was introduced to Marilyn Monroe as a publicity stunt by a journalist who hoped they would quarrel spectacularly. Instead, they made friends, perhaps because each glimpsed the other's vulnerability. 'In repose', Edith said of Marilyn, 'her face was at moments strangely, prophetically tragic, like the face of a beautiful ghost.'[11] However, Edith did not take kindly to the attentions of the gossip columnist Hedda Hopper. When there was an outbreak of rabies in Hollywood, she told everyone the outbreak had been caused by 'Miss Hopper going round biting dogs'.[12]

Although Edith liked George Cukor, she was exasperated by his attempts to make a film out of her book *Fanfare for Elizabeth* (really the story of Anne Boleyn), with Laurence Olivier and Vivien Leigh in the lead roles. Afterwards, she recalled a scriptwriter's contribution, 'This is the scene where you have those Cardinal guys threatening the King with everlasting damnation. And the King says, "That's O.K. by me, boys! Go right ahead. You tell your boss the Pope that I am King of England – and to hell with his everlasting damnation."'[13]

These visits to the United States were the climax of the Sitwell renaissance, but became too exhausting. The health of both siblings was failing, in particular Osbert's. Together, they made a final tour in 1957. Osbert continued to exchange letters and books with American writers with whom he had built lasting friendships, such as Marianne Moore and Lincoln Kirstein of the New York City Ballet – dedicating a book to Kirstein and his wife Fidelma.[14]

Secretly, Osbert Sitwell regarded Evelyn Waugh as his only equal as a writer. Waugh, who guessed at this flattering opinion, pretended to reciprocate. He congratulated Osbert warmly when the autobiography's fourth volume came out, writing from Piers Court on 29 May 1949, 'Very many thanks indeed for *Laughter in the Next Room* . . . an entirely delightful volume.' He described it in less enthusiastic terms to Nancy Mitford. 'Osbert's book is queer, isn't it,' he confided.[15] He thought some of his friend's opinions dangerously progressive.

Yet he paid Osbert the compliment of keeping him informed about his own work. In August 1951, referring to a new novel, he told Osbert, 'It is all Small Arms ('Musketry' to you) and ante-room tippling. I get so obsessed with military dialogue I can't stop.'[16] This was *Men at Arms* which, fortunately, would not make Osbert so jealous as had *Brideshead Revisited*.

In September 1952 Waugh confided to Ann Fleming, a little nervously, that the *New York Times* had commissioned him to write a profile of Osbert. 'Though it is all love & praise it is certain to give deathless offence,' he says. He jokes how he has been tempted to write that, just as Osbert's ancestor styled himself Sitwell Sitwell, 'Sir Osbert should have taken the name Hurt Hurt.' Waugh says he has refrained, to have a shot in the locker 'in case he turns nasty'.[17]

No doubt, the article contained praise. The 'Grand Old Man of English Letters', Osbert's life was one of unbroken enrichment, his latest book always his best, wrote Waugh, recalling how wonderful the Sitwells had been in the 1920s. Yet the portrait's compliments were tongue-in-cheek – 'The bland, patrician features . . . the courteous manner (Mr Turveydrop ameliorates the stern carriage of Sir Leicester Dedlock in this baronet) . . . a hint of alertness and menace.'[18] (Anyone who read Dickens would have known that Mr Turveydrop and Sir Leicester are among the most ludicrously pompous characters in all English fiction.)

Osbert accepted the praise, concealing any resentment he may have felt. He knew enough about writing to realise that Evelyn Waugh was probably the greatest English novelist of the twentieth century, and valued his prickly friendship sufficiently to put up with a certain amount of mockery. Fortunately, Waugh never went any further. He was too fond of staying at Renishaw, which he ranked with other great houses where he was welcome, such as Chatsworth or Longleat.

Chapter 23

DECAY

In 1950 a specialist informed Osbert that he was suffering from Parkinson's disease, possibly due to undiagnosed encephalitis (a viral inflammation of the brain) caused by the Spanish flu that had nearly killed him thirty years before. Because of inadequate medication, Parkinson's was an even worse affliction than it is now. But for some years Osbert managed to lead a reasonably normal life.

In August 1957 Waugh paid him another visit, writing when he got back to Combe Florey, 'Thank you for days of enchantment.'[1] He recalled it a little differently in a letter to the Duchess of Devonshire. 'The talk is mostly of medicines. I just managed to keep my end up on sleeping draughts but Mr Hartley has us all beat by a great [insect] bite in the left foot over which he has consulted two doctors and a chemist.'[2] It was Waugh's last visit.

Despite his increasing disability, Osbert continued to write and went on sending copies of his books to Waugh, who in 1959 thanked him for yet another, *Fee Fi Fo Fum*. This was a reinterpretation in a 1950s setting of English fairy stories, such as Jack and the Beanstalk. Waugh, who had just returned from Africa, adds, 'I was asked to dinner by a native chief in Tanganyika who said "Don't dress. Come in your tatters and rags."'[3]

By now, Osbert fell over constantly. When he lunched at Chatsworth in the summer of 1960, he had to be carried into the dining room by the Duke of Devonshire and Lord Antrim. Ann Fleming, who was present, reported to Waugh that 'during the meal his fork started knocking against his plate, the din was awful, and it was difficult to maintain unembarrassed conversation'.[4]

In October that year he underwent an operation on the brain. The result was encouraging. To some observers, he looked healthy enough, while his speech and handwriting improved. But it was a temporary respite that would last less than three years.

Meanwhile, Edith's feud with David Horner came to a head. In her letters to Sachie she referred to 'Little Lord Fauntleroy', 'the creature' or 'the animal', later claiming that only her newfound religious faith had stopped her from murdering him. She was shocked by his homosexual affairs. It is only fair to say that even observers less biased than Edith found Blossom grotesque, W. H. Auden laughing at him as 'a rose-red cissy, half as old as time'.[5]

Horner returned Edith's loathing, claiming that she had been driven mad by sexual frustration and ought to be in a lunatic asylum. By now her drinking was out of control, she fell frequently and made noisy scenes, all of which he cited in support of his theory. Penelope Sitwell recalls an atmosphere of mutual hatred that was quite terrifying. When Edith went to hospital with a kidney infection, David insisted that Renishaw did not have the resources to look after such a sick woman and gave Osbert an ultimatum – either he or she must go.

In August 1960, Edith was forced out of what had been her home for two decades, even leaving behind Rex Whistler's portrait. Despite her formidable personality, she could not cope with the day-to-day business of life: her finances were in chaos, and she had little ready money. No doubt, her father had supposed Osbert would provide for her, in the way he himself had provided for Aunt Floss. But her brother gave her nothing.

She took refuge at her London club for ladies, the Sesame, saved from bankruptcy by an admirer, Elizabeth Salter, who acted as her unpaid secretary and put her affairs in sufficient order to provide her with an adequate income.

It seems odd that he should behave so cruelly, as in some ways he was a kind man. (Although an agnostic, he had urged Edith to become a Catholic because he thought it might give her peace of mind.) But, ruthless in the pursuit of his own comfort, he would not tolerate the prospect of endless rows. As a friend of Sacheverell, the Byzantinist Sir Steven Runciman, observed, 'The Sitwells could never stop quarrelling with each other.'[6] Yet once they had been so united.

In a poem, 'Serenade to a Sister', Sachie expressed his sadness at being banished from Renishaw, 'the lost paradise'.

> Why
>   cannot I walk into the wood
> We called the wilderness
> Beyond the statues of the warrior and the amazon?
> Why
>   cannot I walk into the wood
> Through the wooden gate
>   where I was often frightened as a child
> And look down to the lake between the trees?[7]

Edith must surely have shared his sense of loss.

Meanwhile, Osbert was far from forgotten in the land of letters. In January 1961, Graham Greene sent him a copy of the recently published *A Burnt-out Case*, inscribed, 'For Osbert with great affection'. Greene was an old if not a close friend, who back in the twenties had told Osbert how much he enjoyed his verse, while Osbert admired his novels.

Early in 1962, *Tales My Father Taught Me*, which Osbert had begun years before, appeared as a postscript to his memoirs. In the final chapter, 'The New Jerusalem', Sir George – cutting the usual ludicrous figure – advises his son to emigrate to Canada or America and build a new Renishaw, a replica of the old. Although suavely amusing, the book was a last vicious kick at his parent – time had not diminished Osbert's hatred. On this occasion, however, more than one reviewer realised the portrait bore little resemblance to reality.

The three Sitwells appeared together at a concert given at the Festival Hall on 9 October 1962 to celebrate Edith's seventy-fifth birthday. In a wheelchair, heavily fortified by alcohol, during the first half Edith read in that beautiful voice some of her poems; these were intermingled with a Rossini sonata, a Mozart divertimento and Benjamin Britten's setting of *Still Falls the Rain*, which was sung by Peter Pears. The second half was a performance of *Façade*, conducted by William Walton.

It was the very last appearance of the 'delightful but deleterious trio'.

⁕

Blossom's nemesis arrived in January 1963, when Osbert engaged Frank Magro as his valet. A Maltese bachelor in his thirties, a clerk in a travel agency and in no way a professional 'gentleman's gentleman', Magro was fascinated by his employer. Catering for Osbert's every whim, he not only washed, shaved and dressed him, but managed his correspondence and read to him – including the twelve volumes of Proust's *À la recherche du temps perdu*, in English. Soon he was promoted to private secretary. Horner, who recognised a rival, detested him.

Magro could be difficult, and his protective attitude to his employer became so irritating that Sacheverell grew to loathe 'the Maltese'. At Renishaw the staff resented his pretensions, refusing to treat him as a 'gentleman'. But Osbert rejected every criticism.

The improvement worked by the brain operation eventually wore off. In London Osbert sometimes went to his club, the St James' in Piccadilly, where he made a tragic spectacle with his ravaged face and staring eyes yet still kept an air of Hanoverian distinction.[8] He never ate at the club, for fear of spilling food over himself. When Magro came to take him home, he would be inserted with difficulty into a huge black overcoat with an astrakhan collar. He began to spend more time at Montegufoni for the sake of the climate.

In 1963 he broke with David Horner, whose promiscuity had been irritating him for some time. A year before, either drunk or chasing a handsome young cook, Blossom had fallen down a flight of stone stairs into a cellar at Montegufoni, cracking his skull and breaking an arm and several ribs. (There were rumours that he had been pushed.) A haemorrhage reduced him to a wreck, and despite a partial recovery he changed almost overnight into a querulous, fiendishly tempered old man who was incapable of controlling his rages. He also grew insanely jealous of Frank Magro. In consequence, when Osbert left for Italy in September he did so without Horner and never saw him again, after more than thirty years of friendship.

Renishaw became increasingly run-down. After the war, Osbert had even contemplated demolishing the ballroom until the house was classified as a building of historical importance in 1951.[9] Roofs leaked, paper flapped on the walls. The gardens fell further into the decay into which they had been let slip during the war, with overgrown flowerbeds and unkempt lawns. Some of the statues were hidden by shrubbery.

During a visit in 1961 to retrieve Edith's belongings, Elizabeth Salter was shocked by the neglect. Two years later, Nancy Mitford and her sister the Duchess of Devonshire found 'a ghostly house', Debo commenting, 'I never saw such ingrained gloom' – they doubted if Reresby would want to take it on.[10]

Osbert was further demoralised by Edith's death in 1964, just before the publication of *Taken Care Of*, her embittered and sometimes spiteful autobiography. If occasionally grotesque, she had been the most gifted of the three, with a streak of genius. Throughout her life she suffered from loneliness and even terror, as he must have known; now that she was dead, did he reproach himself for letting Horner turn her out of Renishaw?

Evelyn Waugh's last letter to Osbert, dated 10 December 1964, was one of sympathy for Edith's death. 'How well I remember climbing those stairs at Pembridge Gardens (?) Square (?) – sitting entranced by her anecdotes.'[11] When Waugh himself died in the spring of 1966, Osbert – now a chair-bound wreck – wrote to his widow Laura to say how sorry he was. In her reply, she said of Evelyn, 'I know he is much happier out of the world.'[12] Osbert may well have envied him.

One consolation during these last years was John Lehmann, who had founded *New Writing* and *The London Magazine*. With the approval of all three he embarked on a study of the Trio as 'leaders of taste in their time'. Its title, *A Nest of Tigers*, was inspired by Edith's joke about herself and her brothers – 'We are as happy as a nest of tigers on the Ganges.' Lehmann let Osbert make corrections to the manuscript, so that the book, eventually published in 1968, ended up as a paean of praise. Osbert, who lived just long enough to have it read to him, was delighted. However, Sachie was incensed by the inclusion of Edith's tale of being sent out when a girl to pawn their mother's false teeth and buy a bottle of whisky. (This was to show that her childhood had not been unlike what she imagined was that of working-class poets.)

Back from Italy, Osbert visited Renishaw for a last time in the summer of 1965. He had grown so attached to Frank Magro while abroad that he let him eat with him in the dining room, which angered other members of staff. Although their employer could not put food into his mouth without Magro's assistance, they refused to serve a valet and, when Osbert ordered them to do so, left en masse. He stayed on for another month, Frank cooking his meals and feeding him in the great red room beneath the family portraits. But the row had upset him so much that he trembled more than ever. He decided it was time to leave – for good.

The last years of Osbert's life were lived out at Montegufoni, nursed by Magro. When he died in 1969 he had become almost blind, slumped in his wheelchair with his head on his chest, muttering inaudibly and forgetting in mid-sentence what he was trying to say. A heart attack finished him off in May. Sachie and Georgia, with their sons Reresby and Francis, were at his deathbed, and he was buried in the Protestant cemetery at Florence.

Sacheverell went on writing for nearly twenty more years. His books still found readers, if a dwindling band, and in 1984 he was made a Companion of Honour. He got on better with Reresby after Georgia's death, occasionally visiting Renishaw. He died aged ninety in 1988.[13]

Today, few people read Osbert's autobiography, and Sachie's *Southern Baroque Art* is a museum piece. Edith continues to have admirers, however – a recent biographer calls her one of 'the great poets of her generation', although not everyone may agree.[14]

Yet it would be wrong to relegate the Trio to the level of their old Bloomsbury rival Lytton Strachey (even less read) and dismiss them as mere minor writers who occasionally had something interesting to say. Instead, they should be seen through Waugh's eyes, as stimulating personalities who made a remarkable impact on their generation and on the taste of their period.

'For all their faults, the Sitwells were a dazzling monument to the English literary scene,' wrote Cyril Connolly, looking back at the twenties.[15] They are well worth studying if we want to understand England in the heady years after the First World War. At the time, they really did seem delightful and deleterious.

Somewhat ironically, Renishaw Hall – which played a vital part in inspiring all three of them – does a better job of preserving their memory than any of their books.

Chapter 24

RENISHAW REBORN

When Osbert left England in 1965, he gave Renishaw to Reresby Sitwell – who, as Sachie's elder son, was ultimate heir to the baronetcy. What made this a little less painful was Osbert's fondness for his nephew. He told friends, 'Renishaw is made for Reresby and Reresby for Renishaw,' and that he liked to 'think of them as belonging to each other'.[1] In the event, Osbert had far more grounds for saying this than he can ever have guessed.

⁂

Born in 1927, Reresby was tall, heavily built and high-coloured. He had the same thick hair as his uncle, to whom physically he bore a certain resemblance, if his voice was not so deep. He had tremendous presence and zest for life, a keen sense of fun, and his laughter filled the room; his arrival at a boring party had the impact of a mass blood transfusion. He was fond of wine, cigars and good conversation, and was an enthusiastic traveller. Because of his appearance, some observers thought him a throwback to the Sitwell squires of the Regency; but he neither hunted nor shot, from dislike of inflicting pain.

Although he could write – as he showed in a book on Mount Athos co-written with John Julius Norwich, the preface to a new edition of *Hortus Sitwellianus* and a fine booklet on Renishaw – he lacked any sense of vocation as a writer, no doubt intimidated by the family's output.

On the other hand, he would always show impeccable taste in pictures, furniture and gardens, together with a strong feeling for family history.

Like Osbert, he loathed Eton, which he remembered as cold and dirty because of the war. In contrast, he enjoyed National Service with the Grenadier Guards, during which he was commissioned and spent nearly three years in occupied Germany. (His company commander Miles Fitzalan-Howard, later Duke of Norfolk, recalled that he was a natural soldier – 'very good with the men'.) After going down from Cambridge and various unsatisfying jobs, he became a wine merchant in a firm whose senior partner was Bruce Shand, father of the future Duchess of Cornwall.

In 1952 Reresby married a beautiful Anglo-Irish girl, Penelope Forbes, who came from a background even more patrician than Lady Ida's. (The Forbes have been noble since 1442 while her uncle, the eighth Earl of Granard, was Master of the Horse to Edward VII and George VI.) Despite her childhood being overshadowed by the death of her father in a motor accident, Penelope became a formidable, resourceful personality, no less colourful than her husband. She was a tall, slim, striking brunette whose intelligence was on a par with her looks – during the war she had worked as a code-breaker.

Unshakably loyal, Penelope gave Reresby rock-like support throughout their long marriage and proved to be the ideal partner for the renewal of Renishaw Hall. She was well equipped to deal with an impossible mother-in-law, brushing aside repeated attempts at interference. (The archives are full of abusive letters from Georgia.) Nor did she take any notice of Sachie's outrage when, asking his granddaughter the name of her dachshund, he was told 'Heinz Sacheverell Sitwell Prickles'.

Penelope never forgot her first visit by herself to Renishaw during the mid-1950s, having recently married Reresby. Osbert gave her a pleasant welcome, as he liked and admired her, while she found him amusing. Yet the atmosphere at lunch was not exactly easy. The new butler, who was in love with his employer, resented beautiful ladies. Nor did the agent seem to like women. After walking by the lakes, she had to clean soot off her shoes and stockings.

The evening was even more daunting. Save in one room, lighting was still provided by oil lamps or candles. After dinner, Edith, her alarmingly Gothic new aunt, announced, 'Dear child, it is time you went to bed,' picking up two huge silver candlesticks, one of which she handed to her. Having led Penelope up stairs and along a pitch-black, seemingly endless corridor to a cavernous bedroom, she left her cowering in the darkness with the single candle.[2]

Despite this unpromising start, the couple fell hopelessly in love with Renishaw, and became devoted to every stone and blade of grass. Years later, Reresby captured its spell perfectly when he wrote of a

> strange compelling atmosphere which seems always to have held a mysterious grip upon all who live or work here, an enchantment that will not appeal to everyone – and may well be tempered by the vagaries of climate – but has led one visitor, the artist Rex Whistler, to declare that Renishaw 'was the most exciting place he knew'.[3]

It was also the most exciting place known by Reresby and his wife. 'Renishaw looks more beautiful in this lovely spring each time we go there,' he wrote to Osbert in March 1966. 'No wonder you found handing it over such a terrible wrench ... I wonder what you will think of some of our minor alterations and re-groupings of furniture? On the whole I think many of the things we have done are what you would have got round to if you were more mobile.'⁴ Yet despite many invitations, Osbert never returned to the place he had loved above all. 'Although I should very much like to see Renishaw again, I cannot see myself travelling to Sheffield under any circumstances,' he explained to Penelope in a letter of January 1968. 'But if I ever made up my mind to come to Renishaw, you and Reresby must be there too.'⁵

For a few years, however, Renishaw had a rival in Reresby's affections – Montegufoni. In August 1968 he wrote to Osbert after learning that he, and not Sachie, would inherit the great Tuscan castello.

> I have to thank you for so many things . . . above all, of course, for Renishaw and all its treasures – so many of them surprises I never expected, the family estates, the farms and the woods I have got to know so well these last few years, all these things and now the promise of more.
>
> Your letter in fact reached me yesterday morning. I should, of course, have written to you at once but, although I never doubted your word, once you had made your decision and told me, yet somehow I felt stunned and unable to marshal my thoughts on paper. All I can say is that, poor Christian as I am, my fervent prayers are that your present comparative improvement in health will long continue and that you will be spared a good many years more to enjoy Montegufoni.⁶

The embittered Blossom still managed to be a nuisance. Suspecting that he was no longer going to inherit Montegufoni as Osbert had once promised, despite having plenty of money he demanded some of Renishaw's more valuable pictures, which he insisted had been given to him. Osbert told his nephew to take no notice.

For some years after Osbert's death Reresby spent a few weeks each summer at Montegufoni, and his enjoyment of the castello's Chianti led him to plant a vineyard in Derbyshire. Finally, however, realising he must choose between Renishaw and Montegufoni, he chose Renishaw. It was a brave choice with a Labour government in power and Denis Healey threatening to 'squeeze the rich until the pips squeaked'. It was also a lucky one. Had he stayed in Tuscany, the flamboyant 'Barone Inglese' up at the castello could well have become a target for kidnappers when the Brigate Rosse – the Italian revolutionary movement – emerged at the end of the decade. Montegufoni was sold in 1976.

To a large extent what Reresby and Penelope did at Renishaw, inside and out, was to turn Sir George's plans into reality. To begin with, however, even to live in the house was a daunting experience. Upon taking over in autumn 1965, they and their young daughter Alexandra had to live with electric light in only a few rooms and no heating. It was so cold that during that first winter they sometimes preferred to read the newspapers in the warmth of the car. It all needed vast expenditure to put right. When heat and light finally came, separate electric circuits were installed to reduce costs.

After modernising the kitchen in the former Preserves Room (the old kitchen, with its copper pots and pans, being kept as a museum) – and after providing seventeen bedrooms with baths – there still remained the problem of staff, the upstairs–downstairs world having vanished with the war. During the 1960s, many owners of great houses who had not yet learned to live without servants abandoned the struggle, selling their homes.

At Renishaw, the problem was solved by staff from the village, finally culminating with the charming Pat and Sheila – renowned for their beautiful frilled aprons and splendid hairstyles – who came in daily to cook as well as clean. They produced (and at the time of writing still produce) meals reminiscent of a good French restaurant.

Until 1979 the butler (unpaid) was Leedham, who did not notice the passage of time, and much to Alexandra Sitwell's embarrassment laid a child's small knife and fork for her on her twenty-first birthday. On retiring, he was replaced by a weekend butler, Philip – otherwise an electrician – who was fascinated by life at the hall. ('There's diamonds as big as pigeons' eggs in there,' he remarked during dinner for a ball at Chatsworth.)

The immediate task, Penelope recalled, was just tidying up. Then she and her husband embarked on a methodical restoration, the first room reclaimed being the ballroom from use as a junk room. It was repainted as a temporary measure by the then cleaners' husbands, and given curtains that Penelope made herself. Sir George's Brustolon chairs were moved into it from the Great Drawing Room, as was *Belisarius in Disgrace*. Most rooms were repapered fairly quickly, but as late as 1975 discoloured paper still flapped on the walls of the Duke's Wing.

Gradually Renishaw became a masterpiece of decoration. The Great Drawing Room was repainted in subtle colours. Instead of being carpeted its wooden floor was stencilled and then varnished by Paul and Janet Czainski with designs inspired by the floor of Empress Maria Feodorovna's state bedroom, which Reresby and Penelope had seen at the Pavlovsk Palace in St Petersburg. An immense Regency colza-oil chandelier from Sir Sitwell's time was converted to electricity, lighting the room as it had never been lit before.

The dining room regained some of its original furnishings. Five of its Chippendale dining chairs were returned from Weston, then joined by three more found at an antique shop in Sheffield, the set being completed by a skilled cabinetmaker.

Another drawing room became 'the Print Room', with eighteenth-century engravings pasted on its walls in place of wallpaper, inspired by one seen in a great Irish house. The walls of the Stone Hall (the old stairwell) were covered with a hundred blue and white plates brought back from China by Osbert. The ghost wing was given electric light, which at last got rid of its uncanny atmosphere.

Penelope went to a London workshop to learn gilding so that she could put life back into faded furniture and picture frames, while the cabinets and commodes were cleaned and renewed. The collection continued to grow, one acquisition being a big Derbyshire Blue John urn of about 1810 that was joined by two Blue John topped tables.

Some of the bedrooms, such as Osbert's, 'Lady Margaret's' or 'the Duke's' needed little refurnishing, but others had been sadly neglected. Mouldering ostrich plumes were removed from the four-poster beds while country house sales were regularly attended to find better tables and chairs. All received new curtains and carpets.

Osbert's study was left untouched. Reresby would sometimes invite one or two guests into it, then read them his uncle's story of the only recorded English vampire, imitating Osbert's deep voice, which made for an unsettling performance. When there alone, he himself thought it had an eerie feeling. One afternoon, leaning out of the study window in a reverie, he suddenly felt a cold hand pressing down on the back of his neck. For a few long seconds he remained petrified, unable to move – only to find that a creeper growing on the wall outside had become detached and fallen on him. As his uncle had written in 'Night', the poem which conjured up the haunting of Renishaw Hall, 'A shudder

from the ivy that entwines/The horror that is felt within its grip . . .'
'Night' was much admired by Reresby, who read it again and again,
feeling it reflected his own sense of hearing faint echoes of what had
happened there long ago.

Renishaw is a benevolent and cheerful dwelling, a welcoming place
of happy memories. Yet, as in most old houses, there have been ghosts.
A blue-haired American lady who had heard the story of the Boy in
Pink complained of not being woken by him – nobody cared to tell
her that she wasn't young or pretty enough. Even so, the middle-aged
pianist Moura Lympany, scarcely a raving beauty, was convinced she
had been kissed by him and seen his beautiful face drifting away.

The Boy was not Renishaw's only phantom, but Philip Ziegler went
too far in claiming that it was infested with ghosts in the way another
house might be by rats. More recently, Simon Jenkins gave a lurid sum-
mary in his *England's Thousand Best Houses*.[7] Even when Jenkins wrote,
however, he was out of date, since they had all gone.

While Reresby did not object to the Boy in Pink, he took drastic
measures to get rid of the others, having the house exorcised first by an
archdeacon, then by a rabbi and finally by Monsignor Alfred Gilbey,
the former Catholic chaplain at Cambridge. He reinforced their min-
istrations with fresh paint, redecorating every room. Since then, there
have been no more hauntings.

A silver plate on the ballroom wall commemorates a ball given by
Reresby and Penelope in 1977 for 700 guests, to celebrate their twenty-
fifth wedding anniversary and also Alexandra's coming out. It was an
epic party on the scale of Sir Sitwell Sitwell's routs. The hall was filled
with flowers, the gardens and statues were floodlit, and the gas flam-
beaux by the main porch had their mantles removed, roaring flames

into the night. The hosts stood at the door to greet guests, Penelope and their daughter Alexandra in ballgowns made by the famous Rahvis sisters.

'The best music I have heard for a long time,' wrote one guest. 'If it had gone on any longer, I should have been dead on my feet. The breakfast and champagne were a great sustenance in the middle of the dancing.' Another thought the party more impressive than the Shah's coronation. It was all paid for by some broken sixteenth-century Maiolica plates, hoarded by Osbert, that Penelope found in a cupboard.

Almost every weekend the couple entertained with house parties in more or less pre-war style, but only changing for dinner on Saturdays. As many as sixteen guests would arrive on Friday in time for dinner. There was always a cheerful welcome from the hosts, who sat on or by the fender in front of the fireplace in the old hall that still served as a drawing room.

Although the guests were no longer predominantly writers and artists as in Osbert's time – even if they often included John Piper and Moura Lympany – they were no less interesting. Among the grander were the aged Duke of Portland, who had a platonic crush on Penelope and drove a car much too small for a duke, and Baron Élie de Rothschild (the colourful owner of Château Lafite) and his wife Liliane, whom Reresby thought 'the most intelligent woman I ever met'. But at meals you might just as well find yourself sitting next to a gardener or a cabinetmaker in black ties.

The diarist James Lees-Milne, who came with his wife Alvilde in 1974, recaptures one such weekend in *Ancient as the Hills*. For years he had longed to see Renishaw, and wished he had done so during Osbert's time, for 'then it must have been more Gothic and gloom-filled than it is now. Reresby and Penelope have brightened it up.' He thought the Chippendale commode 'about the most beautiful piece of furniture in all England'. There were ten other guests, delicious food and 'an old family butler who obliges for house parties but will accept no recompense, no gratuity'.[8]

As for their host and hostess, he thought Penelope beautiful and stately while Reresby was 'a very sweet fellow' who reminded him of Sachie. Even so, Lees-Milne took exception to his 'coarse streak'. When showing them their bedroom, Reresby said to Alvilde Lees-Milne, 'If Jim gets too randy, you can always put the bolster in the middle.'[9] (They realised he knew they were both bisexual.) When Lees-Milne left he presented Penelope with his novel about incest, *Heretics in Love*, carefully writing in his dedication on the fly-leaf that 'this insalubrious tale was written by, and not about me'.

⁕

During these weekends, on the first morning Reresby would take his guests on a tour of the house with a talk that became an increasingly polished performance. (He enjoyed being a travel lecturer, his subjects ranging from ancient Egypt to Robin Hood.) High points of the Renishaw lecture were attributing the other commode in the Great Drawing Room to Chippendale – 'unsigned but the work of the Master *at his very best*' – or how Sargent in his portrait had given Edith a straight nose and Sir George a crooked one, when the reverse was true. All this was spoken in a voice deepened to add solemnity.

The talk included details of family heraldry, such as his forebears the Morleys of Hopewell having borne rabbits on their coat, 'a fine example of canting arms'. There was advice on restoring furniture, and how it is cheaper to use the very best craftsmen just as 'sometimes it is cheaper to eat at Claridges'. Other topics were Robin Hood, about whom he knew a great deal (having written a pamphlet on the subject),[10] and a local crusader and namesake, St Reresby – 'the canonisation is purely local'. There were also some extremely amusing stories in Derbyshire dialect.

Tours of the Renishaw gardens could be equally memorable. After the Second World War these had become almost a jungle, as Osbert lacked the energy to restore them. Their comprehensive re-creation after 1965, with innovations that included planting a hundred species of rose and creating a 'White Garden', was a saga to which the host did full justice.

There were afternoon excursions, sometimes to tour a ducal house – Haddon, Hardwick or Chatsworth – but also to see the Christmas lights at a mining village, or to visit a gigantic black pig who lived contentedly in a small cottage kitchen. Alternatively there might be a picnic near the ruins of Bolsover Castle (of which the guests would already have seen an evocative Piper painting in the hall at Renishaw) or beside the forlorn shell of Sutton Scarsdale, once a glorious Georgian mansion.

At Sutton Scarsdale, during an al fresco lunch, the host would explain that in 1946 his uncle Osbert had bought what was left of the place to save it from demolition, and that he himself had sold it to the Ministry of Works for £200 – which was why the house eventually went to English Heritage. After this Reresby would recount, with gusto and vivid anatomical detail, his theory of how the (presumably) castrated Mr Arkwright and his wife had served as models for D. H. Lawrence when he wrote *Lady Chatterley's Lover*.

In 1984 Reresby published *Hortus Sitwellianus*. This was an elegant new edition of Sir George's *On the Making of Gardens*, with a short foreword by Sacheverell, an introduction consisting of an excerpt from Osbert's memoirs and an essay by Reresby, 'The Gardens at Renishaw'.

Reresby's essay gives us some idea of the sheer magnitude of their restoration, which was very much in the spirit of his grandfather. To begin with, he and Penelope trod carefully: 'When the new owners took over Renishaw in 1965, at first they had to be cautious not to offend their uncle by too dramatic alterations,' writes Reresby. He goes on:

> The destruction of the sunken gardens had to be glossed over but, gradually gaining confidence, they put in hand other minor improvements. So the Water Garden was completed, by paving the unfinished side with coping stones taken from the walls of a derelict orchard. At the same time, a wrought-iron footbridge that had connected the bottom of the wilderness with the South Park and become redundant, was placed to join the 'island' with the 'mainland', so that one can walk from the end of the grass 'causeway' over the tops of the water-lilies on the far side.

He adds, showing his own passionate love for the gardens, 'one of the great minor pleasures of Renishaw is to gaze at the many-coloured water-lilies, opening and closing their flowers according to the time of day, and feed the swarms of coruscating goldfish'.[11]

Sir George might not have liked some innovations, such as the 'Yuccary' in the Orangery (restored in 1999), which houses the National Collection of Yuccas – thirty species of unlovely plants from the deserts of the western United States, some very rare. Nor might he have cared for the dachshund cemetery in Sir Sitwell Sitwell's Gothic temple. Yet he would have been charmed by Reresby's 'Auricula theatres' – tiny display cabinets whose shelves hold pot after pot of these exquisite little flowers.

In 1983 Reresby served as High Sheriff for Derbyshire. Wearing Osbert's court sword and velvet court dress, he swore an oath of loyalty to the Queen before the Lord Lieutenant at Derby Cathedral while trumpeters in the uniform of the old Derbyshire Yeomanry played Haydn's Derbyshire Marches. Again in court dress, he acted as return-ing officer for the general election that year. What pleased him was the sense of continuity from his forebears.

These were the 'golden years' of Mrs Thatcher's premiership, but far from happy ones for many in Derbyshire. The miners who had brought down Mr Heath met their match, and when their strike failed the mines' closure meant widespread misery. On the other hand, lower taxation made it easier to maintain Renishaw, while soot-blackened grass and the red gleam of pit-head lights at night became things of the past.

In 1997 Reresby told the *Sheffield Telegraph*, in an interview for a Piper exhibition, 'I tend to regard Renishaw as the mistress of my old age, beautiful, charming, moody and unpredictable.' By now he had ensured that Renishaw Hall was playing a role in the life of the local countryside, and of Derbyshire as a whole.

Guided tours of the house had started, as well as concerts and plays in the gardens, while a museum with art galleries was created in the stables, with display cases designed by Alec Cobb. The galleries included a Museum of Sitwell Memorabilia and an exhibition of John Piper's works. This contribution to local culture was recognised in 2004 when Sheffield University gave Reresby an honorary doctorate – which delighted him, as the Trio had all received doctorates from Sheffield.

Meanwhile, in Tony Blair's 'Cool Britannia', the lord of the man-ors of Eckington and Barlborough in Derbyshire, of Whiston and Brampton-en-le-Morthen in Yorkshire, remained a Victorian squire who was accepted as such for miles around because of his affability and good nature. He kept up rent dinners, inviting farmers to dine at the hall twice a year so that they could drink Her Majesty's health and pay the rent. An improving landlord, he took a practical interest in his estate's thirty or so farms, regularly inspecting farm buildings. On one occasion during the demolition of a ruined cottage, the arms of Richard III, with their white boar supporters, were found painted on a wattle-and-daub wall – but they crumbled into dust before his eyes.

In old age, Reresby grew to look even more like his uncle. In 1999 the Queen Mother lent four Pipers from her own collection for an exhibition at Renishaw, and soon afterwards lunched at the Sitwells' London house. She was so struck by the resemblance between Reresby and Osbert that – aged ninety-nine – she announced as she left, 'I feel rejuvenated!'

Having suffered a stroke that increasingly slowed him down, Reresby died at the end of March 2009, a fortnight before his eighty-second birthday. Until the end, he remained devoted to Renishaw – I remember him leaving it for London when a shadow of his former self, murmuring as we drove away down the drive, 'Goodbye, dear old house.' A few months before his death, he had left instructions for a great diamond-shaped funeral hatchment with his coat-of-arms to be hung over the north porch when he died – a gesture that would have delighted his grandfather. During the funeral service in Eckington parish church, at Alexandra's request, Osbert's poem 'Night' was read.

Nobody who knew Reresby could disagree with the obituary in *The Times*: 'Fun-loving, flirtatious and gently feudal, he won the love and affection of a wide and diverse circle of friends and tenants.'[12] His monument is a reborn Renishaw Hall – more enduring than any of the Trio's writings.

⁂

In the end, Sir George triumphed, because Reresby and Penelope ensured that his plans were realised while adding much that was their own invention. Together the pair developed every aspect of Renishaw's power to please. Today, even the most casual visitor can sense the spell that it has cast on the generations of Sitwells who have lived there.

Chapter 25

TODAY

In 2009, Reresby's daughter Alexandra Sitwell became the first woman to be squire of Renishaw Hall. A small girl when her parents took possession in 1965, she had at once succumbed to the spell of the landscape as well as that of the house, spending so much time in the Renishaw woods – even sleeping in them at night – that for the first few weeks they did not see her for days on end. From the very beginning, however, she took an enthusiastic part in the house's restoration.

Intent on preserving their achievement inside and out, she is no less determined than they were that Renishaw should survive as a family home (she and her husband Rick Hayward have a son and daughter) and as a monument to the Sitwells. She is also keen to carry on its traditions, provided these are viable in the modern world. One example is presiding over the biennial rent dinners that her father enjoyed so much.

Her carefully considered innovations reflect this determination. Among the first was engaging a new, highly professional archivist, in a programme designed to increase our understanding of the Sitwell family's history and the evolution of Renishaw Hall. One consequence has been the rediscovery of hundreds of letters to Osbert which had been carelessly stuffed into drawers or cupboards. They show that he was in contact with far more writers, artists, musicians and actors than any Bloomsbury can have been, not excepting Virginia Woolf. All of the books in the house – some 25,000 – have been catalogued, which meant taking every single volume off the shelves in the library and in other rooms, listing and reshelving them.

Alexandra has also redecorated the library and the front hall, and many bedrooms, reconfiguring the furniture. Nearly all the paintings on the first and second floors (apart from those in the Duke's Wing) have been rehung. Osbert's collection of twentieth-century art – not just the Pipers and Nevinsons, but the Tchelitchews, Gaudier-Brzeskas and Rex Whistlers – has been framed and are on display. More family portraits have been placed in the dining room, to maximum effect.

At the same time, following in her parents' footsteps and in those of her great-grandfather, the gardens have gone from strength to strength. The present gardener, David Kesteven, has been an enormous help in carrying on the tradition. Alexandra has encouraged him to rediscover and recreate the architecture of the gardens as first laid out by Sir George, reducing climbers on the house and garden walls and opening up vistas into the west park. In addition, with her mother and David, she has redesigned the Fountain Garden and the Ballroom Garden.

Today, thanks to all the work put in over the years by Sir George, by Reresby and Penelope, and more recently by Alexandra, the result is generally acknowledged to be one of the most impressive horticultural ensembles in England, as well as a real plantsman's joy.

In April 2015 it was announced that Renishaw had won the coveted HHA/Christie's Garden of the Year Award, which is annually given by the auction house to a Historic Houses Association member garden after it has been voted a favourite throughout the previous year by the HHA's Friends. (Past winners include Blenheim Palace, Bowood House, Castle Howard and Hever Castle.) The award reflects the amount of enjoyment gained by the garden's many visitors, and the extent of the owner's personal involvement in its maintenance and development.

Each year more and more visitors come to see Renishaw Hall and its gardens. Often they have been drawn by Renishaw's regular appearance on such TV programmes as *Countryfile* or Lynda Bellingham's *Country House Sunday*. The exhibitions in the stable block flourish, and attract an increasing number of visitors.

Just as it was for Rex Whistler, for more than a few people Renishaw is still the most exciting place in England, and continues to cast its extraordinary spell.

OWNERS OF RENISHAW

George Sitwell, 1625–67

Francis Sitwell, 1667–71

George Sitwell, 1671–1723

Francis Sitwell, 1723–53

William Sitwell, 1753–76

Francis Hurt Sitwell, 1776–93

Sir Sitwell Sitwell, 1793–1811

Sir George Sitwell, 1811–53

Sir Reresby Sitwell, 1853–62

Sir George Sitwell, 1862–1925

Sir Osbert Sitwell, 1925–65

Sir Reresby Sitwell, 1965–2009

Alexandra Sitwell (Mrs Rick Hayward), 2009–present

NOTES

Foreword
1. Evelyn Waugh, *Sunday Times*, 7 December 1952.
2. H. Acton, *Memoirs of an Aesthete* (London, Methuen, 1948), p. 208.
3. Osbert Sitwell, *Noble Essences or Courteous Revelations* (London: Macmillan, 1950), p. 41.

Chapter 1: The Cavalier
1. Unless otherwise stated, material quoted in this chapter comes from Sir George Sitwell, *Letters of the Sitwells and Sacheverells*, 2 vols (Scarborough: for George Sitwell, 1900–1), vol. I.
2. Osbert Sitwell, *Left Hand, Right Hand!* (London: Macmillan, 1945), p. 13.
3. The two grants of arms hang in the library at Renishaw.

Chapter 2: 'Mr Justice Sitwell'
1. Sir Reresby Sitwell, *Renishaw Hall and the Sitwells* (Derby: Derbyshire Countryside Ltd, 2001).
2. Unless otherwise stated, material quoted in this chapter comes from Sitwell, *Letters of the Sitwells and Sacheverells*, vol. II.

Chapter 3: A Mathematician
1. Unless otherwise stated, material quoted in this chapter comes from Sitwell, *Letters of the Sitwells and Sacheverells*, vol. II, and Sitwell, *Renishaw Hall and the Sitwells*.

Chapter 4: The Merchant Squire
1. Unless otherwise stated, material quoted in this chapter comes from Sitwell, *Letters of the Sitwells and Sacheverells*, vol. II, and Sitwell, *Renishaw Hall and the Sitwells*.

Chapter 5: Passing on the Torch
1. Unless otherwise stated, material quoted in this chapter comes from Sitwell, *Letters of the Sitwells and Sacheverells*, vols I and II, and Sitwell, *Renishaw Hall and the Sitwells*.

2. Sir George Sitwell, *The Hurts of Haldworth and Their Descendants at Savile Hall, The Ickles and Hesley Hall* (Oxford: University Press, 1930), p. 225.

Chapter 6: A Regency Buck

1. Renishaw Archives (hereafter R.A.), Sir George Sitwell's Red Notebook C, p. 58 (Print Room).
2. Sitwell, *Left Hand, Right Hand!*, p. 17.
3. Joseph Friedman, 'New Light on the Renishaw Commode', *Furniture History Society Journal* 1997, pp. 136–42.
4. E. A. Smith, 'The Yorkshire elections of 1806 and 1807: a study in electoral management', *Northern History* 2 (1967), pp. 62–90.
5. Osbert Sitwell (ed.), *Two Generations* (London: Macmillan, 1940), p. 40.
6. R.A., Box 139, Bundle 2.
7. R.A., Box 139, Bundle 1.

Chapter 7: Ruin?

1. R.A., Box 139, Bundle 1.
2. Sitwell, *Renishaw Hall and the Sitwells*, p. 8.
3. Sitwell, *Two Generations*, p. 62.
4. Ibid., p. 61.
5. Ibid., p. 74.
6. Ibid., pp. 23–4.
7. Ibid., pp. 12–13.
8. Ibid., pp. 130–1.
9. Ibid., pp. 18–20.
10. Ibid., p. 120.
11. R.A., letter (1881) from Georgiana Sitwell to Sir G. Sitwell.
12. Sitwell, *Left Hand, Right Hand!*, p. 18.
13. Sitwell, *Two Generations*, p. 139.
14. Ibid., pp. 145–6.

Chapter 8: Camping in the Wreckage

1. Unless otherwise stated, material quoted in this chapter comes from the diaries of Louisa, Lady Sitwell (R.A., Box X3).

Chapter 9: An Unsung Heroine

1. Sitwell, *Left Hand, Right Hand!*, p. 40.

2. R.A., Box ex 28.
3. Ibid.
4. Ibid.
5. Sitwell, *Left Hand, Right Hand!*, p. 29.
6. Ibid.
7. R.A., Farrer & Co. Box.
8. Edith Sitwell, *Taken Care Of* (London: Hutchinson, 1965), p. 59.
9. Letter from Ethel Smyth, quoted in Appendix D of Sitwell, *Left Hand, Right Hand!*, pp. 261–4.
10. Sitwell, *Left Hand, Right Hand!*, p. 156.
11. R.A., Box 24 c1869/70.
12. Sitwell, *Two Generations*.
13. Sitwell, *Taken Care Of*, p. 67.
14. R.A., OS (oversized) Drawer 2.

Chapter 10: The Golden Years Return?

1. Sitwell, *Left Hand, Right Hand!*, p. 50.
2. Osbert Sitwell, *Great Morning* (London: Macmillan, 1948), p. 50.
3. R.A., Bundle 2.
4. R.A., Box 147.

Chapter 11: A Miserable Marriage

1. Sitwell, *Taken Care Of*, p. 20.
2. Sitwell, *Left Hand, Right Hand!*, p. 223.
3. R.A., Box 147, Bundle 9.
4. Ibid.
5. Sitwell, *Taken Care Of*, pp. 20–1.
6. Osbert Sitwell, *The Scarlet Tree* (London: Macmillan, 1946), p. 20.
7. R.A., Box 565, Bundle 1.
8. Sitwell, *Scarlet Tree*, p. 43.

Chapter 12: Sir George's Italian Cure

1. Sitwell, *Letters of the Sitwells and Sacheverells*, vol. I, p. ii.
2. Reresby Sitwell (ed.), *Hortus Sitwellianus* (Salisbury: Michael Russell, 1984), p. 3.
3. Ibid., pp. 36–8.
4. Ibid., p. 109.

5. R.A., Box X13, Green Note Book 1907–10, p. 100.

6. Ibid., p. 13.

7. Ibid., p. 58.

8. Sitwell, *Hortus Sitwellianus*, p. 33.

9. R.A., Box X13, Green Note Book 1907–10, p. 110.

10. R.A., Box X13, Bundle 1, card No. 64.

11. R.A., Box X13, Green Note Book 1907–10, p. 125.

12. Ibid., p. 75.

13. In the Val di Pesa, in the Chianti.

14. R.A., Box 532/1; also in Sitwell, *Great Morning*, p. 51.

15. R.A., Box 470, Bundle 4.

Chapter 13: A New Renishaw

1. Sitwell, *Hortus Sitwellianus*, p. 15.

2. Ibid.

3. R.A., Sir G. Sitwell, *The Story of an Old Garden*, Box 100 (ex X48).

4. David Kesteven, *Renishaw Hall Gardens* (Derby: Abbey, 2010), p. 10.

5. R.A., Box X13, Green Note Book 1907–10, p. 106.

6. Clayre Percy and Jane Ridley (eds), *The Letters of Edwin Lutyens to his Wife, Lady Emily*, (London: HarperCollins, 1985), p. 157.

7. Renamed *Madonna with Two Saints Adoring the Child*, today this is in the Pierpont Morgan Library, New York.

8. R.A., Box 13. opp. p. 104.

9. Sitwell, *Hortus Sitwellianus*, p. 20.

Chapter 14: Renishaw Children

1. Sitwell, *Left Hand, Right Hand!*, p. 104

2. Ibid., p. 111.

3. Osbert Sitwell, 'A Door that Shuts', in *Selected Poems, Old and New* (London: Duckworth, 1943), p. 66.

4. Sitwell, *Taken Care Of*, p. 32.

5. Sacheverell Sitwell, *All Summer in a Day* (London: Duckworth, 1926), p. 79.

6. Victoria Glendinning, *Edith Sitwell: A Unicorn Among Lions* (London: Weidenfeld & Nicolson, 1981), p. 39.

7. Sacheverell Sitwell, *For Want of the Golden City* (London: Thames & Hudson, 1973), p. 417.

8. Sacheverell Sitwell, *Splendours and Miseries* (London: Faber, 1943), p. 242.

9. Sitwell, *Taken Care Of*, p. 41.

10. Percy and Ridley, *Letters of Edwin Lutyens*, p. 157.

11. R.A., Box 408/6.

12. Sitwell, *Scarlet Tree*, p. 305.

13. Sitwell, *Great Morning*, p. 96.

14. Elizabeth Salter, *The Last Years of a Rebel: A Memoir of Edith Sitwell* (London: Bodley Head, 1967), p. 91.

15. Richard Greene, *Edith Sitwell: Avant Garde Poet, English Genius* (London: Virago, 2011), pp. 105–6.

Chapter 15: Leaving the Nest

1. Sitwell, *Great Morning*, p. 13.

2. Ibid., p. 141.

3. Ibid., p. 228.

4. Ibid., p. 13.

5. J. Pearson, *Façades: Edith, Osbert and Sacheverell Sitwell* (London: Macmillan, 1978), p. 72.

6. Richard Greene (ed.), *Selected Letters of Edith Sitwell* (London: Virago, 2007), No. 18.

Chapter 16: The Great War, and Lady Ida's Ordeal

1. Philip Ziegler, *Osbert Sitwell* (London: Chatto & Windus, 1998), p. 54.

2. Osbert Sitwell, *Laughter in the Next Room* (London: Macmillan, 1949), p. 78.

3. R.A., Box 565, Bundle 1.

4. Ibid.

5. Ibid.

6. Greene, *Selected Letters*, No. 21.

7. Sitwell, *Taken Care Of*, p. 20.

8. Sitwell, *Splendours and Miseries*, p. 242.

9. Sitwell, *For Want of the Golden City*, p. 292.

10. Sitwell, *Laughter in the Next Room*, pp. 79–85.

11. Ibid., p. 105.

12. Sitwell, *Selected Poems, Old and New*, p. 157.

13. Sitwell, *Laughter in the Next Room*, p. 113.

14. Derek Parker (ed.), *Sacheverell Sitwell: A Symposium* (London: B. Rota, 1975), p.76.

15. Grover Smith (ed.), *Letters of Aldous Huxley* (London: Chatto & Windus, 1969), p. 141.

16. Sitwell, *Left Hand, Right Hand!*, p. 4.

Chapter 17: 'Sitwellianism'

1. Acton, *Memoirs of an Aesthete*, p. 129.
2. Barry Day (ed.), *The Complete Verse of Noël Coward* (London: Methuen, 2011), p. 53.
3. Cecil Beaton, *The Wandering Years* (London: Weidenfeld & Nicolson, 1961), p. 163.
4. Nigel Nicolson and Joanne Trautmann (eds), *The Letters of Virginia Woolf*, 6 vols (Richmond: Hogarth Press, 1975–80), vol. III, p. 428.
5. Gabriele Finaldi and Michael Kitson, *Discovering the Italian Baroque: The Denis Mahon Collection* (London: Yale University Press, 1997), p. 12.
6. Parker, *Sacheverell Sitwell: A Symposium*, p. 16.
7. Ibid., p. 62.
8. Rebecca West, 'Two Kinds of Memory', in *The Strange Necessity: Essays and Reviews* (London: Jonathan Cape, 1928).
9. Allan Wade (ed.), *The Letters of W. B. Yeats* (New York: Macmillan, 1955), p. 776.
10. Anthony Powell, *Messengers of Day* (New York: Holt, Rinehart and Winston, 1978), p. 38.
11. Penelope Middleboe (ed.), *Edith Olivier From Her Journals 1924–48* (London: Weidenfeld & Nicolson, 1989), p. 98.
12. Nicolson and Trautmann, *The Letters of Virginia Woolf*, vol. III.
13. Ibid.
14. R. L. Mégroz, *The Three Sitwells: A Biographical and Critical Study* (London: Grant Richards Press, 1927).
15. Powell, *Messengers of Day*, p. 35.
16. Cyril Connolly, *The Evening Colonnade* (London: David Bruce and Watson, 1973), p. 300.

Chapter 18: Rivalry with Bloomsbsury

1. Ziegler, *Osbert Sitwell*, p. 1.
2. Parker, *Sacheverell Sitwell: A Symposium*, p. 16.
3. Ibid., p. 4.
4. Ziegler, *Osbert Sitwell*, p. 101.

5. Nicolson and Trautmann, *Letters of Virginia Woolf*, vol. VI, p. 466.

6. Sitwell, *Left Hand, Right Hand!*, p. 19.

7. R.A., Bundle 510.

8. R.A., Bundle 9.

9. Salter, *Last Years of a Rebel*, p. 58.

10. Glendinning, *Edith Sitwell*, pp. 194–5.

11. Sitwell, *For Want of the Golden City*, p. 277.

12. Wyndham Lewis, *The Apes of God* (London: Arthur Press, 1930), p. 322.

13. Glendinning, *Edith Sitwell*, p. 85.

Chapter 19: Renishaw as Patronage

1. Parker, *Sacheverell Sitwell: A Symposium*, p. 12.

2. R.A., Box 501, Bundle 3.

3. Ibid.

4. Greene, *Selected Letters*, No. 65.

5. Sarah Bradford, *Sacheverell Sitwell: Splendours and Miseries* (London: Sinclair-Stevenson, 1993), p. 128.

6. Salter, *Last Years of a Rebel*, p. 60.

7. Peter Quennell, *The Marble Foot* (London: Collins, 1976), p. 131–2.

8. Rupert Hart-Davis (ed.), *Siegfried Sassoon: Diaries 1920–22* (London: Faber, 1981), pp. 75–8.

9. Middleboe, *Edith Olivier*, pp. 79–80.

10. Beverley Nichols, *The Sweet and Twenties* (London: Weidenfeld & Nicolson, 1958).

11. Powell, *Messengers of Day*, p. 164.

12. Christabel Aberconway, *A Wiser Woman? A Book of Memories* (London: Hutchinson, 1966), p. 8.

13. Percy and Ridley, *Letters of Edwin Lutyens*, p. 411.

14. Sir Peter Quennell, personal communication from a stay at Renishaw in 1978.

15. Salter, *Last Years of a Rebel*, p. 186.

16. Michael Davie (ed.), *The Diaries of Evelyn Waugh* (London: Weidenfeld & Nicolson, 1976), pp. 329–30.

17. Ziegler, *Osbert Sitwell*, p. 160.

18. Sitwell, *Laughter in the Next Room*, p. 313.

Chapter 20: Marking Time in the Thirties

1. Middleboe, *Edith Olivier*, pp. 79–80.
2. Sir George Sitwell, *Idle Fancies in Prose and Verse: Being Eight Short Lyrics with a Preface and Postscript* (Oxford: Shakespeare Head Press, 1938), p. vi.
3. Hugo Vickers, *Cecil Beaton* (London: Weidenfeld & Nicolson, 1985), p. 166.
4. Letter from Sir George Sitwell to Reresby Sitwell, 28 November 1936, courtesy of Penelope, Lady Sitwell.
5. R.A., Box 537/ Bundle 13.
6. Letter from Sir George Sitwell to Reresby Sitwell, 19 July 1937, courtesy of Penelope, Lady Sitwell.
7. Pearson, *Façades*, p. 323.
8. Sitwell, *Idle Fancies*, pp. 71–2.
9. R.A., Box 501/ Bundle 3.
10. Letter from Sir George Sitwell to Reresby Sitwell, 26 November 1939, courtesy of Penelope, Lady Sitwell.
11. H.M. to author at a luncheon given by Sir Steven Runciman at the Athenaeum, June 1998.

Chapter 21: Renishaw and the Second World War

1. Ziegler, *Osbert Sitwell*, p. 240.
2. Bryher, *The Days of Mars: A Memoir, 1940–1946* (New York: Harcourt Brace Jovanovich, 1972), p. 22.
3. Sitwell, *Taken Care Of*, p. 151.
4. Ziegler, *Osbert Sitwell*, p. 253.
5. Quoted by George Orwell in *Tribune*, 31 December 1943.
6. R.A., Box 502.
7. R.A., Box 511.
8. R.A., Box 65.
9. Ibid.
10. *Sunday Times*, 22 March 1964.
11. Reresby Sitwell, personal communication.
12. Sitwell, *Renishaw Hall and the Sitwells*, p. 11.
13. Alec Guinness, *Blessings in Disguise* (London: Hamish Hamilton, 1985), p. 148.
14. R.A., Box 511/5.
15. Mark Amory (ed.), *The Letters of Evelyn Waugh* (London: Weidenfeld & Nicolson, 1980), p. 163.
16. R.A., Box 511/5.

17. R.A., Box 528/5.
18. Charlotte Mosley (ed.), *The Letters of Nancy Mitford and Evelyn Waugh* (London: Hodder, 1996), p. 16.
19. *Diary*, May 1933, quoted in Vickers, *Cecil Beaton*, p. 166.
20. Mosley, *Letters*, p. 13.
21. Bryher, *Days of Mars*, pp. 174–5.
22. Cyril Connolly in *Horizon* XVI (No. 90), July 1947.

Chapter 22: The Sitwell Renaissance

1. Osbert Sitwell, *Demos the Emperor* (London: Macmillan, 1949).
2. Ziegler, *Osbert Sitwell*, p. 320.
3. R.A., Box 532/6.
4. Ziegler, *Osbert Sitwell*, p. 308.
5. R.A., Box 567/1.
6. Sitwell, *For Want of the Golden City*, p. 417.
7. Sitwell, *Hortus Sitwellianus*, p. 13; Sitwell, *Renishaw Hall and the Sitwells*, p. 11.
8. John Lehmann, *A Nest of Tigers* (London: Macmillan, 1969), p. 243.
9. Mosley, *The Letters of Nancy Mitford and Evelyen Waugh*, pp. 113–17.
10. Pearson, *Façades*, p. 401.
11. Sitwell, *Taken Care Of*, p. 183.
12. Glendinning, *Edith Sitwell*, p. 200.
13. Salter, *Last Years of a Rebel*, p. 155.
14. Osbert Sitwell, *On the Continent: A Book of Iniquities* (London: Macmillan, 1958). Dedicated to the Kirsteins.
15. Amory, *Letters of Evelyn Waugh*, p. 204.
16. R.A., Box 571/4.
17. Amory, *Letters of Evelyn Waugh*, p. 380.
18. *New York Times Magazine*, 30 November 1952.

Chapter 23: Decay

1. R.A., Box 571/10.
2. Amory, *Letters of Evelyn Waugh*, p. 493.
3. R.A., Box 571/12.
4. Mark Amory (ed.), *The Letters of Ann Fleming* (London: The Harvill Press, 1985), p. 264.
5. Thekla Clark, *Wystan and Chester* (London: Faber, 1995), pp. 27–8.
6. Sir Steven Runciman, personal communication.

7. S. Sitwell, *Serenade to a Sister*, Brackley, Northamptonshire, 1974.
8. Personal observation (the author was a member of the St James').
9. R.A., Box 158, Bundle 6.
10. Mosley, *Letters*, p. 484.
11. R.A., Box 572/2.
12. Ibid.
13. Bradford, *Sacheverell Sitwell: Splendours and Miseries*.
14. Greene, *Edith Sitwell*.
15. Pearson, *Façades*, p. 190.

Chapter 24: Renishaw Reborn

1. R.A., letter (8 October 1966) from Osbert Sitwell to Derek Morley, courtesy of Penelope, Lady Sitwell.
2. Penelope, Lady Sitwell, personal communication.
3. Sitwell, *Renishaw Hall and the Sitwells*, p. 2.
4. R.A., letter from Reresby Sitwell to Osbert Sitwell, courtesy of Penelope, Lady Sitwell.
5. Ibid.
6. R.A., New Acquisitions Shelf 1.
7. Simon Jenkins, *England's Thousand Best Houses* (London: Allen Lane, 2003).
8. James Lees-Milne, *Ancient as the Hills: Diaries, 1973–1974* (London: John Murray, 1997).
9. Ibid.
10. Reresby Sitwell, 'Robin Hood's Bow', lecture (Renishaw, 1996).
11. Sitwell, *Hortus Sitwellianus*, p. 123.
12. *The Times*, 1 April 2009.

INDEX